*Critical Incidents
in Group Therapy*

# Critical Incidents in Group Therapy

**Jeremiah Donigian**
*State University of New York, College at Brockport*
**Richard Malnati**
*Temple University*

*Brooks/Cole Publishing Company*
*Monterey, California*

**Brooks/Cole Publishing Company**
A Division of Wadsworth, Inc.
©1987 by Wadsworth, Inc., Belmont, California 94002. All rights reserved. No part of this book may be reproduced, stored in a retrieval system, or transcribed, in any form or by any means—electronic, mechanical, photocopying, recording, or otherwise—without the prior written permisson of the publisher, Brooks/Cole Publishing Company, Monterey, California 93940, a division of Wadsworth, Inc.

Printed in the United States of America
10 9 8 7 6 5 4 3 2 1

**Library of Congress Cataloging-in-Publication Data**
Donigian, Jeremiah [date]
    Critical incidents in group therapy.

    Bibliography: p.
    Includes index.
    1. Group psychotherapy. 2. Critical incident technique. I. Malnati, Richard J. II. Title.
[DNLM: 1. Psychotherapy, Group. WM 430 D683c]
RC488.D66 1987 616.89'152 86-1011
ISBN 0-534-06282-2


Sponsoring Editor: *Claire Verduin*
Editorial Assistant: *Linda Ruth Wright*
Production Editor: *S.M. Bailey*
Manuscript Editor: *Nancy A. Tramontin*
Permissions Editor: *Carline Haga*
Interior and Cover Design: *Katherine Minerva*
Typesetting: *Instant Type, Monterey, California*
Printing and Binding: *Malloy Lithographing, Inc., Ann Arbor, Michigan*

*To our wives, Anna and Diane,*
*and our children, Melissa, Rebecca, Renneé, and Aimee,*
*all of whom comprise our primary group.*

This text grew out of our shared concerns as teachers of group thera-pists. Its earliest roots were grounded in the observations we made of our students as they struggled with their own evolution from students to group therapists. As they faced their first group sessions, we noted the anxiety students experienced as they encountered the variety of events that occurred during the therapy sessions. The personal effect such occurrences had on students would prove to present barriers to their own personal growth, which could only be lifted after they had gained a greater understanding of the theoretical assumptions which could guide them through each new situation. The most frequently asked questions pertained to what the students could do to understand their roles, as group therapists, to support them through these critical moments.

These inquiries only served to underscore the value for therapists of having a sound theoretical understanding of the dynamics of therapy groups. This led quite naturally to a study of the thought processes that proponents of different theoretical orientations undertake while they approach critical moments in the group's process. As we viewed it, the pivotal moment in the therapeutic process occurred at the juncture where the therapist's creative, scientific, and learned knowledge unit-ed. This happened when a connection between the therapist's knowl-edge gained from experience combined with the therapist's intellectual inquiry and study. Such a connection is often viewed by students of group therapy to be a spontaneous creative response. While the more experienced, theoretically grounded therapists will appear to respond to such occurrences without much hesitation, it is at this moment that students tend to question their abilities. This may lead to a crisis for students; the experienced therapist, however, will move to a greater level of therapeutic effect.

This text was written in response to students' need to develop a theoretical rationale that will sustain and guide them as they perform their work with therapy groups. We have chosen six incidents that can occur in a group therapy session, to explore the theoretical issues and the differing resolutions of them by the therapist. Selection of these incidents by no means implies that they supersede others in importance. We chose those incidents that occurred most frequently in the groups we and our students faced over the years as we worked as group therapists and teachers of group therapists.

After we identified the six incidents, we presented them to experienced group therapists, each of whom was a proponent of a different theoretical orientation. We asked them to respond to each critical incident and explain the thought processes they went through that determined their particular responses to the incident. The therapists have presented their explanations in a "here and now" fashion that gives the effect of immediacy. In this way, students will have the feeling of being right there with the therapists as their mentors, permitting them to be privy to the therapists' innermost thoughts. The ultimate purpose of this approach is not to ascertain which intervention was the best one; the purpose is to help students understand, from the vantage point of experienced group therapists, the rationale that supported their action, to understand why they chose the particular method of intervention, and to gain insight into how experienced group therapists project the anticipated consequences of their choices.

We are gratefully indebted to Drs. Thomas E. Bratter, William R. Coulson, Albert Ellis, Herbert Hampshire, Guy J. Manaster, and Mirriam F. Polster for their willingness to share their responses to each of the critical incidents. We wish to extend special thanks to our colleague and friend, Dr. David Kendall, who contributed the background for three of the theory chapters (Chapters 4, 5, and 6). We also thank Dr. Rosemarie Winstanley for her many helpful suggestions in the revision of our manuscript. In addition, we thank the following reviewers, who made many valuable suggestions: Avraham Scherman, University of Oklahoma; Donald J. Dellario, Boston University; Gerald Corey, California State University, Fullerton; Nicholas Colangelo, University of Iowa; Wayne Lanning, University of Wyoming; James Gumaer, Virginia Commonwealth University; Jack A. Duncan, Virginia Commonwealth University; José George Iglesias, Pima Community College (Tucson, Arizona); Dennis J. Haubrich, Ryerson Polytechnical Institute (Toronto); John Harper, Mississippi State University; and Sheldon Rose, University of Wisconsin. Finally, we wish to acknowledge the very significant role Claire Verduin played as our most patient and understanding editor.

*Jeremiah Donigian*
*Richard Malnati*

# CONTENTS

**Introduction   1**

$\mathcal{P}$*art One: Selected Theories of Group Therapy   7*

Introduction   7

**Chapter One: Client-Centered Therapy   9**

Background   9

*Nature of Human Beings   10*
*Self-Concept   10*

Key Concepts   12

*External Variables   12*
*Group Member Variables   13*
*Therapist Variables   13*

Therapist Role and Techniques   14

*Setting the Climate   15*
*Acceptance of the Group   15*
*Acceptance of the Individual   16*
*Empathic Understanding   16*
*Use of Feelings or Therapist Self-Disclosure   16*
*Confrontation and Feedback   17*
*Therapist Expression of Personal Problems   17*
*Avoidance of Interpretive or Process Comments   17*
*Avoidance of Planning and Exercises   18*

Group Processes   18

*Milling Around   18*
*Resistance to Personal Expression or Exploration   18*
*Description of Past Feelings   19*
*Expression of Negative Feelings   19*
*Expression and Exploration of Personally Meaningful Material   19*
*Expression of Immediate Interpersonal Feelings in the Group   20*
*The Development of a Healing Capacity in the Group   20*
*Self-Acceptance and the Beginning of Change   20*
*The Cracking of Facades   20*
*The Individual Receives Feedback   20*
*Confrontation   21*
*Helping Relationships Outside the Group Sessions   21*
*The Basic Encounter   21*
*Expression of Positive Feelings and Closeness   21*
*Behavior Changes in the Group   22*

Summary   22


**Chapter Two: Gestalt Therapy   23**

Background   23
Key Concepts   24

*Risk-Taking   26*

Therapist Role and Techniques   26

*Making the Rounds   28*
*Games of Dialogue   28*
*The Hot Seat   28*
*Role Reversals   29*

Group Processes   29
Summary   30


**Chapter Three: Individual Psychology   31**

Background   31
Key Concepts   33

*Social Interest   33*
*Holism   33*
*Self-Determination   34*

*Goal Orientation   34*
*Family Constellation   35*
*Inferiority Feelings   35*
*Life Style   36*

Therapist Role and Techniques   37
Group Processes   38
Summary   40


**Chapter Four: Rational-Emotive Therapy   41**

Background   41

Key Concepts   44

   *A-B-C-D-E Construct   44*
   *Homework   45*
   *Three Basic "Musts"   45*
   *Rationality/Irrationality   46*
   *Hedonism   46*

Therapist Role and Techniques   47
Group Processes   50
Summary   52


**Chapter Five: Reality Therapy   55**

Background   55
Key Concepts   56

   *Involvement   56*
   *Feeling Worthwhile   56*
   *Responsibility   57*
   *Denial   57*

Therapist Role and Techniques   58
Group Processes   58

   *Stage 1—Therapist Involvement   58*
   *Stage 2—Focus on Present Behavior   59*
   *Stage 3—Evaluation of Behaviors   59*
   *Stage 4—Developing Positive Responsible Behavior   60*
   *Stage 5—Commitment   60*
   *Stage 6—No Excuses Accepted   60*
   *Stage 7—Avoid Punishment   61*

Summary   61


**Chapter Six: Transactional Analysis   63**

Background   63
Key Concepts   67

*Ego States   67*
*Exclusion/Contamination   68*
*Transactions   69*
*Games   70*
*Script/Counterscript   70*

Therapist Role and Techniques   71

*Interrogation   72*
*Specification   72*
*Confrontation   72*
*Explanation   72*
*Illustration   73*
*Confirmation   73*
*Interpretation   73*
*Crystallization   73*

Group Processes   74

*Therapeutic Processes   74*
*Contractual Agreements   74*
*Group Structure   75*
*Analyses   75*

Summary   76


*P*art Two: Theoretical Practitioners' Responses to Specific Critical Incidents   79

Introduction   79


**Chapter Seven: The Initial Session   81**

Incident #1   81

*Client-Centered Therapy   82*

*Gestalt Therapy 83*
*Individual Psychology 85*
*Rational-Emotive Therapy 87*
*Reality Therapy 91*
*Transactional Analysis 92*

Theory Evaluation Form 94


**Chapter Eight: Group Attack of the Therapist 95**

Incident #2 95

*Client-Centered Therapy 97*
*Gestalt Therapy 100*
*Individual Psychology 103*
*Rational-Emotive Therapy 105*
*Reality Therapy 109*
*Transactional Analysis 110*

Theory Evaluation Form 114


**Chapter Nine: Mass Group Denial 115**

Incident #3 115

*Client-Centered Therapy 116*
*Gestalt Therapy 119*
*Individual Psychology 121*
*Rational-Emotive Therapy 123*
*Reality Therapy 128*
*Transactional Analysis 130*

Theory Evaluation Form 131


**Chapter Ten: A Member Chooses to Leave 133**

Incident #4 133

*Client-Centered Therapy 135*
*Gestalt Therapy 136*
*Individual Psychology 139*
*Rational-Emotive Therapy 141*
*Reality Therapy 146*

*Transactional Analysis*  147

Theory Evaluation Form  151


**Chapter Eleven: A Deep Disclosure Near Session Termination  153**

Incident #5  153

*Client-Centered Therapy*  155
*Gestalt Therapy*  158
*Individual Psychology*  163
*Rational-Emotive Therapy*  166
*Reality Therapy*  172
*Transactional Analysis*  175

Theory Evaluation Form  179


**Chapter Twelve: A Member Maintains Distance  181**

Incident #6  181

*Client-Centered Therapy*  183
*Gestalt Therapy*  184
*Individual Psychology*  187
*Rational-Emotive Therapy*  189
*Reality Therapy*  192
*Transactional Analysis*  195

Theory Evaluation Form  197


*P*art Three: *Where Have We Come?*  199


**Chapter Thirteen: Congruence of Theory with Practice  201**

Client-Centered Therapy  202
Gestalt Therapy  203
Individual Psychology  204
Rational-Emotive Therapy  205
Reality Therapy  206
Transactional Analysis  207
Conclusion  208

## Chapter Fourteen: Comparison of Theoretical Practitioners' Interventions    209

Critical Incident #1    210

Summary of Critical Incident #1    211

Critical Incident #2    211

Summary of Critical Incident #2    213

Critical Incident #3    213

Summary of Critical Incident #3    215

Critical Incident #4    215

Issue of Dealing with Member Termination    216
Summary of Critical Incident #4    217

Critical Incident #5    217

Session Closure and Preparation for Subsequent Session    219
Summary of Critical Incident #5

Critical Incident #6

Summary of Critical Incident #6    221

Primary Intervention Assessment    221
Conclusion    223

## Chapter Fifteen: Considerations in Developing Your Theory of Group Therapy    225

Steps to Developing a Theory    225

Elements of Group Behavior    227
Elements of Member Behavior    227
Elements of Therapist Behavior    227

Conclusion    228


References    229
Index    235

# INTRODUCTION

This book's emphasis on the translation of group therapy theory into practice begins with an examination of the value and role of theoretical background for group therapists in their practice. It is our hope that as students gain a knowledge of differing theoretical approaches, they will develop their own rationale of group leadership and group therapy.

There are moments during the life of a therapy group when critical incidents evolve as natural consequences of group development. These incidents can either present potential barriers or potential opportunities for the group's growth. In this way, the incidents are viewed as *critical.* The manner in which group leaders—the therapists—choose to manage such critical incidents will determine the extent to which the incidents affect group development. These moments (which often appear unannounced) can prove to be true tests even for experienced group leaders who have a firm theoretical base from which to operate. For neophyte group trainees, these moments can generate enough anxiety to immobilize them as they face the situation with uncertainty and trepidation. It is at such critical moments that group-therapist trainees most frequently question their supervisors about what action they should take and what rationale should support their intervention. These inquiries arise as students attempt to bring about an integration of theory with practice.

Other writers have grappled with the relationship of theory and practice. Howard Kiefer (1980) addressed the question in this way:

> Nothing is true in theory and false in practice, or vice versa; however coherent and free from self contradiction, no theory is adequate which fails to account for what happens in practice, unless it somehow is theoretically explained, understood, or fitted into a larger context, (it) remains a faculty mystery. Davey is right on insisting that the final test of any theory is whether it *works* in the sense that its implications and predictions are consistent with events. But completely unexplained events, completely unaccounted for facts, or what might be called raw data must be as meaningless to a man as to a rabbit—without the context of theory, they are at best, things processed by the senses, not grasped by the mind. This means that theory is the intellectual twin of practice, not its opponent; its verbal description and explanation not something separate and wholly other.

In his effort to pinpoint the origin and purpose of theory, Charles Clevenger (1982) allows that theory serves a very functional purpose. It provides a vehicle for bringing together independent observations and placing them in a systematic relationship that permits them to gain a significant and utilitarian value. Still further, Samuel Osipow (1973, 2–3) offers that the role of theory "permits, by deduction, predictions to be made about other events in the framework under observation." He adds that "a good theory clarifies events and leads to further predictions about related events."

Clearly, we have evidence supporting the need for group therapists to have experienced group participation; to be intellectually aware of the various events (the whats) that occur in the group and to note the ways they evolve. Therapists must organize observed events into some systematic order, thereby developing an explanation for the predictability of their occurence. With this knowledge, therapists will not find the group process a mystery, and they will be able to develop leadership styles consistent with desired therapeutic outcomes.

Some students of group therapy will develop their own personal theories; others will develop a rationale supporting their approach to group therapy. Such a rationale should address the role and technique of the therapist, the therapy process, and the nature of group therapy. For example, Irvin Yalom (1985, x) prefaces his book by describing what he perceives as the "front" from the "core" of group therapy. The "front" is much like a facade; it is the "trappings, the form, the techniques, the specialized language, and the aura surrounding each of the schools of therapy." He adds that "the core consists of those aspects of the experiences which are intrinsic to the therapeutic process—that is, the bare boned mechanisms of change." Yalom believes that the "front" has a significant part to play (for example, the charismatic quality of the therapist) in the initial stages of the group; but in the absence or neglect of the "core" of therapy, the therapeutic process is without substance and change is superficial. It is this "core" to which we address our thoughts.

This book results from our belief that students need to develop their "core." They must first realize that effective group leadership demands that they have an intellectual support base from which to function and that this base be comprised of general guidelines to assist them as they practice group therapy. These guidelines should be sufficiently broad and flexible to accommodate the dynamic process of group therapy. If the guidelines are too rigid, they will limit the variety of intervention strategies available to the therapist.

It is our position that students of group therapy can gain a great deal by studying, observing, and even experiencing various theoretical approaches  to group therapy. In so doing, students can begin to recognize how they are affected emotionally and intellectually by each therapist's technique and methodology as well as by accompanying theory. The foundation for one's rationale for leadership style and group development evolves from such experiences. In fact, as students read the chapters on theory, they will discover that all theoretical modes presented have some other theory as their antecedent. Perhaps students will be motivated to do as Yalom has done: to separate the *front* from the *core* of each of the theories presented in this text, and begin to develop a rationale that will guide them as they assume their role as group therapists.

The text is designed to illustrate how theory is translated into practice by the proponents of those theories. Its uniqueness in this regard, however, relies heavily upon the emphasis we place upon how the theoretical practitioners manage each of the critical incidents they encounter.

In its broadest perspective, this text provides the student of group leadership with comparative approaches for dealing with critical incidents that arise in group therapy. Students will find they are not forced to extrapolate how the theoretical approach might be applied, but will be able to follow the actual thought processes of the theorists as the incident is confronted.

The text shows the amount of variability or license practitioners have in interpreting the theoretical principles they follow as they encounter specific situations.

This text also reverses a trend that depicts competitiveness among various theoretical approaches, which can make students look for the *right* or *wrong* approach. It is our belief that students will instead find there are a variety of ways to deal effectively with critical incidents that occur in a therapy group. Thus, for aspiring practitioners, effectiveness will be shown to be a matter of *choice* and *blend* and not an issue of which theory is best.

Finally, and perhaps in a more idealistic sense, this text provides students the learning derived from experiencing various theories, which ultimately could provide the impetus to develop a theoretical system most effective for themselves.

The text is organized into three parts. Part I describes each of the selected theories in group therapy utilized throughout the text. Each chapter follows a relatively simple format. Brief explanations of the background of the theoretical development of its proponents, or founder, open each chapter. This is followed by an examination of the fundamental principles that undergird the theory, its key concepts, the role of the therapist, and the rationale for the techniques utilized, and finally, group processes. We have made no analysis or interpretation of the theories presented in each chapter. Our primary purpose in Part I is to provide readers with a common base of understanding and a refer-ral source as they undertake Part II.

Part II provides the central core of the text. Each chapter presents a hypothetical critical incident occuring in a group therapy session. This is followed by responses from each of the theoretical practitioners. Since it is generally accepted that theoretical principles are subject to the individual interpretation of the practitioner, we encourage each of our theoretical practitioners to engage in that liberty. The response process to each incident was structured in order to assure a certain amount of continuity in the way each of the theoretical practitioners dealt with the issue. The procedures they followed asked them to:

1. explain the thought processes they used to guide them as they selected their particular response, including what aspects about the incident prompted them to take the action they did;
2. explain why they chose one particular intervention method over any other they may have considered;
3. state what consequences they anticipated from their action; and
4. point out what was the most glaring or outstanding condition of the incident, which they in turn identified as lending itself most readily to the theory (or its principle) they espoused.

If a therapist believed that the incident would not fit into or would not occur in one of the theoretical frameworks, they were asked to explain this position and show why an issue was not expected to occur.

Part II also initiates the students' direct participation in becoming aware of their theory of group therapy. Students respond to the same sequence of questions addressed by the theoretical practitioners, and at the end of each section, complete a series of *Theory Evaluation Forms* designed to further highlight their evolving theory of group therapy.

Part III integrates the first two parts of the text, similar to the "capping" process of a typical group therapy session. We examine whether or not our theoretical practitioners' therapy interventions were congruent with the rationale of their respective theories. We also compare and contrast the interventions made by each of the theoretical practitioners to highlight the similarities and differences of the approaches. Finally, we conclude by offering students guidelines by which they may begin to develop a more explicit theory of group therapy of their own.

# PART ONE

# Selected Theories of Group Therapy

## *Introduction*

The first part of this book, chapters 1–6, provides the student with the primary principles that undergird each of the theories used by their respective theoretical practitioners in dealing with the critical situations in Part II. Our purpose is not to teach theory per se, but to offer the essence of a theory that will guide its proponent as a group therapist. This introduction to theory examines the theorists' beliefs about the nature of human conflict and its sources, the role of the therapist, the therapist's use of techniques, the role of group members upon each other, and a sense of the group process that occurs.

Students interested in acquiring a broader knowledge of one or more of the theoretical perspectives should consult the reference section at the back of this book for further reading.

# CHAPTER ONE

# Client-Centered Therapy

## Background

The name most synonymous with client-centered group therapy is Carl Rogers. In 1942 Rogers published *Counseling and Psychotherapy*, which contained the elements of a theory that was later to be more fully developed in his book, *Client-Centered Therapy* (1951). Client-centered therapy is an approach that grew from Rogers's experiences as a therapist. In 1946, Rogers, along with his associates at the counseling center at the University of Chicago, applied the principles of their individual therapy to individuals together in a group (Rogers 1951). It was at this moment that client-centered *group* therapy was begun. By the early 1960s, Rogers was devoting more of his clinical efforts and time to group therapy. In 1970, he wrote that group therapy has supplanted individual therapy as the primary focus of his professional life.

Client-centered group therapy is also known as *basic encounter group therapy* and *intensive experiential group therapy* (Rogers 1967); in this book, we will use "client-centered group therapy" to avoid any confusion with other forms of encounter groups.

Searching for a theory of client-centered *group* therapy per se is a futile exercise. Rogers (1979) has stated that he is "not attempting to build a high level abstract theory." However, in 1959 he extensively delineated his theory regarding individual therapy, personality, and interpersonal relationships. These formulations provide the threads supporting Rogers's rationale for client-centered group therapy. Actually, Rogers (1970) went so far as to say that his approach to group therapy does not differ in any fundamental philosophical way from his approach to individual therapy.

Rogers's client-centered approach to therapy grew out of his experiences as a therapist and an amalgam of thoughts distilled from theorists such as Rank, Buber, Lewin, Maslow, Combs, and Snygg. This unique blend of personal experiences and thoughts appears as a reflection of humanistic, existential-experiential, and phenomenological thinking. In order to appreciate how this translated into Rogers's brand of group therapy, we will examine the critical constructs that Rogers identified as the guidance system for his work as a therapist.

## Nature of Human Beings

Rogers holds that all human beings have the tendency to move toward actualization. It is *the* motivating force that urges humans toward activities of maintenance and growth. This belief in the inherent capacity of individuals to take charge of their lives is crucial to Rogers's form of therapy. He asserts that trusting in a client's basic ability to care for self is an extension of his position that people are much wiser than they think. It is society that has to be faulted for creating the barriers that keep individuals from realizing their full capabilities. Therefore, through therapy, people can learn to regain trust in themselves and to take responsibility for their lives. Consequently, Rogers tries to keep a very low profile in the therapeutic relationship; he works only to facilitate the release of the already existing growth potential in his clients.

## Self-Concept

In most therapeutic modalities, understanding the nature of self-concept plays a significant role. In no other does it play a more important part than in client-centered therapy. Rogers (1959) devoted much thought to explaining how the self develops and how it ultimately affects human behavior. He went to great lengths to describe it and the constructs that reflect it.

Self-concept, according to Rogers, is a person's ability to perceive and differentiate the personal "I" from an internal frame of reference, and to recognize the "I" as experienced from interpersonal relationships. Rogers refers to the development of a self-concept as a "fluid process." It is the way individuals differentiate themselves from others in their social relationships.

Rogers's constructs of congruence and incongruence related to the way the self is perceived and the way it is experienced in social relationships. If one's internal perception of self is consistent with the way in which projected self is *experienced* within interpersonal relationships then a person is referred to as being *congruent.* However, should a discrepancy exist between the *idea* of one's self-perception and the projected experience (self-perception gained from social interactions) then it is said that this person is experiencing incongruency, or is *incongruent.*

Rogers offers that there are a number of ways by which an individual's self-concept is realized and, subsequently, the way a person functions. These constructs function much like needs. The way in which a person chooses to meet them determines the extent of the individual's growth and health. We will highlight four of the constructs to further explain Rogers's theories.

Rogers (1959, 208) states that early in an individual's development, the individual acquires the desire for a form of affirmation, labeled *positive regard.* This construct consists of "such attitudes as warmth, liking, respect, sympathy, and acceptance." Positive regard is a bilateral process; there is both a receiver and a giver. If a person experiences any of these attitudes coming from someone, then the individual is said to be in a state or condition of positive regard. Conversely, should a person experience liking or accepting of another person, then the individual experiences what it is like to perceive another in positive regard.

Should a person state "I accept you as a worthwhile human being without reservation or hesitation," it would be a demonstration of *unconditional positive regard.* The significance of this construct rests in its communication of total acceptance of an individual's strengths and limitations, never emphasizing one over the other.

With the first two constructs, the primary sources for determining one's self-worth are external; socially derived and dependent upon another person. Rogers believes there are also internal frames of reference from which an individual may draw feelings or perceptions of self-worth. The first of these is *positive self-regard.* It is the ability of an individual to refer to internal resources for feelings of warmth, acceptance, and respect, without relying on sources external to the self for positive attitudes.

Finally, individuals also have the capacity to hold themselves in a state of *unconditional self-regard.* For this process, the individuals do not discriminate between their own strengths and weaknesses; nor do they dwell on one over the other. In effect, this construct explains what is often referred to as self-acceptance.

These constructs provide a crucial aspect of the theory. Rogers believes that individuals who are fully functioning are able to rely on internal sources of self-reinforcement; they are less dependent upon others for determining self-worth and self-acceptance. It is only when they lose sight of these internal support systems and become totally dependent upon others that an unhealthy state of affairs exists. For example, if I am dependent solely on receiving positive feelings about myself from those around me, then I will focus my energies on trying to meet their expectations. This creates an imbalance in the self-system in which states of *conditional* positive regard and conditional self-regard exist.

Turning inwardly for support will not help me either since what exists within me are feelings of unworthiness. Thus begins a vicious cycle that could have me depending on others for self-worth; not receiving their *positive* regard, I will then turn inwardly for *positive self-regard*, but not having that within my "self" system, I can find myself again turning outwardly. The resulting image that I project to others, however, may more than likely be one lacking in self-respect. Others, then, will have nothing to respond to other than my behavior, which reflects these nonpositive feelings toward myself. They, in turn, may have no reason to hold me in positive regard, thereby sending me behavioral messages that reaffirm how I already see myself.

Conversely, should I realize that I cannot please everybody by meeting all their expectations all of the time and should I accept both my strengths and limitations, as well as feel free to be selective of the feedback from others, without dwelling on either the positive or negative, then what exists is a state of unconditional positive self-regard. As I project this image of myself outwardly through behaviors, the likelihood is strong that others will see me this way and thus respond in a way that says that they hold me in *unconditional regard.*

## $\mathcal{K}$ey Concepts

The key concepts that support or guide client-centered group therapy can be viewed through three variables: (1) external variables, (2) group member variables, and (3) group therapist variables.

### External Variables

Rogers (1970) first recognized that most encounter groups have *external variables* that separate them from other forms of group therapy. For example, the number of members generally involved in a client-centered group is not less than 8 or more than 18. Structure is very limited; allowance is made for the group to choose its own goals and personal directions. The group therapist works primarily to facilitate members to express their feelings and thoughts. Finally, there is a major emphasis for the therapist and members to pay attention to what is occurring at the moment of interpersonal interaction. This is referred to as immediacy.

## Group Member Variables

Rogers (1970) has developed eight hypotheses that are common to most encounter groups. We can refer to them simply as the ingredients that must exist in order for client-centered therapy to work. They are:

1. The *need for safety* must be met before members will feel free to express themselves and lower their defenses. The leader should establish a psychological climate in which members can feel safe to interact intensively.
2. *Psychological and emotional intimacy* develops as a product of a safe psychological climate. This is evidenced as members begin to share and express their feelings about themselves and those they hold toward others.
3. *Mutual trust* evolves from the personal disclosures that have been made, and this may be evidenced in the form of each member's movement toward greater self-acceptance.
4. *Risk taking* develops as defenses give way. Personal attitudes, values, and behaviors are open to examination and possible change. Evidence of this be seen as traditional ways of thinking and behaving give way to new.
5. *Psychological openness* for individual differences (of self and others) develops. This is evidenced as members work to understand each other.
6. The process of *feedback* develops and becomes more evident. Members more openly share information regarding how they perceive each other. This contributes to self-knowledge by learning how one appears to others and the impact one has in interpersonal relationships.
7. Members become more *creative* and *imaginative* as a result of their newly found freedom. As a consequence, individuals find reinforcement for dealing with their immediate social environment in new and different ways.
8. As a result of the social reinforcement received for the new behaviors, members can be expected, at least temporarily, to *transfer* these behaviors to their interpersonal relationships with others outside of the immediate counseling group.

## Therapist Variables

The third and final level regards the therapist. Rogers (1970) believes that a therapist's attitudes and philosophy play a significant role as he or she leads a group.

First and foremost, a therapist must trust the group to develop its own potential and that of its individual members. It follows closely that there must also be trust in the group process. Therefore, a role of the therapist, much as the therapist in individual therapy, is that of facilitator of the process.

The therapist must also believe that the group can set its own direction and thereby be capable of taking care of itself. By this, it is meant that the group can recognize that there are barriers to movement or growth, which must be dealt with before the group can move toward a healthier state. But a group therapist should recognize the uniqueness of each group and understand that no two will begin or end the same way in their readiness to grow and move toward healthier states. Some groups will begin by being very resistant to expressing feelings and will thus move very slowly; others may be expressive from the outset and move rapidly.

The client-centered therapist should not enter into a group session with any specific goals for the group. The only thing that the therapist can expect to occur is that the process will always be the same; there will be movement, although it may not be translated into a successful experience for the group.

While there is much reliance upon group process as being the primary force in the group, the *way* the client-centered group therapist facilitates that process is a key variable in the life of the group. There are a variety of behaviors in which the therapist engages to help move the group. They include empathic listening, disclosure of feelings, a willingness to share personal issues that are distressing, facilitating rather than directing the group, and maintaining a low profile in one's role as a therapist. To this latter point, Rogers has stated that he sees himself more as a participant in the group and therefore tries to avoid emphasizing his role as its therapist. He believes that by so doing, the group will be more inclined to take responsibility for its own growth and development and rely less on him as the force for doing so.

Rogers adds that he wants the *whole* person to be present in the group. By this he means that members should bring both their cognitive and affective dimensions to the group in order that he, as a facilitator, can work to help them express and grow in both their ideas and feelings.

## Therapist Role and Techniques

The role of the therapist and techniques is a difficult category to address directly since Rogers has long been on record that he prefers not to use techniques or gimmickry in his work as a group therapist. In fact, Robert Coulson, in his book *Groups, Gimmicks, and Instant Gurus* (1972), has addressed this area directly. However, if it can be said that whatever a group therapist does can be viewed as being a technique, then, by definition, the very act of not employing any techniques, in and of itself, is a technique (to do nothing, is to do something). The client-centered group therapist performs certain functions in helping the group move toward a state of self-awareness.

## Setting the Climate

The way group therapists proceed to establish the emotional climate is most critical. By being transparent, that is, allowing for their own feelings and thoughts to be shared with the group and trying to remain flexible, receptive, and relaxed, therapists hope to convey to members that it is okay to feel free to be one's self. This modeling activity is also carried over to the way the group therapist *listens* to the members. The therapist tries to convey to group members that each is important and that what each has to say is significant. Rogers (1970) refers to this as *validating* the person. During this listening process, the group therapist is less inclined to be listening to the story line of the presenter and is more likely to seek out the meaning behind the words and identify the feelings the speaker is trying to convey.

By listening in this manner, the group therapist will communicate to each of the members that regardless of what is said, how emotionally deep or ridiculous, this is a safe place to say it and at least there is one person (the therapist) who respects them and acknowledges that what was said had significant meaning to the person who said it.

Psychological and emotional safety is provided in another way. Deep emotional disclosures or unspoken feelings can be painful and freeing experiences. Client-centered group therapists try to communicate to the member that they are psychologically with the group member during this critical moment. It is important that group members feel that someone is there who is psychologically and emotionally strong enough to support them when they face a crisis in the group.

## Acceptance of the Group

Acceptance of the group communicates to its members that the therapist indeed trusts them to come up with their own direction. This even takes into consideration whether or not they are at a point in their own individual readiness to deal with emotional issues. By not imposing expectations on the group, the therapist also facilitates the members to experience freedom to be creative and expressive. The end product can be a discovery of new and different ways to cope effectively with themselves and others, thereby developing a sense of personal independence and self-reliance.

## Acceptance of the Individual

Acceptance of the individual is the therapist's way of communicating a readiness to accept the members as they are with no hidden expectations. This granting of permission from the therapist to the group members to choose whatever level of active commitment to the group they want is the first step toward facilitating self-acceptance. It follows, therefore, that as self-acceptance increases, greater risking behavior will be demonstrated, along with acceptance of individual differences as each person's unique qualities surface. Acceptance of the individual also helps facilitate members to develop their *whole* selves. Accepting the members where they are (intellectually involved or emotionally distant, for example), reassures members and allows them to feel free to enter the group, eventually at an emotional level, should they choose.

## Empathic Understanding

Rogers (1970) has acknowledged empathic understanding to be his most significant and most frequently used activity as a group therapist. By trying to grasp the specific meaning of what a member of the group is saying, the therapist will facilitate member-to-member understanding. What one member *intends* to communicate is made clear for the others, thereby avoiding misunderstandings. By illuminating the interactive process, the therapist helps to avoid the confusion that often arises: participants on both sides of the interaction become so invested in their side of an issue that they fail to state clearly their position. In some ways, then, empathic understanding can be viewed as the means by which the therapist helps the group stay focused on the issues at hand and develop a sense of congruency.

## Use of Feelings or Therapist Self-Disclosure

To achieve the objective of helping participants develop a *wholeness* about their person, a therapist can demonstrate, through modeling, the way to be expressive of one's feelings and how to trust them. Therapists should be responsive to both negative and positive affective states that exist within themselves. There is spontaneity or immediacy attached to this way of behaving. Rogers refers to it as an intuitive feeling not consciously derived. By behaving in this manner, the therapist is also helping the group to move toward a level of psychological and emotional intimacy. It is as though permission is being granted to share aloud the feelings that one is experiencing at that moment within the group. There is also an underlying assumption that there is trust in the group and, therefore, that the group will also hold in positive regard the person expressing the feelings.

## Confrontation and Feedback

Confrontation and feedback helps participants learn about themselves, their self-concept, by communicating the way a member's behavior(s) are experienced by the therapist. The focus clearly must be upon behavior that can be changed by the participants, and not an attack upon their personhood or the defenses over which they may have little control. The feedback can also provide information about how a participant's behavior presents a self-image to the other persons in the interactive exchange.

The leader can anticipate that the feedback will facilitate group process. It may induce interaction. It may also precipitate distress in the person receiving the feedback. In some cases, if the person receiving feedback appears to be overwhelmed by the process, the leader should allow the person to break emotional contact by acknowledging the fact that they may need to withdraw from the encounter.

## Therapist Expression of Personal Problems

In order to function maximally as a facilitator of group process, Rogers believes he must divest himself of those stressful personal issues to which he may be attending while he is at the same time leading the group. Rogers believes that unless he does so, such personal material will interfere with his ability to listen effectively. He cautions that the group therapist must be careful not to use the group to meet the therapist's own personal needs. However, there may be times when it would help the group to know that the therapist is experiencing difficulties and that it is not the group's fault.

## Avoidance of Interpretive or Process Comments

It is Rogers's belief that observations made by the therapist about the group process tend to make the group self-conscious and slow it down because the members feel as though they are being examined. It also tends to separate the group therapist from the members. This obviating works counter to Rogers's efforts to maintain a low profile and to allow the group members to develop their own sense of responsibility and direction.

It follows that Rogers also avoids attempts to interpret the reasons behind an individual's behaviors. He submits that, at best, it would be an educated guess. Furthermore, such behavior on the part of the therapist has elements of authoritativeness, something Rogers wants to avoid projecting.

## Avoidance of Planning and Exercises

Rogers emphasizes the need for the group to evolve naturally and to let the facilitative processes occur spontaneously. He views the use of preplanned activities or exercises as a resource of last resort. If role-playing, body contact, or psychodrama are used, they should evolve naturally from the group and be designed to meet the needs of the members at that moment in time. In fact, Rogers submits that an exercise that may be truly spontaneous in one group might not be in another, since it may not work or have the same desired effect.

# Group Processes

It must be emphasized that a client-centered group session is highly interactive, with great reliance upon the members to provide the group's motivation and direction. Furthermore, the group therapist is very conscious of and dependent upon the process of the group. On the surface, it may appear as though the group therapist is very passive and doing very little. Nothing could be further from the truth. The therapist, in fact, is very actively listening as well as observing the group's process patterns. Rogers (1967), has identified 15 developmental patterns or stages that a group can be expected to go through, each with its own unique characteristic and effect upon the group's growth and development. These stages are presented below in the order they usually occur.

## Milling Around

Milling around usually occurs immediately upon the leader's disclosure that this group is very unique, that members can expect virtually no direction from the therapist, and that they have some very unusual freedoms. The characteristics of this stage are awkward silence, confusion, cocktail-party conversation, politeness, some expression of frustration about what is expected or what the members should do, and a great lack of continuity between member-to-member statements. Usually during this period, members will try to identify roles, determine who the leader is, establish the group's purpose, and explore norms.

## Resistance to Personal Expression or Exploration

Members will generally present their public selves during the milling period. However, as some individuals begin to disclose personal material, others can be expected to respond with mixed feelings. Their own sense of insecurity may direct them to behave in ways that would mask the fear they experience as pressure mounts for them to disclose their own deep feelings. Such fear may manifest itself through questions regarding group trust, the reality of the group situation versus that of the "real" world, or by the presentation of an image of being all-knowing or emotionally distant from that which is occurring in the group.

## Description of Past Feelings

As time moves on, the expression of personal feelings tends to become the predominant issue. However, unresolved ambivalence between the group's trustworthiness and risk of self-disclosure is still present. Usually a safer route will be taken. Members will often move toward discussing their feelings at an intellectual level by examining encounters they have had with individuals outside the group. This reference to emotional experiences that have occurred in the past are *current* at an intellectual level, but truly exemplify feelings that exist in the *there and then*, as opposed to the *here and now* of the group.

## Expression of Negative Feelings

It can be generally expected that group members will attack, criticize, or present nonsupportive statements to one another. This behavior may manifest itself in a way that reflects anger toward a member for remaining aloof or distant (that is, not adhering to group norms). It may also be reflected in an attack upon the leader for not measuring up to the group's role expectations. Whatever the case, the astute observer will readily recognize that these feelings are very genuine and have a *here and now* quality. The feelings are personal and current as they occur in the group. Rogers has theorized that either the members are testing the trustworthiness of the group and their freedom of expression, or they are finding it easier to express negative feelings out of fear that positive ones, such as "I have warm feelings toward you," could be dangerous because they could leave them vulnerable and open to rejection.

## Expression and Exploration of Personally Meaningful Material

The developmental sequence continues with some members beginning to disclose personally significant material to the others. Rogers believes that this may result from members' growing view of the group as their own, in which they can have some say in what they want to make of it. Another variable, which to Rogers facilitates the occurrence of this dynamic, is the development of a climate of trust, leaving individuals free to take some risk. This evolves, in part, from having earlier experienced and expressed negative feelings without dire consequences.

## Expression of Immediate Interpersonal Feelings in the Group

Sooner or later, member-to-member interaction will lead to the expression of feelings one has for the other. The immediacy, the here and now, of the expression of feelings usually is the end result of an increasing climate of trust. The feelings can be positive or negative. For example: "I didn't like you at first because you reminded me of my ex-spouse," or "Your openness allows me to feel very close to you, and I like that."

## The Development of a Healing Capacity in the Group

Certain group members will demonstrate naturally and quite spontaneously abilities to be helpful to other members who have been expressing their own difficulties. Rogers believes that group members are a valuable source of assistance in the therapeutic process for other members.

## Self-Acceptance and the Beginning of Change

The early stages of change are characterized by the demonstration of self-acceptance. In this phase of the group's development, members begin to make statements about themselves that reflect awareness of their own personal attitudes, values, behaviors, and role perceptions, and their willingness to come to terms with them.

## The Cracking of Facades

The group will reach a point where being open, genuine, and honest is the most important group norm. As the group reaches this point, members become intolerant of members who do not conform. Their disdain for superficial and intellectual approaches to interpersonal relating is evidenced by behaviors that can range from sensitive recognition and nudging of a reluctant member to outright attacks that often can appear quite violent in their effect.

## The Individual Receives Feedback

During the life of the group, group members are given information about the way they are perceived by each other. Usually such information leads to new and deeper levels of self-awareness. Feedback can be warm and supportive, conveying positive messages about the way a person is perceived. Feedback can also be nonsupportive, conveying a negative message to the individual.

## Confrontation

Confrontation is an extension, or added dimension, of the feedback process that is addressed to a member's incongruent behavior. It generally is directed at an individual demonstrating feelings or thoughts that are not consistent with their demonstrated behavior. This phase of the process will usually occur later in the life of the group, and not in its earlier periods. The interpersonal transactions that illustrate this stage occur as one member offers a statement that is straightforward and on the level (often called "leveling") about a fellow member's unappreciated behavior or about behavior that is not consistent with the member's expressed intended messages. Confrontation is often an unsettling experience for the persons involved and at times for the group as a whole, but it is a necessary part of the group's process.

## Helping Relationships Outside the Group Sessions

Group process does not stop the moment a group session ends. Members will often form subgroups that meet outside of the regularly scheduled sessions. Frequently such subgroups, comprised of two or more members, will meet to provide help and support to one another as they experience the advent of new self-perceptions that evolve from being in the regular group. Often it is through such subgroups that individuals are able to come to personal acceptance and actualization of themselves.

## The Basic Encounter

The intensity of the interaction among members over a period of time eventually leads to deeper emotional levels in their relationships with one another. The extraordinarily close and direct contact, which normally is not attained in everyday life, contributes to the change-producing dimensions of the group experience. The emotional tone of the group is heavy; often interspersed with both fears and expressions of attachment to one another, which usually are qualified by statements that they have never felt this way toward another person before.

## Expression of Positive Feelings and Closeness

One can expect that as the group's life continues, feelings of warmth, unity, group spirit, and trust evolve. These are manifestations of the realness of the members, which includes the expression of negative and positive feelings.

### Behavior Changes in the Group

Some definitive behavior changes occur as the group matures or moves towards termination. Physical gestures are altered, and individuals present themselves as relaxed, open physically, and able to deal with each other in ways that reflect acceptance of other members. Voice tones are congruent and express feeling. Word choices are carefully made in order to express thoughtfulness and straight messages, as well as offering help. Individuals also appear to listen intently in ways that reflect interest in understanding the other person accurately. There also appears to be a spontaneity in the way members respond to one another, as though it were a demonstration of being free from the intellectual inhibitions that blocked them during the very early stages of the group.

## Summary

In client-centered group therapy, the therapist's primary objective is to help members become aware of themselves and to translate this awareness into behavior that reflects self-responsibility, instead of feeling controlled by the environment. This is achieved largely through what has been referred to as the basic encounter.

The client-centered group is highly interactive, with much reliance upon the members to provide its motivation and direction. In striking contrast to other approaches to group therapy, the therapist maintains a very low profile and will be a participant-member. By so doing, it places an additional burden upon the members to take responsibility for the group's movement.

By adhering to the belief that *group process* remains the same regardless of the group's composition, the therapist can be effective and, in fact, remain different from the other members. By trusting and understanding that a group must go through various developmental stages, the therapist can actively participate as a member, while simultaneously working as a facilitator of that process. By attending to the *way* things are happening in the group, the therapist helps members deal with resistance and feedback, contend with confrontation, provide empathic understanding, and model such qualities as vulnerability, transparency, and genuine and trusting feelings. It is important to realize that these are among the qualities that reflect the realness of being human and through which the client-centered therapist helps members experience behaving in new ways. By providing for such experiences within the group, members will learn the behaviors that will enable them to deal effectively with their lives.

# CHAPTER TWO

# Gestalt Therapy

## Background

A discussion of Gestalt therapy accurately begins with an introduction to Frederick Perls, the founder and developer of its basic principles. The history and evolution of Gestalt therapy is well-documented and has received considerable attention. Frederick Perls received his M.D. in 1921 and went on to receive further training in psychoanalysis. In 1926, he worked with Professor Kurt Goldstein and received his first exposure to Gestalt psychology. In 1942, his formalized theories on applying the principles of Gestalt psychology to personality development and psychotherapy were published in a manuscript titled *Ego Hunger and Aggression* (later in book form, 1947).

Gestalt therapy differs from Gestalt psychology, developed originally by Wolfgang Kohler and Kurt Wertheimer. These classical Gestalt psychologists developed a theory of perception that attempted to explain an individual's perceptual process by understanding the interrelationships between the *form* of the object being observed and the way in which the person was *perceiving* it. It was a conscious effort to show that the perceiver was not only reacting to *situations*, but had partial responsibility for how such situations were perceived (their form). These perceptions, in turn, affected how the observer dealt with the situations. Wallen (1970, 8) explained that the significant difference between Gestalt psychology and Gestalt therapy was that "the academic Gestalt psychologist never attempted to employ the various principles of Gestalt formation . . . to organic perceptions, to the perceptions of one's own feelings, emotions, and bodily sensations. He never really managed to integrate the facts of motivation with the facts of perception."

Gestalt therapy was also a movement away from the psychoanalytical and behavioristic approaches to therapy. In 1951, when Frederick Perls, Paul Goodman, and Ralph Hefferline published *Gestalt Therapy*, it marked their attempt to construct a unique blend of certain psychoanalytic principles with those of existential and phenomenological thought with a humanistic orientation. The cultural and social aspects of the 1960s allowed for the addition of a humanistic flavor to clinical and counseling psychology, and marked the period when Perls's work received its greatest acceptance and popularity. His book *Gestalt Therapy Verbatim* (1969) has become the pillar upon which Gestalt therapy has developed.

Frederick Perls referred to group psychotherapy sessions as workshops. The Gestalt Workshop group typically consists of a therapist and five to eight group members meeting on a weekly basis. Meeting times are usually an hour and a half but may range from one to three hours. Some weekend workshops are conducted for as long as 20 hours. It is not unusual for a single therapist to work with a group of 16 people, but two therapists usually lead groups numbering eight or more. Workshop sessions tend to be longer in duration as the size of the group increases.

## *K*ey Concepts

Fundamental to Gestalt therapy is the belief that people are striving for *completeness* or *perfection*. Translated, this means that "there are values in living that persons know from their own experiences or from their observations of others to be valuable and enhancing: spontaneity, sensory awareness, freedom of movement, emotional responsiveness and expressiveness, enjoyment, ease, flexibility in relating, direct contact and emotional closeness with others, intimacy, competency, immediacy and presence, self-support, and creativity" (Fagan & Shepherd 1970, 1–2). It is the way in which people view the world that blocks or impedes achievement of such growth and "experiencing of life." The objective of therapy is to free a person from these barriers to effective living.

Critical to the process of helping clients remove these barriers, are the concepts of *here and now*. Gestalt therapy does not concern itself with personal histories. It holds disdain for the *should's, could's* and *ought-to-be's*, which are brought about through attempting to meet expectations of societal roles and norms. Perls has often referred to this as top-dog and under-dog aspects of the personality. The top-dog is the moralizer; its specialty is telling the individuals what they should or ought to do, it is the boss and also condemns. The under-dog tries to counter the top-dog by excuses, apologizing, and behaving defensively. For the Gestalt therapist, the way to resolve the dispute between the top-dog and the under-dog is referred to as *integration*. The therapist attempts to get the two arguing sides to cease striving for control. Bridging the gap, or unifying the two sides of the personality, is intended to overcome the split caused by these two struggling sides and make the person whole. Gestalt therapy urges individuals to experience the present, while developing a self-support system and avoiding manipulative behaviors designed to gain environmental support.

The existential dimension of Gestalt therapy is emphasized here. The therapist's role is to create a "continuum of awareness" (Perls 1969b, 51). It is through this moment-to-moment awareness that the member realizes there is some unfinished business (that is, recognizes incompleteness). The tendency, according to Perls, is for individuals to mask this incompleteness by intellectualizing. He writes that this flight away from the present may be seen as "jumping like a grasshopper from experience to experience" (Perls 1969b, 51). Thus, one never stays long enough to complete the business at hand. Gestalt therapists, therefore, minimize the *why* of behavior and emphasize the *what, how,* and *now*. Perls's famous statement "lose your mind and come to your senses," (1969b, 9) tries to get members to focus on the *now* of their experience.

Conceptually, *focusing* plays a significant role in Gestalt therapy. Focusing means the therapist is attending to members' behaviors at the moment, including voice modulations and changes in body posture. The focusing process involves the therapist's search for the inconsistencies in the members' verbal and nonverbal behaviors that prevent achievement of completeness. This process requires the therapist to confront members when incongruencies are noted in the therapeutic situation. By "cutting through the garbage" (Perls 1969a), the therapist forces members to deal with the immediacy of the problem. Member denial or avoidance of exhibited discrepancies of verbal and nonverbal behavior is usually futile, since the therapist continually focuses members on the very moment the encounter is being experienced. In short, members are forced to face themselves squarely and are not allowed to escape, short of withdrawing (Perls 1969b).

Closely related to the focusing process is the concept of responsibility. This is exemplified by insisting that members make "I" statements, that they take ownership for their behavior in dealing with life and not blame others for the way they act. Learning to be responsible rids members of the temptation to lean on role expectations set forth by society.

### Risk-Taking

Taking ownership and responsibility for one's behavior can present risks to the individual. This element of *risk-taking* is another important concept in Gestalt therapy. To take a risk requires a willingness to take chances; to experiment in order to move toward understanding one's self more fully. How the therapist allows for members' risk-taking and what it means is best explained by Joseph Zinker (1977, 18): "even though I respect the validity of his [the member's] experience, I am tempted to whet his appetite toward a formulation of new visual or cognitive or motoric perspectives of himself. The new perspective or dimension does not have to be dramatic; it merely needs to move the existing system into a highly fresher view of itself." There is some anxiety in this, for the member is being asked to view the experience of self from a novel perspective, a break from the comfort of old ways. It becomes a task of the therapist to help the member recognize that anxiety is a part of life (Levitsky & Simkin 1972) and the way toward becoming whole is to face anxiety, which often is in the form of resistance to change, rather than take flight from it.

Finally, in order for people to be totally integrated, they must be willing to accept themselves as who they are in order to be *authentic*. It is important for members to become aware of their thoughts and feelings, and ways of experiencing the environment. Zinker (1977, 19) expresses best what Gestalt therapy means when he states: "it stands for all that is in front of me, for all that promises completeness of experiencing, for the things to come which are awesome, frightening, tearful, moving, unfamiliar, archetypical, growthful....One needs 'juice' to make creations and if the juice is not in the person's feelings or language, then it is surely somewhere in his body" (19).

It is the communicating of being alive and just *being* rather than playing at life to which authenticity refers. In other words, a person must feel free to be angry, sad, happy, and to fully experience the complete range of living.

## Therapist Role and Techniques

A fundamental concern of Gestalt therapy is to identify "the nature of complete functioning and completed experience...which suggests an underlying question which the therapist asks both himself and the patient: 'What is the nature of complete living?' " (Levitsky & Simkin

1972, 245). Attending to this primary issue creates the basis for Gestalt therapy's method and techniques. From the point of view of the Gestalt therapist, however, techniques are simply that. They are to be viewed "merely as convenient means, useful tools for our purposes but having no sacrosanct qualities" (Levitsky & Perls 1970, 140).

Clearly then, techniques are not the focus of the therapist. Instead, what is important are the purposes that techniques serve. Thus, the emphasis of Gestalt therapy falls upon the therapist's ability to be creative, to work freely and to utilize "his prime instrument—himself" (Polster & Polster 1973, 21). Similarly, Zinker (1977, 17) has viewed Gestalt as being "Creative Therapy."

It would be a contradiction to impose upon Gestalt therapists the techniques they "should employ in therapy." However, Levitsky and Perls (1970, 140) have identified techniques that are centered around two sets of guidelines, referred to as "rules" and "games." While there are a limited number of rules, there is no definitive limit to the list of games.

Close examination indicates that these techniques are extensions of the basic concepts of Gestalt therapy, thus giving them a valid reason for existing. In addition to the basic rules discussed earlier of now, "I" language, the awareness continuum—or the *how* of experiencing, there are three additional rules: (1) I and thou, (2) no gossiping, and (3) asking questions (Levitsky & Perls 1970).

The *I and thou* rule is intended to state emphatically that communication involves two people, the sender and the receiver. Members are made aware that they arc to *be talking to* and not *talking at* the listener.

The purpose of the *no gossiping* rule is to help the members recognize their feelings. It insists that the person speak directly to an individual who is present and not about a member who is not.

The final rule, *asking questions*, is grounded in the belief that behind nearly every question is a statement. The therapist, therefore, is urged to help members recognize the difference between a manipulative type of question that is not truly seeking an answer versus questions that are genuine or legitimate ones, such as inquiring how a person may be feeling at a given moment.

The forum in which the basic techniques of Gestalt therapy are utilized is called the *experiment*. The experiment in Gestalt therapy is designed to facilitate members' effective dealing with barriers "without sacrificing the immediacy of experience" (Polster & Polster 1973, 234). The members are allowed to act out unresolved feelings in a relatively safe environment, which supports risk-taking behavior. During this period of experimenting, the therapist relies upon creative processes to select the techniques that for that moment seem to offer the most help to the individual members in dealing with unfinished business (such as anger toward another person).

As stated earlier, there are an indefinite number of "games" in Gestalt therapy. The following list illustrates only a limited sampling of the type of "games" a Gestalt therapist may employ.

## Making the Rounds

Making the rounds often functions as an ice breaker in Gestalt groups. The event that usually precipitates the use of this technique is a statement by a member that he or she does not like anyone in the group. Such an individual, in fact, may be avoiding facing feelings they are experiencing right at the moment regarding themselves. The therapist may direct members to express how they feel about each of the other members and what it is about these other members that affects them that way. By so doing, the members are *focusing* on the experience right then and there at the moment of confrontation. In this way, they are able to gain insight into their own feelings, as well as how they perceive others.

## Games of Dialogue

Earlier, we presented the theory of top-dog and under-dog. These are the dualities within individuals that tell them what they *should* do (top-dog) and that make excuses for why they did not get the job done (under-dog). This split within individuals manifests itself in a variety of ways. It is the therapist's task to identify the behavior when it occurs. At that moment, the therapist will direct members to actually engage in dialogue between these two parts of themselves. If the conflict is between a group member and a person outside the group, the individual may be instructed to engage in a dialogue between themselves and the other person by imagining the other person is actually there. The members would address the person, imagine the response they would receive, and then reply to the response. The game does not have to rely upon dialogue between persons. It can also involve various parts of the body, such as right hand versus left hand.

## The Hot Seat

Perhaps the hot seat is the technique for which Gestalt therapy is best known. The title "hot seat" is derived from a situation in which a chair is placed directly in front of and facing the therapist, who in turn invites any group members choosing to "work" to sit in the chair. The objective is to get group members to face their problems as they are presently experiencing them. They are not allowed to talk about them (intellectualize). By revealing their personal material in front of the group, there is an added intensity of *experiencing* something that cannot be discounted, thereby increasing self-awareness. Furthermore, the therapist *focuses* the members on the unfinished business by interacting with them directly. Almost appearing unmerciful at times, the therapist will aggressively confront members to deal with their problems.

Polster and Polster (1973) have developed an additional dimension to the concept of the "hot seat." They refer to it as the "floating hot seat." It is designed to take advantage of the phenomenon of universality by encouraging group members to participate spontaneously in the sharing and disclosing begun by the member who is in the "hot seat." The net result is that group member participation is increased.

### Role Reversals

The use of role reversals encourages group members to play out roles they generally suppress. Perls believes that often individuals' overt behaviors actually represent just the opposite of what are underlying tendencies. For example, members may say they do not like to get angry. Their present behaviors show them to be timid and nonassertive, and they complain people do not respect them. The therapist, in this case, may ask members to behave in just the opposite of the way they have in the past: that is, to express their anger and their feelings about not being respected. It is through risking this experience, which has been so marked by anxiety, that members come in contact with a dimension of their being that they have long suppressed.

## Group Processes

Although the Gestalt workshop group is more therapist-centered than client-centered practices, the therapist makes it immediately apparent that group members must take responsibility for their own behavior. There is less reliance, formally, upon the interactive behavior of and between members than upon the therapist for directing a member's actions. There is no prearranged plot. Instead, the therapist observes and detects the specific behaviors in which members are engaged. The therapist then points out the behaviors to the members, who can choose to work or not work. It is at this point that the therapist's creative skills are needed to select the technique that will enable members to experience the meaning of their behaviors. The therapist, relying heavily upon intuition, may choose to disregard the presence of other members momentarily, and work one-to-one with the individual whose behavior is being dealt with. Or, the therapist may choose to direct one participant to turn and work directly with each group member through the use of experiments or exercises designed to emphasize those behaviors that have been blocking the member from functioning fully.

The Gestalt therapist believes that an inextricable relationship exists between the working member and other group members. Through their identifications and projections with the working member, other members gain from observing their peers' experiences. Similarly, for the person in the "hot seat," the presence of the group provides an implied support that facilitates risk-taking. As a result, the heightened experience leads to personal growth for the individual and for the other members. The therapist is aware of this dynamic and employs it fully by helping the client to stay in the here and now by confronting individuals about incongruencies, and by pointing out ineffective ways in which they have chosen to deal with their lives.

There is no effort by the therapist to interpret "discoveries" made by group members. Interpretation is appealing to the rational side of participants and could help them avoid taking responsibility for their behavior. Instead, the therapist attempts to help members learn how to take full ownership for their actions and gain greater self-trust and self-reliance through the process of confrontation or by employing the rules or games of Gestalt therapy.

## Summary

Taking responsibility for one's self is a primary task for each member in a Gestalt therapy group. There is little reliance upon member-to-member interaction, unless it is directed by the group therapist. Usually, group members are expected to volunteer the problem they wish to work on. From that point on, the relationship is between each member and therapist. The group therapist will employ a variety of techniques to assist the member in resolving unfinished business.

As working members present unfinished business, the other members will often vicariously experience, through identification, segments of their own unfinished business. Thus, the group lends itself to being a forum for therapy, where support is provided for members to carry out their own individual experiments.

During the experimentation process, the therapist attends very carefully to members' physical as well as verbal cues. The therapist actively confronts members' incongruencies. The members are forced to communicate in the here and now. Staying in the present does not allow the participants to talk about the past or search for the "why" of their behavior. Energy is directed toward experiencing in the present. The therapist continually works to help participants accept that reality is now and that it is counterproductive to establish controls over the present to regulate the future.

Since change (like aging) is inevitable, the participant is encouraged to accept what *is* as opposed to what *should be*. As a consequence, each member will realize that nothing is permanent and that there are those things for which one can be responsible and those things for which one is not.

# CHAPTER THREE

# *Individual Psychology*

## *Background*

Alfred Adler, who like many others broke away from Sigmund Freud, developed an approach to human behavior that stresses the social aspects of living as they relate to mental health. The heavy emphasis on social involvement may seem in conflict with the term "individual psychology" until we realize that the origin of the term is German, and meant to convey the concepts of the uniqueness and indivisibility of the human organism, and not separateness or isolation from other people. In fact, one of the most persistent areas of disagreement between Adler and Freud stemmed from their beliefs about the basic motivation of people. Do sexual instincts determine social behavior, for instance, or does social interest determine sexual responses?

Adler believed that social interest is the primary force that influences not only sexual behavior but all other human behavior as well. Infants are born into a social atmosphere and become increasingly aware, as they grow and develop, that their survival demands certain kinds of social behavior, and they are, in fact, totally dependent for many years on the adults who surround them. As time passes, they devise and revise *the way* they view their worlds, and their behavioral responses are attempts at effectively coping with such interpretations. These unique views about the nature of life and its meanings both result from, and contribute to, each individual's self-appraisal, in a never-ending cycle of evaluation and interpretation.

At birth, the worldly environment seems so overwhelming to individuals that a profound feeling of inadequacy and inferiority must inevitably develop. From that day on, according to Adlerians, people become goal-oriented, both physically and psychologically. So, if, as adults, they want to know what causes them to act in a certain way, they must focus on their current objectives, rather than on some historical events. This does not mean, of course, that people always reach their objectives, or that their objectives are always productive ones. Nor does it negate the premise that their early recollections of childhood and their ordinal position within the family constellation do not affect their achievement levels. If these past experiences have been very painful, their current outlook, and therefore, their social responses, may be twisted and warped.

Since human beings tend to define self-concept in terms of their perceptions of, and comparisons with others, the most significant parts of their environment are the people who provide models for them. That is, all human behavior is socially motivated by the basic task of striving to find a satisfactory niche among fellow humans. The nature of that niche depends in turn on perceptions individuals have of those humans and of the environment in which they all function. That sought-after niche, and those perceptions, though continually in a state of some flux, acquire a basic stability that becomes the model and guide by which individuals conduct their lives.

Even so, Adler maintained that the human personality is much more than a passive recipient and responder to external influences. The outlook individuals have on life is the result of their unique and idiosyncratic *interpretation* of their environment, and two people under the same environmental influences may create substantially different interpretations. To this extent, Adler says individuals are the creators of their world view and their lifestyle, and therefore, capable of changing and developing their own destiny. For individuals who are motivated toward making productive modifications in their attitudes and behaviors, this approach is an obviously optimistic one.

The Adlerian emphasis on social interest and the necessity for harmonious social living indicates a high priority for group work, even though Adler himself wrote little about group potentialities. His death in 1937 preceded the tremendous group therapy movement that began after World War II. However, a large number of his disciples, such as Rudolph Dreikurs, Helene Papanek, Donald Dinkmeyer, and Heinz and

Rowena Ansbacher, have made substantial use of group processes in their writings and practices.

Much of Adlerian group therapy is preventive, educational, and developmental in nature, as maladjustment is usually considered to be closely related to faulty interpretations of one's environment, misguided or distorted forms of compensation for feelings of inferiority, and goals that are inappropriate to social living. Since individuals can have conscious control over all of these phenomena, the therapeutic process is largely one of cognitve examination of their attitudes, values, goals, lifestyle, and self-esteem. Emotions are viewed as tools that people create in order to reach certain social goals, and are therefore not the primary focus in Adlerian groups.

# Key Concepts

## Social Interest

Social interest connotes a feeling of identity with humanity, a sense of belongingness believed to exist innately in every human being but which needs to be developed and nurtured. The ideas of social interest, social feeling, and social cooperation, are both practical and idealistic, and both desirable and realistic.

Like most members of the animal kingdom, humans, as a species, naturally strive for self-preservation. In addition, humans have cognitive powers that encourage them beyond mere self-preservation; they want to *advance* themselves. By virtue of their intelligence, humans have a choice: they can strive for their goals in a "survival of the fittest" manner, or they can behave cooperatively in a community effort. To use the former method is both painful and destructive, and totally illusory because of its self-defeating consequences. When individuals correct the faulty thinking that leads to destructive attitudes and actions, and instead encourage the emergence of a feeling of intimate belongingness to each other, they will greatly diminish the feelings of alienation and loneliness that engulf them and lead to maladjustment and unhappiness. They will then emphasize the importance of sharing, equality, interest in others, responsibility, and cooperation.

Dreikurs (1950, 9) wrote that "the social interest has no fixed objective. Much more truly may it be said to create an attitude of life, a desire to cooperate with others in some way and to master the situations of life. Social interest is the expression of our capacity for give and take."

## Holism

The human psyche is perceived by Adlerians to be an integrated whole, and any attempts at factoring out self-contained, separate parts for study are erroneous methods of investigation. Even though human beings may often *appear* to be inconsistent and incongruent, they really are quite constant and congruent in terms of their intentions, and in terms of the behaviors they believe will lead to the fulfillment of those intentions. Because therapists as observers are by definition outside of the human psyche (or individual system), it is their lack of understanding of how that system is operating at a given point in time that causes confusion.

This holistic approach also applies to Adlerian groups. When some part of the group undergoes changes, the whole group system is forced to adjust itself in order to regain its own sense of consistency and congruency. "We consider the group an open system which is different from the sum of its units, the individual members," Helene Papanek wrote (1964, 43). Any change in the group is followed by a change in its units, the individual patients, and vice-versa; each member can influence and change the group.

## Self-Determination

Individual Psychology has a firm belief in the strength and in the creative powers of individuals to determine their own destiny. People make choices and act on those choices in accordance with their own subjectively determined goals, and they must take responsibility for their choices. While this is an awesome challenge, it also provides individuals with continuing opportunities to make new and different choices, and thus to alter the outcomes of their existence.

In a group setting, the concept of self-determination becomes very important. With such an outlook the group therapist can encourage members to examine, with the help of each other, their goals, choices, and convictions, including their origins and potential revisions. But the decisions must always remain with each member, and must be based not on past causality but rather on future goals.

## Goal Orientation

Dreikurs (1950, 11) wrote that according to Adler, all living things seek a goal. With regard to man in particular, Alfred Adler declares that it is impossible for us to understand his behavior and actions unless we know his goal. The Adlerian belief that cognitive power (as opposed to emotional power) dominates the human system, makes individuals' conscious determination of goals a priority in all therapeutic endeavvors. While past and present behaviors are necessarily goal-oriented, the *understanding* of those goals may not always be conscious. Rather, the goals may have been developed as a response to childhood experiences, and somewhat habitually continued into adulthood even though inappropriate.

Dreikurs describes two fundamental kinds of goals. The first is a *life style goal* that develops in early childhood and emanates from significant childhood experiences, primarily related to family interactions. This goal results in a general pattern of thinking and behaving whereby the individual begins to live life according to certain subjectively developed principles. Within this general pattern, the second form of goals, *situational goals,* are created and acted upon daily. Though sometimes difficult for an observer to discern, these situational goals fit somehow into the life style goal, according to the "private logics" of the individual (Dreikurs 1971, 3:52).

In an Adlerian group, identifying the goal orientation of members is an underlying task of the therapist and helps members understand both their present behavior and their future conduct. The emphasis is placed on the *purpose* that behavior serves rather than on the causes from which it developed. In other words, in order to find the causes of behavior, Adlerians look to the results of that behavior. The desire for that result (the goal) is the real cause of the behavior.

## Family Constellation

Individual Psychology puts significant emphasis on early childhood recollections as a major factor in the attitudes individuals acquire and the goals they seek. Since the family is the focal point for most such experiences, the nature of the family system and how individuals view their role in that system is pertinent to an adequate understanding of current functioning. Adlerians believe, for example, that different ordi nal positions in family births can have quite significant influences on individual development. Sibling rivalry, for the purpose of gaining parental and environmental support and approval, for example, is a common phenomenon, especially among successively born children close in age. These early family experiences, then tend to exert much influence on the manner in which life is perceived and lived by each person.

Accurate perceptions of the family constellation can be therapeutic to members of a therapy group. Becoming cognitively aware of how one is currently influenced by past relationships can help participants to resist those influences if they so choose. In addition, the group members may perceive helpful similarities between their family constellation and the group setting of which they are now a part.

## Inferiority Feelings

Born with total dependence into a world of overwhelming size and power, young children soon become aware of their relative inferiority to the environment. In order to survive, appropriate coping behaviors must be learned, which are responses derived from the way children perceive their environment. Adlerians believe that the nature and quality of such responses are largely influenced by the kind of parenting that is provided. Thus, there is a heavy emphasis on parent education. Even so, with societal reinforcement of feelings of inferiority and the general lack of parenting skills in the public domain, a large number of children grow up with feelings of inadequacy and behaviors that are highly self-defeating as responses to those feelings.

These responses are often mistaken attempts to equalize the balance of power—to prove to oneself and significant others that one is indeed not inferior, but rather *belongs* in an integral way to the social milieu. The tendency, however, is to overcompensate. "Whenever an attempt is made to compensate for an inferiority feeling, this is never done merely by actual compensation, but always leads to overcompensation." (Dreikurs 1950, 30–31).

Often, because of inadequate adult responses to such behavior in childhood, children grow up clutching the same kinds of responses that enabled them to survive an earlier age, but which are quite inappropriate in adulthood. The inferiority feelings may persist, even while feelings of equality or superiority may be communicated. These feelings of inadequacy about oneself can have harsh social consequences. "The behavior of all children and all adults establishes the general validity of the following law: The natural social interest of every human being reaches its limits when feelings of inferiority arise....As soon as an individual inferiority feeling is established, development of the social interest becomes impaired. One cannot develop a feeling of belonging if one considers oneself looked down upon" (Dreikurs 1950, 20).

The impact of this concept on Adlerian group functioning is important. Since, to some degree at least, there seems to be a universal feeling of inadequacy in people, it may be that the recognition of this common characteristic tends to act as a unifying principle for group participants. From this cohesive force, members would be encouraged to provide the mutual help that will, in fact, exhibit their social interest while also improving their self-concepts. According to Adler, these two facets are inseparable.

## Life Style

As individuals develop, they create perceptions of both themselves and the world outside. They then respond according to their unique interpretations of those perceptions. The consistent, purposeful direction of these responses defines their life style. "It is a set of ideas, schemata, and, not as in common parlance, habitual modes of behaving. Schematically, the life style may be seen as a syllogism: 'I am...' 'The world is...' 'Therefore...' And whatever the case may be, it is in terms of the proposition which follows the 'therefore' that the person thinks, feels, perceives, dreams, recollects, emotes, behaves, etc." (Allen 1971, 5).

The life style, then, evolves from a goal-oriented cognitive process and gives each individual's life some stability and consistent direction. This is true even though the person at times appears to act incongruently. In such cases, Adler believed that the observer is inadequately comprehending the individual's gestalt, not that the individual is behaving or thinking inconsistently.

It is often difficult to see one's life style clearly, whether you are that person or an observer. "As long as a person is in a favorable situation, we cannot see his style of life clearly. In new situations, however, where he is confronted with difficulties, the style of life appears clearly and distinctly" (Adler 1956, 173). Since group counseling situations tend to be strange and anxiety-producing for most people, the life style, along with its characteristic modes of behavior and attitudes, becomes readily apparent to the skilled Adlerian group leader. Because it is thoroughly ingrained from childhood, it is also very resistant to change. Nevertheless, a basic understanding of one's life style, along with group encouragement and personal motivation, can provide an individual with all the tools needed to make significant modifications.

## *Therapist Role and Techniques*

The Adlerian group therapists are both models of effective living and strategists and technicians. They are highly involved both in and with the group, and strive to be appropriately creative and spontaneous. They are free to use whatever methods seem to be in the best interests of the group's basic goal: the improvement of members' self-esteem and the simultaneous enhancement of their social interest and value. As such, the therapists' basic *attitudes* are of primary importance.

Thus, therapists must approach the group in a genuine spirit of equality and, in every way possible, encourage each group member to follow suit. They must communicate a high degree of empathy and respect, as well as honesty, openness, and congruency. Adlerian group therapists believe that their actions do indeed speak more influentially than words, but when both are employed congruently, the impact is infinitely greater. Therefore, while their attitudes, behaviors, and communication skills are basic to adequate modeling, they are usually insufficient for the therapeutic needs of the group. Other more technical and professional competencies are required as well.

Donald Dinkmeyer, W.L. Pew, and Donald Dinkmeyer, Jr. (1979) have described several such competencies. They involve an understanding of group development and processes, a comprehension of human nature and behavior from an Adlerian point of view, and the possession of a variety of specific techniques and strategies to further the goals of the group.

Initially, the group must gain structure in some way and acquire some purposes for its existence. Adlerian therapists usually take a substantial amount of responsibility for encouraging the development of a structure that they believe will facilitate the attainment of the group's goals. These goals may be more specific than improvement of self-esteem and enhancement of social interest, but these more basic goals are always kept in mind and never knowingly violated. Within this broad framework, therapists often allow group members to determine sub-goals that are meaningful to the members. In both cases, therapists help members attain a facilitative structure and meaningful goals by both showing and telling them facilitative aspects of the communication process and encouraging them to act likewise. They may use verbal and non-verbal exercises to accomplish this, or they may wish to utilize the natural unfolding of the group's interaction to point out helpful approaches, behaviors, and responses.

Since social interest is a primary focus of Adlerian groups, the therapists' early role must also stress the building of positive relationships between the therapist and members, and among members themselves. The therapist tries to help the participants identify their human similarities and develop a cohesive bond that will encourage the open sharing of life styles, feelings, and individual goals, as well as development of the skills and courage necessary to give helpful feedback.

While Adlerian group therapists do not have a specific methodology common to all Adlerians and are therefore free to be spontaneous and creative, their responses must be preceded by certain learned skills and abilities, such as thematic listening and behavioral interpretation. In addition, they must be able to confront individuals emphatically, head off destructive elements, recognize and focus on group assets and positive feedback, paraphrase and clarify issues, and summarize group content and processes. They must also be astute observers and interpreters of nonverbal behavior and adequate diagnosticians. Belief in the holistic and goal-oriented purposes of all behavior, and in the human ability and necessity of self-determination and decision-making, guides therapists in their verbal and cognitive interventions.

## *Group Processes*

The Adlerian philosophy, dominated as it is by concepts such as social interest, life style, goal orientation, holism, human worth and dignity, and self-determination, mandates the development of certain group processes. Such groups must be expected to stress the development of a social climate wherein social interest could be positively expressed. But Adler also believed that while social interest is inherent and innate in all of us, it needs to be environmentally nurtured or it may remain forever dormant. Thus, the initial thrust of an Adlerian group is not only to develop a structure conducive to such nurturing but to help, in every way possible, the participants to experience their innate interests in social cooperation. This may be accomplished through didactic instruction, group exercises, or the therapist's interpretations to the group of their own interactive behaviors; often, some unique combination of all of these methods is utilized.

Since many individuals have learned faulty behaviors and made faulty assumptions about themselves and the world as a result of early childhood and family experiences, an adequate feeling of self-esteem and social interest cannot be expected at the start of a group. In the process of developing that self-esteem and social interest, each participant's current style of life will eventually emerge amid the interaction, and becomes important resource material for subsequent sessions. As group cohesion is developed, members will begin to take more and more risks, in accordance with the model set by the therapist. Honest and caring feedback results. "The whole process can be described as a cycle that is being set in motion and in which (a) perceptions and beliefs change, (b) courage and belonging enable one to try on new behaviors, (c) involvement and risking are rewarded by acceptance and belonging, (d) fear of making a mistake is replaced by the courage to be imperfect, which reduces anxiety and insecurity, and (e) as self-esteem and feeling of worth develop, the person is able to try additional change" (Dinkmeyer et al. 1979, 141).

The social interest that is deliberately developed in the group is the sine qua non (the essential factor) around which the group becomes and remains therapeutic. Feelings of belongingness, acceptance, support, and worthiness are basic to action; before individuals can adequately test out the reality of old and new behavior, they must feel a basic sense of security and self-esteem.

Adlerian group members are continually urged to investigate the meanings of behaviors, to become aware of their own motivations and to guess at the motivations of others. Such investigations bring some insights, which can then be tested, either within the group or with group support. "There are four phases to Adlerian Group Counseling: (1) the establishment and maintenance of an appropriate counseling relationship; (2) psychological investigation or analysis; (3) insight; (4) reorientation of goals." (Hansen, Warner & Smith 1976, 59).

While Adlerian group therapists are free to create their own evaluative instruments to assess the progress of group participants, much of the assessment is subjective and pragmatic. Adler contended that significant progress occurs as each participant continues to gain more self-confidence and simultaneously reaches out to help others. These goals represent the self-esteem and social interest concerns of the Adlerian viewpoint. Group feedback to each member, and the results of each member's "reality-testing" efforts both within and outside the group, help to provide the validation by which both individual and group progress can be assessed.

## *Summary*

Like many other approaches to group counseling, the relationships of the group members to each other, and of each to the therapist, are highly significant in Individual Psychology. For some participants, a strong attachment to the group is enough to stimulate both their thought processes and desired behavioral changes; for others, additional activities are necessary, and the leader may incorporate didactic instruction, group exercises, and specific homework assignments into the process.

It is the end result that is important, not the particular methodology utilized. This does not mean that "anything goes," but that it is the basic and general *attitude* of group therapists that is crucial. Therapists must be a model for behavior that is to be encouraged by the participants—models of positive self-esteem and of social interest and social caring. *How* they behave when they present themselves is much more important than *what* they specifically do.

Initially, the group therapists must somehow try to influence the direction of the group toward a cooperative, caring social climate that acts as both its own reward and as the basis for risk-taking and reality-testing for the participants. During this continuous process, the material focuses primarily on the goals and life styles of the participants, with the aim of acquiring insights and understandings that will stimulate productive actions. These actions may result in the modification either of goals or of some aspect of a self-defeating life style.

While group therapists may use special techniques, such as group exercises, to help them accomplish their goals, Adlerian principles stress the cognitive domain as the controlling force in life. Early and continuously as individuals develop, they intellectually interpret their environment and cognitively create a life style designed to further their goals. In the process, their emotions become tools with which to further these goals, and are thus generated in line with their intentions. Such often heard comments as "I can't help it; that's the way I feel," would likely be challenged in an Adlerian group, possibly with a didactic explanation such as "Emotions cannot make one do something that one does not want to do." This lack of emphasis on the basic significance of emotions, in and of themselves, is a major distinguishing difference between Adlerian group therapy and many other common approaches.

# CHAPTER FOUR

# Rational-Emotive Therapy

## Background

In the mid-1950s, Albert Ellis formulated a new approach to personality change, which he termed Rational-Emotive Therapy (RET). Trained in psychoanalytic procedures, Ellis had become increasingly disenchanted with the inefficiency and general ineffectiveness of psychoanalysis, and began searching for a more efficient and helpful approach. RET was an outgrowth of this search and the result of his previous training, his clinical experiences, and his logical and scientific thinking.

According to this approach, people have an innate tendency to pursue happiness and pleasure, but also a strong predisposition to engage in self-defeating behaviors. The words "tendency" and "predisposition" are significant in that they do not represent a deterministic philosophy. Rather, they indicate that while we may be pulled in these directions by our biological inheritance, it is possible—with desire and hard work—to overcome such psychological gravity. So it is that some people seem passively to accept an existence of unhappiness and pain, while others are motivated to overcome their self-defeating tendencies and to behave primarily in self-enhancing ways.

Whichever choice is made though, it is reached through a highly cognitive process whereby individuals *condition themselves* to think and act and emote according to their idiosyncratic belief systems. That is, whatever individuals *believe* to be true about a certain event or condition governs their emotional reaction to that situation. Such beliefs may in fact be rational, that is, reality-based and provable, or irrational, fantasized and unprovable.

Because our goals tend to be rational, but our means of achieving them often irrational and self-defeating, we become frustrated and inappropriately emotional when presented with such a situation. That is, not only do we become frustrated about a given situation, but we overreact and become frustrated about our frustration, eventually engaging in what Ellis terms "awfulizing" behavior. We blow things way out of proportion; we tell ourselves we "just can't take anymore." At this point we become emotionally disturbed, not because of what others have done to us, or because the situation is truly horrendous, but because we have talked ourselves into such a state that we have become emotionally immobilized.

It is this self-talk (a cognitive process) that Ellis sees as the culprit when it is insane and irrational, but as the antidote when it is sane and rational. That is, since people talk themselves *into* emotional disturbances, they can also talk themselves *out* of them. However, since we have a strong predisposition to think crookedly and to create our own misery, the antidote is often most effectively applied with outside help.

This help can be given in the form of group activities, and RET practitioners are often quite involved in leading such groups. Ellis has described four kinds of groups available to RET participants: family groups, regular weekly group therapy sessions, marathon sessions, and workshops (1974, 17). While the format may vary in each of these settings, the basic principles of RET remain the unifying force. These principles stress that "significant personality changes...come about when the individual clearly sees, acknowledges, and works very hard at surrendering or minimizing his peurile demandingness...." (Ellis 1974, 15). In a very real sense, that often means a radical change in an individual's philosophy about life itself, as what was once "terrible" now becomes "inconvenient," and what was once "intolerable" now becomes "unpleasant."

Thus, as situations are perceived in less upsetting ways, and with less upsetting words, the individual perceiving the situations becomes correspondingly less upset. Then, as this new perception of life pervades more and more of one's life situations, it becomes a permanent fixture in the individual's life, resulting in basic personality change.

As noted, earlier, however, the tendency toward self-defeating behavior is strong and not easily overcome. In addition to this biological predisposition, cultural and educational influences can likewise encourage unhealthy beliefs, feelings, and actions. These influences too often foster and model irrational ideas and belief systems, especially in the immature young child who is understandably quite gullible and suggestible. Once these ideas take hold, they become very resistant to change because our natural tendency is to reindoctrinate ourselves with these ideas as we grow older. And, even if we *do* modify our philosophies and our irrational belief systems at a cognitive and emotive level, behavioral change can be exceedingly difficult. Therefore, homework assignments are commmonly given in RET, so that a congruence will emerge between the thinking and feeling processes, and behavioral activities.

The general goal of this cognitive–emotive–behavioral approach to philosophical reorientation and personality change is "to internalize a rational philosophy of life just as he [the client] originally learned and internalized the irrational views of his parents and his community" (Ellis 1962, 95). More specifically, this means creating a way of life that affords us a reasonable degree of happiness and enjoyment. The RET therapist thus tries to help clients accept and accomplish the following objectives (Ellis 1979, 54–57):

1. A healthy outlook toward *oneself*. Ellis uses the terms self-acceptance, self-interest, and self-direction. According to his view, people open themselves up to irrational conclusions when they rate their self-worth according to their earthly achievements. People are worthy because they are alive; and because they are unique and separate individuals, they are interested primarily in themselves. Rational thinking would, therefore, induce them to take responsibility for the direction of their own lives.

2. A healthy outlook toward *others*. Even though rational people are basically self-oriented, there is also a strong predisposition to live in a group atmosphere. Therefore, if people completely ignore others' self-interests, irresolvable conflicts are likely to arise, some of which will result in a defeat of *our own* self-interests. Some degree of help and cooperation with others is therefore in our best interests—healthy and rational. This often calls for an attitude of tolerance and flexibility whereby we accept others' rights and behaviors precisely because we accept our own. We allow both others and ourselves the leeway to make mistakes and to learn from them, and we do not insist on such rigid rules that we become immobilized and self-defeating.

3. A healthy outlook toward *reality*. There are few guarantees in life. We live in an uncertain world, full of both tragedy and pleasure, much of it not under our control. Mature and healthy people accept this reality—and make the best of it by choosing to view life as adventure-

some and creative rather than as fearsome and routine. These individuals know that risk taking is a part of life and that mistakes sometimes result. Yet this does not deter them; in fact, it spurs them forward. They attack life and thereby control what they can, instead of letting life attack them and thereby controlling very little.

4. A healthy outlook toward the *future*. Emotionally and rationally secure people are committed to life and to the preservation of happiness. They are absorbed in daily living and are optimistic about their future. At the same time, they are aware that life is a struggle, sometimes requiring exhaustive work and striving just to stay even. Since they are both optimistic and realistic, they do not have expectations that are impossible to attain, but they do recognize the possible rewards of diligence and commitment. Thus, they are able to act objectively, rationally, and systematically when this behavior is called for. They do not negate their emotions, but tend to exhibit control over them when they are appropriate to the situation.

# Key Concepts

## A-B-C-D-E Construct

This construct is Rational-Emotive Therapy's best-known and most basic precept. The letters A through E represent both a theory of human behavior and personality change and a basic cognitive method of clinical practice. The first letter, A, symbolizes an *Activating Event* or *Experience* of some significant stimulus that triggers an emotional reaction or *Consequence* (represented by letter C).

According to RET, it is inaccurate to say that A *causes* C because it is unlikely that everyone would react the same way to that activating event. Rather, it must be how a given individual *perceives* A that causes a specific reaction. That is, what a person *believes* about the occurrence of A is really what causes C. This *belief* is represented by the letter B. When this belief system is based on irrational and unprovable ideas and thoughts on a given subject, it can lead to inappropriate and dysfunctional emotions and behaviors.

When this happens, RET therapists must help their group members to actively and forcefully *Dispute* (D) these irrational beliefs about A. The therapist accomplishes this by: (1) vigorously challenging the client to prove the validity of those beliefs, (2) serving as a model for other group members to do the same for each other, and (3) teaching members how to challenge their own belief system to help sort out facts from unrealistic hypotheses.

This disputing process will eventually lead to a new and more realistic understanding of one's self-defeating tendencies and behaviors, and will result in new cognitive insights that represent the *Effects* (E) of this disputation.

## Homework

Assignments for work done outside the counseling session are common in RET. These assignments may be cognitive, emotive, behavioral, or a combination of these. For example, group members may be asked to utilize the Self-Help Report Form that helps them to go through the A-B-C-D-E cognitive process described earlier; they may then be asked to explain how they used this process to help themselves when the group reconvenes the following session.

Or members may be assigned an emotive task such as rational-emotive imagery. This kind of assignment may first be practiced in the group with the expectation that further practice be tried between sessions. This technique might involve closing one's eyes and imagining oneself encountering an emotional situation, and then consciously working at changing the original inappropriate feelings to more appropriate ones that befit the situation.

The therapist may also recommend a behavioral assignment. For example, the therapist may suggest that the member perform an observable action outside the session, such as a shy member initiating a conversation with intimates, acquaintances, or strangers, determined by the individual's idiosyncratic problem area.

In theory, there is no limit to the amounts and kinds of homework that can be given to group members. Assignments outside of the group are important in helping irrational ideas, inappropriate emotions, and self-defeating behaviors that may be temporarily changed during the group sessions and become more permanent through the reinforcement of continuous and successful practice outside the group setting.

## Three Basic "Musts"

In some of Ellis's early writings, he listed numerous irrational beliefs that led in varying ways to emotional disturbances. These have more recently been consolidated into three basic "musts" with which individuals indoctrinate themselves (Ellis & Whitely 1979, 46). These are:

(1) "I *must* (or *should* or *ought*) perform well and/or be approved by significant others. It is *awful* (or *horrible* or *terrible*) if I don't! I can't *Stand it*. I am a pretty *rotten* person when I fail in this respect!" (2) "You *must* treat me considerately and fairly. It is horrible if you don't! When you fail me, you are a bad individual, and I can't bear you and your crummy behavior!" (3) "Conditions *must* be the way I want them to be, and it is *terrible* when they are not! I *can't stand* living in such an awful world. It is an utterly abominable place!"

According to Ellis, it is this childish and unrealistic demandingness—this *must*abatory thinking—that is at the root of virtually every emotional disturbance. Obviously, these three "musts" have many derivatives and subcategories with which the group leader and group members may work.

## Rationality/Irrationality

Rational-Emotive Therapy defines "rationality" essentially as goal-enhancing behavior, and "irrationality" as goal-defeating behavior. More specifically, "the term *rational,* as used in RET, refers to people's (1) setting up or choosing for themselves certain basic values, purposes, goals, or ideals, and then (2) using efficient, flexible, scientific logico-empirical ways of attempting to achieve such values and goals and to avoid contradictory or self-defeating results" (Ellis & Whiteley 1979, 40).

It is significant to note that these goals are not chosen by the therapist, but rather by the members themselves. The degree of rationality is then determined by the extent to which group members' behaviors move them most effectively and efficiently in the direction they want to go. Even so, at the most basic "want" level, Ellis sees almost universal similarities among people, even though their specific goals may differ greatly. That is, most people desire to live a long life, to engage in some form of intimacy with others, to be socially productive, to become involved in some forms of recreational activities, and to be generally happy in all the above pursuits.

Rational thinking, emoting, and behaving, then, represent a process through which such pursuits can be attained, while irrational behaviors, thoughts, and emotions lead to a defeat of such pursuits. The practice of RET emphasizes the use of scientific methodological thinking to challenge those belief systems that lead to goal-defeating results. "The essence of the scientific method is exactly this: to set up a series of hypotheses, to see what results they lead to, and then to debate or challenge these hypotheses if the results seem to bee poor" (Ellis & Whiteley 1979, 69).

## Hedonism

As mentioned above, nearly all humans are basically hedonistic; that is, they seek pleasure and happiness. Unfortunately, however, there are often occasions when they have to choose between short-term pleasure and long-term happiness. RET perceives most people as striving for long-term happiness; but many of these people seem to *demand* short-term pleasure as well. When these goals are incompatible, the end result can only be varying degrees of frustration, often culminating in irrational behavior and inappropriate emoting.

If individuals consciously choose short-term pleasure in a given circumstance and are willing to take the probable long-term consequences without whining and moaning, then their behavior and thinking may well be termed rational. However, the desire to attain both long-range happiness and short-range pleasure is very strong, and although our basic values usually favor the long-term principle, our behavior leans toward the short-term.

According to Ellis, the low frustration tolerance that is often at the root of this self-defeating behavior inhibits people from reaching their long-range goals. This desire to avoid immediate pain and discomfort comes from our wishes to take the easiest way out, which may well have its basis in our biological predisposition toward self-defeating behavior. And this is why people must be vigorously challenged, and taught to challenge themselves and each other, to overcome their various forms of irrationality. Individuals can in this way work to change their philosophy and emotional states as well as their behavior, so that this tendency to defeat themselves will be intensely combatted on all fronts.

## Therapist Role and Techniques

The therapist's role in RET groups, is active, directive, and authoritative; there is little question as to who is in charge. In varying ways and at different times, the therapist acts as teacher, catalyst, confronter, efficiency expert, model, observer, and scientist. She or he must have a great deal of common sense, understand and be able to use the principles of logic and of human behavior, be well-versed in the RET approach, and be unafraid of debating, disputing, confronting, and challenging group members. The therapists' attitudes must reflect an unconditional acceptance of each and every member and a willingness to communicate respect by being open, honest, straightforward, and genuine in relationships with the group. Yet relationship-building is only a means to an end, a way for therapists to get their foot in the door, a way of showing their care so that group members will open themselves up to the therapists' influence, which comes in the form of interventions, interruptions, and modeling. The real therapeutic value lies in the technique through which group members learn to challenge their irrational assumptions and beliefs, and to engage in alternative behaviors that are goal-enhancing rather than goal-defeating.

RET breaks down these techniques or methods into three rather distinct classifications—cognitive, emotive, and behavioral. The cognitive methods used in RET most distinguish it from other forms of therapy. Ellis has written that "all told, RET therapists tend to use perhaps 40 or 50 regular techniques and theoretically, cognitive-oriented therapists have a dozen or more major procedures at their disposal" (Ellis & Whiteley 1979, 66–67). When broken down into sub-categories and specific treatment forms, more than 200 types of interventions could be labeled "cognitive." And, since RET is highly eclectic, pragmatic, and individualistically oriented, therapists and group leaders are free to create and experiment with techniques, as long as they remain generally consistent with the basic theoretical and philosophic outlook of RET.

The most fundamental cognitive method stems from the A-B-C-D-E construct discussed earlier. Through this technique, group members are taught how to challenge and dispute their irrational beliefs and assumptions. The therapists, of course, are the primary teachers and may engage in some very didactic activities in so doing. In addition, the therapists may work one-on-one with some or all group members and, in the process, model what they want members to learn. Then, as members begin to challenge and dispute themselves and each other, the therapists act as supervisors to this process.

Often some form of cognitive homework is given to specific group members, as deemed appropriate. In an effort to help members gain greater understanding of the constructs they are learning, such homework may include the use of books, recordings, and films, or it may be a creative endeavor that addresses the idiosyncratic situation of each of the members. One of the more common and formal methods involves the "DIBS" technique (Disputing Irrational Beliefs), in which members work on one particular irrational belief at a time and learn how to dispute it. Then, they continue such disputing—a few minutes a day, over several weeks, for example—at home, until the message is sufficiently internalized.

Other cognitive techniques favored by Ellis include the use of mental imagery, bibliotherapy, and teaching as learning. All of these can be employed in numerous ways in group counseling. Since our minds are involved in the creation of illogical assumptions, the use of imagery to block out these self-defeating thoughts and pictures by creating or strengthening more self-enhancing ones is often highly useful. Bibliotherapy as a cognitive tool is often used to help group members gain a deeper understanding of the cognitive concepts they are learning about through reading relevant books and articles. Another technique, teaching as learning, can be most useful in a group setting. As indicated above, one of the goals of RET is to teach the group members to help each other so that, in the process, members will learn how to help themselves more effectively and efficiently.

RET uses several emotive techniques designed to elicit feelings among group members. Perhaps the most basic, though ambiguous, technique is that of unconditional acceptance. This, of course, is an attitude that must be conveyed to members at a feeling level; to merely say it does not communicate it. The therapists must be able to separate persons from their behaviors, to accept individuals totally precisely because they are human, while still being able to attack the irrational beliefs that are causing individuals problems.

Role playing is another technique that can be used to evoke feelings. The therapist (or any member) may suggest such an activity in order to give members some corrective practice before they go out and try it on their own. The ways in which role playing can be effectively utilized are limited only by the creativity of the group participants.

The process of therapist modeling can also be highly effective in producing a feeling of fairness and congruence. Asking members to accomplish what their therapists are unable or unwilling to do is seldom therapeutic. But when therapists show that they can and do effectively use those principles they have espoused, it encourages members to work even harder and more productively.

Sometimes emotions can be stirred by suggesting that a member make new self-statements that are more rational. Or, the emotional intensity of old but basically rational self-statements can be increased by challenging the process the member(s) used to arrive at such self-statements. By making these statements more affective, they appear more believable and can be more easily internalized. In a similar vein, verbalizing self-statements in a less affective manner decreases their believability and internalization.

Imagery is used as both a cognitive technique and an emotive one. By asking members to create in their minds a very emotional picture, the participant can develop a highly emotional state which the therapist can then work with in the immediate moment. In addition, members can be taught to bring themselves to such a state so that they might practice gaining control of these emotions.

Finally, Ellis has developed shame-attacking exercises whereby members are assigned tasks, to be performed either in or outside the group, to combat feelings of shame and humiliation that often accompany other feelings of inadequacy, and serve only needlessly to heighten their anxieties. Members are asked to do something ridiculous or shameful, and to then evaluate the results—which are inevitably less horrifying than they had been telling themselves. Thus, members learn to put themselves into a more rational perspective, to laugh at themselves, to take themselves less seriously, and thereby to decrease their anxieties and disturbances.

The behavioral techniques of RET represent the third mode of therapist influence. Even if the cognitive and emotive methods are working well, the forces against rationality are so strong that individuals will likely revert back to old illogical behavior—unless they are induced to frequently practice the new behavior.

Most of the methods common to behavior therapy are useful in RET. Often they are given in the form of work outside the group, after having been initiated and practiced in the safer atmosphere of the group; for it is unlikely that permanent change will occur otherwise. The suggested behaviors are always put into a cognitive framework, usually involving the RET concepts of irrationality, demandingness, and *must*abatory thinking. What is likely to work, and for whom, is usually the criterion for the use of behavioral techniques. As with the cognitive methods, the number of possible assignments is virtually limitless.

However, since some of these assignments can be quite uncomfortable and frightening, the use of operant conditioning is sometimes employed. The principle behind this technique suggests that in order for a desired or learned behavior to continue to occur, it must be followed by a satisfactory experience. RET therapists, therefore, encourage members whose anxieties make assignments difficult to carry out to reward themselves—*after* they have carried out their specified tasks. And if further encouragement is needed, some equally distasteful punishments can be effected if their tasks are not completed within a specified time.

## Group Processes

As mentioned earlier, Ellis has described four types of groups that RET theorists utilize: workshops, family groups, marathons, and general weekly sessions. While there are obviously some procedural variations that result from differences in makeup and structure, the general principles of RET encompass them all. We will examine the latter two groups, with an emphasis on general weekly sessions, since they correspond most closely to the groups discussed in this book.

While there is no set procedure that every RET group therapist must use, it is fair to assume that the therapists will be quite active and directive from the beginning. For example, after a general welcome and basic orientation at the beginning of the first session, therapists ask members to introduce themselves and to state their goals. Follow-up questions are asked, with ever-increasing challenges toward more personalized and risking information. For marathon sessions, Ellis (Burton 1970, 112–27) has suggested asking questions such as "What bothers you most right now?" or "What are you most ashamed of at present?" or "Think of something risky you can do at this moment and do it."

RET therapists do not necessarily wait for volunteers to respond. They may call upon particular individuals or ask silent ones why they did not speak or act. For those who seem shy or ashamed or embarrassed, this may signal the need for some shame-attacking exercises at a later time.

The point is that therapists do not usually sit silently by and allow the group to grope and drift while searching for something meaningful to talk about. Instead they are likely to direct and structure the process in an effort to make the group as therapeutic and efficient as possible. If the therapists feel that relationship-building activities or exercises are warranted, they will suggest them—knowing that the most significant therapy will occur when the members start dealing with their irrational thoughts and behaviors.

During these early hours of therapy, the questions and activities initiated by the therapists encourage interaction among the members. However, the therapists are usually careful to limit any given transaction to a few minutes in order neither to allow anyone to monopolize the group nor to forget the main purpose of the group, which is to attack irrationality and to replace it with goal-enhancing thoughts and behaviors. During these early moments, group members learn many things about each other that are useful in the more meaningful activities that occur later on.

Thus, while the therapist is usually quite active in *structuring* group activities, these activities are designed to encourage group interaction. In order to utilize the principles of RET on each other's behalfs, group members must learn these principles first. The therapist can help members accomplish this task by assigning outside reading, films, demonstrations, and through didactic instructions and modeling. As has been suggested earlier, *how* individual RET therapists accomplish this task is much less important than *that* they accomplish it.

Whatever methods or combinations of methods the therapists choose to aid the members' awareness of the RET approach, it is inevitable that they will model its use within the group. As members learn through cognition, observation, and experiences, they are encouraged to use these RET principles with each other. This peer assistance often arises spontaneously; if it does not, therapists can initiate activities to stimulate it. For example, a therapist might ask a member to specify someone in the group in need of help, and to join that member in the center of the group by applying RET helping principles in a one-to-one confrontation. If or when the pair begins to stumble, the therapist can ask other group members to help out.

In such situations, therapists maintain control over the process and act as supervisors to the helpers. When members' attempts at helping become ineffective or inefficient, the therapist can interrupt, intervene, and influence the process and direction of the interactions. Such interventions are necessary precisely because the group *helpers* are, at any given moment, subject to the same irrational beliefs, and inappropriate emotions and behaving, as those they are trying to help. Thus, out of ignorance or misapplication of principles or unrecognized self-defeating thoughts, group members can sometimes lead each other astray, even while their intentions are quite the opposite. As they practice and gain experience session after session, their ability to help can be expected to improve considerably. This allows the therapists to become less directly active as therapist and more indirectly active as teachers, reinforcers, and monitors of the helping process.

As mentioned earlier, assigning homework activities is common in RET groups. Members are encouraged to create and suggest such assignments for their peers. Usually the therapist discusses with the members appropriate kinds of homework. Correction or discussion of homework also occurs in subsequent sessions. Weekly RET sessions usually last from 2 to 2-½ hours. The percentage of time spent discussing, correcting, and suggesting homework assignments will vary considerably, according to the members' stage of development.

## Summary

People are born with strong tendencies toward both rational, self-*enhancing* behavior and thought processes, and irrational, self-*defeating* behavior and thought processes. Humans' wishes, desires, and goals tend to be pleasure-oriented and rational but their means of achieving them often takes them further away from those goals. We are often impatient and unwilling to endure short-term discomfort in order to gain long-term happiness. Believing we can always have both is an unreasonable and unrealistic belief, but one that is often reinforced through our culture and educational process.

To desire complete and everlasting joy and happiness is not irrational; it is merely human. However, to expect and *demand* such a perpetual outcome is not only irrational, it can lead to tremendous emotional trouble and inappropriate behavior when that demand is not fulfilled. This childish demandingness arises out of a self-defeating belief system that RET seeks to challenge.

Ellis has recently categorized 12 irrational ideas, which he believes to be the basis for nearly all emotional disturbances, into three major *musts:* (1) I must be totally competent and approved of; (2) others must treat me fairly or they are bad people; (3) living conditions must be the way I want them to be. These demands and their derivatives and corollaries set the stage for such immobilizing feelings as hate, depression, anxiety, and guilt. And, since these feelings are largely nonproductive, people commonly feel guilty about feeling guilty, depressed about feeling depressed, and so on. In other words, we continually reindoctrinate ourselves with our own irrational thoughts, feelings, and behaviors.

RET approaches this problem at all three levels but emphasizes cognition. Thus, the irrational beliefs of an individual are recognized, challenged, and attacked in a logical, scientific manner. Rather than accepting the common argument that a certain experience or event *causes* an emotional reaction, the RET practitioner would try to persuade an individual that the event was only a catalyst that awakened an irrational belief *about* the event. It is that belief that truly causes the emotional reaction; thus, that belief must be challenged and seen for what it is, if the reaction is to subside and change. In this way, RET promotes a whole new outlook on life, a new approach to emotional dysfunctioning, and a new philosophy for everyday living.

In an RET group, members learn how to help each other through this rational, emotive approach. They learn to recognize irrational ideas and to connect them to dysfunctional emotions and inappropriate behaviors. Group therapists are usually quite active in structuring and directing group interactions and activities in the most effective and efficient manner. Their methods of teaching the approach may vary according to style, but the members must learn the A-B-C-D-E model if the group is to be minimally effective.

The use of homework assignments is also part of the RET group process. These assignments are created by members and the therapist to fit the particular needs of each individual, and may be cognitive, emotive, or behavioral. In this way, the RET approach is very eclectic and quite pragmatic, utilizing its own specific theory of personality change, but also using methods often associated with many other approaches.

# CHAPTER FIVE

# Reality Therapy

## Background

The principal proponent and founder of Reality Therapy is William Glasser. A psychiatrist, Glasser took issue with the basic concepts of psychoanalytic counseling and, in fact, outlined in 1965 six primary ways in which his approach to therapy differed from traditional therapy. Much like other systems of psychotherapy, Reality Therapy was born out of individual therapy, with its principles later applied to group situations.

Reality Therapy has a very rational appeal, and no small wonder that it should. It avoids dealing with history, feelings, and attitudes; instead, it deals directly with behaviors. It emphasizes what is happening in the present and demands that group members learn how to take responsibility for their actions. There is a great emphasis on the teacher-learner, or pedagogical, relationship that exists between group member and therapist. The primary objective of Reality Therapy is to *teach* members to behave in responsible ways. The ultimate consequence of such action, it is believed, leads to successful living.

# *Key Concepts*

The fundamental premise underlying Reality Therapy is that people who suffer personal, psychological, or irrational problems have not adequately met their basic needs. These fundamental needs are to love, to be loved, and to feel worthwhile. Glasser believes that a person who is in need of help has *chosen inappropriate ways* to satisfy their needs. The consequence of this leads to symptoms that reflect the degree to which these needs are not met. Conversely, as needs are satisfied through appropriate behaviors, the tension they created is reduced.

## Involvement

Involvement represents a crucial component to Reality Therapy. It is, according to Glasser (1965, 26) a process whereby a client or member finds another "person with whom he can become emotionally involved, someone he can care about and who he can be convinced cares about him. . . . " This relationship with at least one other person represents the process by which love needs are met. Without this significant person, one's basic needs will not be fulfilled. It is very important that this other person be in touch with reality and be able to fulfill his or her own needs within the world.

According to Glasser, learning to fulfill one's needs appropriately begins in early infancy. "A person who does not learn as a little child to give and receive love may spend the rest of his life unsuccessfully trying to love" (1965, 13). For Glasser, love is synonymous with involvement. The extent to which individuals involve themselves in loving ways with others is a reflection of the degree to which their need for love is fulfilled. Generally, individuals who become involved with others will be successful, while those who remain uninvolved will feel alienated, and experience anguish, and will see themselves as unsuccessful or as *failures.*

## Feeling Worthwhile

Just as significant as giving and receiving love is the need to feel *worthwhile.* Individuals who hold themselves as being worthy believe that what they do with their life is worthwhile and that their very existence does make the difference. This is an inner-care belief system that is projected behaviorally in actions that reflect self-respect. It is not the stereotypical, conceited, egotistical, or narcissistic self-involvement that is referred to here. In fact, it is just the opposite. Persons whose needs are filled in regard to their own self-worth will generally be capable of extending respect toward others and engaging in loving relationships.

According to Glasser, the key to gaining self-worth is to abide by the norms of society. For example, behavior that reflects meeting the standards of morality, and expectations of others' productive work, are the means by which the needs for self-worth and love are met.

Glasser contends that both needs must be met in order for a person to be free from others. Individuals can have strong feelings of self-worth, but not have their love need fulfilled. This would mean they would still be in pain and discomfort. In essence, the two needs (love and worthiness), though independent of each other, must both be fulfilled if individuals are to function free of anguish.

## Responsibility

A critical factor in meeting the basic needs of individuals is *responsibility*. Glasser believes that it plays a significant role in personality development, and that it is the parents' task to demonstrate to their children how to be responsible. By so doing, children will develop their own sense of self-worth. This ultimately leads to what Glasser refers to as "success identity." It results from learning effective ways to satisfy basic needs. The parents of such children not only allowed their offspring to experience activities on their own, they demonstrated love and care through disciplining their children; teaching them right from wrong, and in effect, providing them with appropriate role models. This form of involvement helps to develop *success identity*.

Conversely, a child's feelings of being unloved and unworthy leads to irresponsible behavior and creates a *failure identity*. Parents of children who have developed a failure identity have acted irresponsibly themselves because they have not become involved with their children. Perhaps they choose the "easy way out" when faced with disciplining their children. They tended to "give in" to their children's every wish, rather than taking stands that may not have immediately pleased their children. Individuals with failure identities manifest them in a variety of unrealistic ways in an effort to reduce their pain or discomfort. These behaviors range from emotional disturbances, such as mild depression, to full blown psychotic episodes. They may take the form of behavior problems that are antisocial (such as alcoholism, drug abuse, and the like) and physical responses manifested as illness (such as ulcers, hypertension, headaches, backaches).

## Denial

Glasser refers to such behaviors or symptoms as *denial*. It is believed that while these symptoms may hold validity for the group member, they are, in fact, excuses for not facing reality of the individual's situation. Responsible and involved behavior would not lead to these conditions, or, at the very least, would allow a person with a success identity to face these afflictions responsibly and not use them as excuses for behaving irresponsibly.

Reality Therapy draws its name from its effort to help group members quit *denying* the reality of their world and to help them realize that they must learn to meet their needs within the norms of society. However, therapy extends beyond helping the group members to accept the reality of their environment. It helps them learn behaviors that will enable them to fulfill their needs in the real world, thereby reducing stress. The objective of therapy is to get group members to eliminate established but inappropriate coping behaviors from their responses and add new, more effective ones.

# Therapist Role and Techniques

We must preface this section by stating that it is peculiar to Reality Therapy that group leader's role and therapist techniques are synonymous with group process. Glasser has identified seven developmental stages of therapy. These same stages are reflective of the roles and techniques that the therapist must employ in order to facilitate members' growth to responsible living. Consequently, the therapist's role, group techniques, and group processes will be presented simultaneously.

In order to be effective, the therapist must employ these techniques in a developmental sequence. To ignore them is to doom the therapeutic process to failure.

# Group Processes

## Stage 1—Therapist Involvement

The most significant ingredient in Reality Therapy for the therapist is to develop a warm, intimate, and emotional relationship with each group member. It is the lack of such involvement with another person that has brought the group member to seek help. This is the most difficult and trying period in therapy. The therapist must demonstrate his or her emotional regard for group members and be willing to suffer through their difficulties with them. The objective is to get each of the members to move away from self-involvement and self-focus to involvement with another.

Members are encouraged to trust that someone does care about them and feel they are important. The therapist helps members accomplish this by acknowledging that whatever feelings or thoughts individual members choose to disclose are significant and of interest to the therapist. Two things are accomplished in this process. First, members feel validated through involvement with significant others, and, second, through modeling, the therapist demonstrates to other group members the way to move outside of self-involvement to involvement with another. It is the immediacy of this interaction between group member and therapist that allows the member to experience involvement with another in a warm, accepting, and nonpunitive atmosphere. Conditions are present to maximize the chance for success in developing responsible behavior. By so doing, the member is given the opportunity to develop a sense of self-worth.

## Stage 2—Focus on Present Behavior

Reality Therapy holds little value in delving into history. While it may make for an interesting story line, it provides excuses for members to avoid taking responsibility for their present situation. Instead, the therapist works to get the members to focus on their present behavior. The effort here is to help members recognize that their current lot in life is the consequence of their behaviors.

Although members may press to discuss the feelings that are attendant with their behaviors, the therapist's task is to downplay them as much as possible, short of denying their significance, and to attempt to focus members' attention on their behavior. It is only through the altering of behaviors that members can achieve success identity. Therefore, the therapist makes efforts to help members develop responsible behaviors and recognize the consequences of their actions. It is important to remember that one of the objectives of Reality Therapy is to help members assume responsibility for their behaviors. The underlying premise is that members have developed a repertoire of behaviors that have allowed them to avoid their responsibilities, and that this has evolved as a matter of choice. That is to say, members have *chosen* to engage in the self-defeating behaviors. It is even quite possible that they no longer consciously realize that they have made the decision to behave as they do. Therefore, the therapist must work to focus members on what they are presently doing as opposed to why they are doing it in order to help members become *aware* of the control they do have over their behaviors and that ultimately the consequences of such responsible action are not as painful as those of irresponsible behaviors. Within the group setting, members can practice the new responsible behaviors that lead to involvement with others.

## Stage 3—Evaluation of Behaviors

In the process of helping members to develop responsibility, there comes a moment when they must examine and evaluate their behavior in terms of its effectiveness for meeting their needs. How responsible are their behaviors? It would be counterproductive if the therapist made that determination. It is the therapist's task, however, to keep members focused on the fact that they have made behavioral choices and to realize that the resulting consequences of their acts is their responsibility.

## Stage 4—Developing Positive Responsible Behavior

After members have evaluated their behaviors and accepted them as irresponsible, they must take the responsibility to want to change. Then they must develop, with help from the group, a positive plan of action. This plan should be realistic. Often members who have had failure identities do not know how to plan effective ways for coping with life. The therapist and the group, therefore, help the member develop a step-by-step program of action, with each step maximizing the chance for success. By assuring the achievement of each sub-goal, the member is provided the opportunity to experience success. This experience helps the member avoid fear of rejection and does not allow a confirmation of a low sense of self-worth.

## Stage 5—Commitment

The next step in the process requires members to develop a commitment to their plan of action. This is often not an easy task, for each member's identity with failure is strong. Commitment is in the form of a pronouncement (much like a contract) which members have made out loud to the therapist or the group and from which it becomes hard to back out. It necessitates an involvement with another that heretofore was missing. Therapists are aware that members' failure identity had kept them in self-central positions; however, a commitment to change, through implementing a plan of action, creates pressure to move away from an inner-directed self-focus to an outer-directed other-focus. Achieving *success* can be enhanced since it would be difficult to quit (fail) on a plan of action that has been announced to others. It is through commitment, then, that one can reverse the failure identity process and develop a success identity.

## Stage 6—No Excuses Accepted

On the face of it, it would be easy to believe that members may fail to meet their commitment. This is especially so since members have lived failure identities, where commitments and involvement with others were virtually nonexistent. Yet, it is precisely the type of reasoning that could defeat the efforts of the therapist. The therapist must develop a very hard line. Once a commitment is made, no excuse is valid. The members must not be allowed to explore *why* they have not fulfilled their commitments. Instead, the therapist's actions must state to the members, "I care enough about you, believe in you, and value you enough that I am not going to buy into allowing you to experience failure again." The objective is not to reduce the tension but to maintain it so the members will learn that the only relief is through positive action. Further, it is precisely at such times that the therapist may say, "Okay, your plan failed, what do you want to do about it now?" In the therapist's response, no acknowledgement was made to explore the excuses or reasons why the plan failed.

If individual members have failed a plan of action, they may need to reassess it to see if it is still realistic. If it is, the plan may require a renewed commitment. If it is not, then an alternate plan, oriented to achieving the same objective, may be needed. Again, the therapist avoids delving into why the first plan did not work but helps the members recommend themselves to the new one.

## Stage 7—Avoid Punishment

Group members who have developed a failure identity have learned to accept punishment. In fact, it might be said that they expect it. It is virtually a form of negative reinforcement, confirming their sense of worthlessness and the belief that no one cares. Thereby, it moves members to avoid involvement with others. The purpose of this stage is to allow members to experience the consequences of failure in order to accomplish their plan of action, learn to take responsibility for it, and learn how to reevaluate the situation free from punitive measure imposed from another.

Glasser (1965, 50) wrote about the process of facing reality through this kind of therapy:

> Our basic job as therapists is to become involved with the patient and then get him to face reality. When confronted with reality by the therapist with whom he is involved, he is forced again and again to decide whether or not he wishes to take the responsible path. Reality may be painful, and may be harsh, it may be dangerous, but it changes slowly. All any man can hope to do is to struggle with it in a responsible way by doing right and enjoying the pleasure or suffering the pain that may follow.

## Summary

An observer of a Reality Therapy session will see that it appears to be more akin to a discussion group than a therapy group. Where Gestalt Therapy focuses upon here-and-now behaviors and Client-Centered Therapy attends to the group's present experiencing, Reality Therapy attends more to the progress of each group member's efforts to work toward achieving a success identity, by overcoming actions affiliated with noninvolvement and low self-worth. The group session is used as an opportunity for each member to move outside and away from a self-centered focus, toward a focus on another. The group therapist acts both as a role model for, and facilitator of, members to experience a realistic caring involvement with other persons. Through mutual caring and continual focus upon developing responsible behaviors, group members are encouraged to assist each other to avoid irresponsible behavior. The group therapist engages in a pedagogical relationship with members, directing discussion and using the influence of the group to help members adhere to group norms (the lack of which was one of the very reasons for a person's difficulty).

The group therapist will also directly confront members if they are avoiding responsibility for their behaviors by identifying their denial. Again, this action on the part of the therapist acts as a model for members to involve themselves with another person in a responsible way. The ultimate goal of Reality Therapy is to help members take what they have learned from their group experience and apply it to other parts of their life.

# CHAPTER SIX

# Transactional Analysis

## Background

At the moment of birth, infants automatically adopt a healthy attitude toward both themselves and others—an attitude of basic trust and worthiness which Transactional Analysis (TA) describes as "I'm Okay— You're Okay." Thereafter, however, that view is continually modified according to their interactions (transactions) with others. Until approximately age six—while children are in the initial stages of building this personal view of themselves and their world—their personality is most easily influenced. After that time, their energies are channeled primarily into activities and behavior designed to confirm and reinforce this learned viewpoint.

Such is the basic position taken by Eric Berne, generally agreed to be the creator of this approach to human development and change. Berne, a psychiatrist trained in analytic procedures, developed and organized his ideas in the early 1950s. With the help of interested colleagues in his home area of San Francisco, he refined and modified these ideas, which soon began to influence other mental health workers in other parts of the country and world. Finally, in 1966, four years before his untimely death, Berne formally applied his approach to the group mode in his book, *Principles of Group Treatment.*

The success of TA is perhaps most attributable to its practical emphasis on actual behavior and applied concepts, in contrast to the more traditional psychiatric emphasis on the unconscious and inferential aspects of personality. What can be *seen* and *explained* in terms that are personally meaningful in day-to-day living is certainly more likely to be accepted by people than the more complicated and mysterious elements of psychoanalysis. This explains a large part of the general acceptance of this approach.

Transactional Analysis's approach to personality development stresses that growing children have both physiological and psychological needs, each of which requires transactions with others in order to be met. In their earliest years, when the development of their self-esteem and other-esteem is most pliable and easily influenced, these "others" are primarily adults, usually the parents. If their transactions with these adults are in keeping with the reinforcement of the "I'm Okay—You're Okay" life view, children develop into reasonably healthy adults, able to initiate and sustain productive relationships.

However, if the transactions are of a nature that suggests a more negative view of the self and the world, other life views may become dominant in a child's mind. Perhaps the most socially destructive view is "I'm Okay—You're Not Okay." This individual's earliest transactions with significant adults may have been so punishing that the outside world can only be seen in negative terms when compared with oneself. Some degree of obnoxious, antisocial, revengeful, and perhaps paranoid behavior can be the result of such an outlook.

A third life view, "I'm Not Okay—You're Not Okay," is a viewpoint centered in despair and hopelessness. Not only may one's earliest transactions have encouraged and reinforced an outlook of unworthiness about oneself, but in fact, the whole rest of the world may look lousy as well. Depression, boredom, and a general lack of energy and enthusiasm might well characterize someone with this life attitude.

The fourth life view, "I'm Not Okay—You're Okay," may well be the prevalent outlook in our social system, and perhaps even most socially productive. It is probably not as personally fulfilling or relaxing as the basic birth outlook of "We're All Okay" but it can create a competitive, striving personality, anxious to contribute to society in a way that gains the feeling of "Okayness" attributed to others but not oneself.

Unfortunately, in order to gain that feeling of worthiness in comparison to others, most of us resort to playing social "games" that are uniquely and idiosyncratically designed to give us the "strokes" we believe are needed for our psychological survival. And the strokes we attempt to get, through manipulation and game playing in our transactions with others, are in accord with the view that we learned through our earliest transactions with others.

Strokes, in TA terms, are simply indications from outside sources that one is a unique human being, that one counts in some way, that one has an impact on his or her world, that one's life has some individual meaning. If an individual has come to believe that he or she is basically "Not-Okay," then the strokes that are sought may well be negative ones; that is, the games that are created and played will be programmed to reward the individual with a reinforcement of the existing feelings of unworthiness. The search for strokes is an essential aspect of everyone's makeup, and can have positive, negative, or mixed elements. Since this search is action-oriented, in that it requires transactions with others, it can be observed and analyzed so that one's basic life view may be identified by others who are aware of such processes. Both insight and actual behavior, then, are cornerstones of the TA model, and both of them are vital to the proper functioning of a TA group.

The need for outside sources of reinforcement to reaffirm one's basic life position necessitates the structuring of one's time to actively seek those strokes. Transactional Analysis identifies six basic avenues that are useful, though not necessarily healthy, in this endeavor.

An individual may *withdraw* into his or her own fantasy world, and thereby provide to oneself those strokes unable to be found in the outside world. Such a withdrawal from transactions with others in favor of talking to and stroking oneself is tantamount to an isolationist position and hardly conducive to a healthy personality when carried to extremes.

The use of *rituals* also provides us the means to gain strokes. Even such an automatic response as "How are you today?" indicates a real, though perhaps superficial, recognition of one's personhood; such rituals may take on even greater importance when they are withheld, as when one is snubbed. Unimportant as such transactions may first appear, they often represent highly significant strokes to people who structure their time largely in an effort to obtain such ritualistic responses.

*Pastimes* represent another significant avenue for gaining attention and recognition. "Passing the time of day" might be a way to paraphrase this method. It would include various types of discussion sessions about such external issues as politics, sports, and economics. Entering into such discussions may give one a sense of belonging, being cared about, being listened to, and being considered important enough to be talked with.

A fourth way of putting oneself in a position to gain strokes is through *activities* of various kinds. Our work is one such activity, but participation in sporting events or organizations may be even more valuable to some individuals. The transactions that take place while engaging in such activities may be vital to the affirmation of many, and may be accomplished verbally, nonverbally, or paralinguistically (tone of voice, hesitation of speech, or emphasis of certain words).

Perhaps the most-discussed but least understood or recognized form of stroke-getting is through the use of *games*, which Berne has often humorously but meaningfully detailed in *Games People Play*. These games are designed by the participants to result in victories according to the basic life position of Okayness that each participant holds. For example, if an individual's series of transactions (which make up a game) conveys both direct and subtle messages of a controlling nature, then the recipients of such messages must desire to get *their* strokes by being controlled. If these recipients are unable to get the strokes to match their perceptions of their life position in this way, they will cease to respond according to the rules of the sender's game, and that game will end. Those individuals who see game-playing as their primary means for receiving strokes will then seek out other persons more willing to play by their rules, and for whom those rules will provide the strokes they deem necessary to continue their "racket" of basic life view. The recognition and analysis of such maneuvering—which takes place through transactions within the group—is a vital part of the therapeutic strategy of TA counseling.

The final avenue for receiving strokes is *intimacy*, which Berne sharply distinguishes from pseudo-intimacy (Berne 1966, 231–232). According to Berne, real intimacy is a game-free exchange of transactions, affective and spontaneous in nature. Such exchanges rarely occur in group settings, perhaps due to the inability of most participants to program themselves internally when they respond, as contrasted with considering how they will "look" in front of others. This tendency of individuals to inhibit themselves (which comes from socialization experiences) takes away from the authenticity of the transaction, and thus becomes another game. Real intimacy is perhaps its own reward in that it provides strokes on an "I'm Okay-You're Okay" basis.

These six methods, then, constitute the means by which individuals structure their time in order to put themselves in the most advantageous positions to receive the amounts and kinds of strokes they feel they need to reinforce and confirm their destiny and role in life. This life script (personality) in turn was prepared primarily in the first few years of life, through transactions of both a verbal and nonverbal nature with the external world. How individuals *use* their personalities to conduct transactions with others is explained in terms of ego states.

All individuals contain three such ego states: Child, Parent, and Adult. These ego states represent the dominant forces affecting an individual's behaviors at a given point in time. An understanding of these ego states and how they function in transactions between group members, and between group members and the group leader, is necessary to the proper functioning of a TA group. Since transactions of individuals with the outside world (as represented by significant others in one's group) both determine and reinforce their life style, as exhibited in behavior and personality, it is understandable why TA proponents put such a premium on group therapy, where here-and-now transactions can be immediately recognized and analyzed. The insight acquired through such group analysis enables each individual to make the desired behavior changes.

# Key Concepts

## Ego States

According to TA principles, each of us is driven, at different times and in different places, by one of three internal command stations known as Child, Parent, and Adult. Although these ego states may be aware of each other's existence, only one of them can be in charge at a given moment in time. The commands given by these ego states are also very different, and occasionally there will be internal challenges for dominance in a given situation.

The Child is the first ego state to develop and, in fact, is inherent at birth in the form of the Natural Child. The Natural Child is a sub-part of the Child ego state and represents the uncontrolled, untrained, undisciplined, and nonsocialized part of the personality—the part that totally seeks its own spontaneous pleasure, without regard to social dictates. Soon after the infant is born, however, he or she must begin to curb some of these natural tendencies, and to adapt to the demands of more powerful others. This develops into the Adapted Child—that part of the personality that responds to training, learning, and authority. A third part of the Child ego state, known as the Little Professor, begins to develop during the preschool years. The behavior of this aspect of the Child reflects the beginning of rational, logical, evaluative thinking, and is the forerunner of such behavior in the adult. According to TA, the Child ego state is the most significant part of the personality, as it is the foundation upon which self-esteem is built.

The Parent ego state is quite well-developed by the time a child enters school. It represents the assimilated dictates of right and wrong and appropriateness that all children acquire through messages from parents and other authority figures. It is sometimes all too recognizable by parents who see their own questionable behaviors and verbalizations mimicked by their young children. Such messages are internalized and often carried into adulthood, regardless of their objective accuracy.

Prejudices and traditions are passed from generation to generation in this way, since the Parent ego state is nonperceptive and nonthinking. It assumes the truth of past mandates and judgments, and acts similarly to a conscience. It is as if we have tape recordings being played over and over in our heads, and to the extent to which these recordings shut out current, more accurate information, they may be destructive. It should also be recognized that Parent material contains elements from all three ego states of one's own parents, as well as from other significant adults in our past—all of whom received *their* parental mandates from the three ego states of important people in *their* background, and so on.

As indicated earlier, the Child's Little Professor is the earliest forerunner of the Adult ego state. The Adult is that part of the personality that assimilates and evaluates information, makes decisions, and deals in facts, logic, questions, and outcomes. It is rational and bases its behavior on current data it has collected. Unlike the Parent and Child ego states, which focus mostly on emotions and the past, the Adult's emphasis is cognitive and current. Since the most impersonal Adult ego state is usually more acceptable to others in interpersonal transactions, the Child and Parent states sometimes try to disguise themselves as Adults in an attempt to deliver a message with as little risk as possible. For example, a teenager, upon arriving home late at night, might be asked this outwardly Adult question from his or her parents: "What time were you supposed to be home?" Chances are, however, that it is the parent's *Parent* ego state doing the talking and that the real message is "You're late! And I want an explanation!" It is quite likely that the receiver will see through the disguise, though, and the subsequent responses will indicate whether or not a game is about to be played.

All three ego states are useful at different times; the appropriateness of their use, according to the situation, is the key criterion. Overuse of any one or two to the exclusion of another can be detrimental to interpersonal functioning.

## Exclusion/Contamination

The terms *exclusion* and *contamination* relate to the malformation and malfunction of the ego states described above. In some cases, usually due to inadequate parenting, individuals get stuck in one or two ego states and have great difficulty activating the other(s). The exclusion of an ego state greatly increases the chances of such individuals being avoided, chastised, or patronized in situations where the activation of the excluded ego state(s) would be appropriate. In other cases, the ego states may not be adequately separated within the personality structure, causing such rapid changes from one to another that an observer might question the stability of such an individual. Ideally, the ego state will be flexible enough be to called upon without too much delay, but without being so fluid that it becomes difficult to distinguish one from another.

Contamination occurs when one ego state gains too much influence over another. Usually, this happens when the Child or Parent intrudes upon the Adult. For example, when it is appropriate for the Adult to assess a situation objectively, but objectivity is clouded by a bias that has been accepted as fact, but which in reality represents a strong parental prejudice, contamination has occured.

## Transactions

As indicated earlier, transactions are utilized as attempts to gain the recognition and attention considered necessary for physiological survival. Such transactions begin at the moment of birth and continue thereafter as the desire for psychological stroking gains greater emphasis as persons approach adulthood. For the most part, however, adults desire strokes to confirm the life view of "Okayness" that they formed as very young children. The young children's transactions form the personality basis that they will attempt to confirm in adulthood. Obviously, therefore, individuals' earliest transactions are much more significant to their development than are the later ones that may well serve as reinforcers of rigidity. When looked upon in this manner, it is not difficult to understand why group members will go to great lengths to avoid change, and how game playing contributes to that avoidance behavior. The recognition and analysis of such games thus becomes the heart and soul of the process in a TA group.

The interactions or transactions that occur between people can be of three basic types: complementary, crossed, or ulterior (crooked). These transactions result from whichever ego state is in control of a person's behavior at a given point in time.

When clear messages are emitted from an ego state that is clearly recognized by both sender and receiver, and when the receiver responds from the appropriate ego state, the transaction is said to be complementary. For example, if person "A" makes an Adult remark to person "B's" Adult ego state, and the latter responds with an Adult remark (Adult ego state to Adult ego state) there has been a *complementary* transaction, and communication is likely to continue.

However, if person "A" sends a message from the Adult ego state to person "B's" Adult ego state, but "B's" Parent or Child ego responds, then there has been a *crossed* transaction, and communication is likely to deteriorate or end. In this case, at least one of the participants may become confused, angry, or suspicious, and since the transaction has produced strokes for only one of the players, the unrewarded person will desire to structure his or her time in different ways.

An *ulterior* transaction occurs when a significant message is being sent at a subtle or hidden level, alongside another message being sent at a clear and open level. In other words, the most important message is disguised to lessen the risk for the sender (and perhaps for the receiver, if both understand the game being played). If the sender's disguised message is uncovered, and if it should prove to be embarrassing or somehow destructive, then the sender can always find a defense in that the *actual words spoken* clearly conveyed an innocent message. Often the hidden message is emitted through nonverbal gestures, facial expressions, or tone of voice, making it very difficult to "convict" one or both communicators in terms of their intentions.

## Games

While the concept of games was described in an earlier section, it needs further recognition here, since it plays an important role in transactional analysis. Berne describes a game as "a series of ulterior transactions with a gimmick, leading to a usually well-concealed but well-defined pay-off" (1966, 207). Since the acquisition of strokes is a basic motivation of TA theory, games are only played when all players are receiving the strokes they need to confirm their accepted life position. "In effect, there are no real losers in games that people play with one another; both partners receive the payoff they seek" (Hansen, Warner, & Smith 1976, 189). The importance of games and game-analysis in TA groups has been further noted by Berne in his discussion of time-structuring options open to people in their quest for strokes: "Since the experienced transactional therapist will quickly break up rituals and pastimes to move on to games, and since, on the other hand, real intimacy rarely occurs in groups, most of the proceedings of transactional groups will consist of games and game-analysis" (1966, 231).

## Script/Counterscript

Once the individuals have begun to solidify their life position (feelings of personal "Okayness" in comparison to the rest of the world), they make life plans to fit that perception. This script is similar to that of a play in which the actor knows how the play is to conclude and works diligently to behave throughout the play in a manner appropriate to that predetermined ending (life position). In real life, however, the script is usually an unconscious plan, although the individual may be just as diligent as the actor in making it come out according to the script. Unfortunately, such scripts are commonly written in early childhood, when the indiviudal is quite incapable of making such serious, and often tragic, commitments.

If growing children are subjected to a significant number of important ulterior transactions, they may develop alternate scripts to use upon occasion. That is, if inconsistent or garbled or misunderstood messages were received, or if they were told one rule, but saw an opposing rule modeled, a counterscript might result. At times, then, in trying to implement *everything* taught, individuals could take on a Jekyll-Hyde character that would permit the inclusion of contradictory parental mandates and injunctions.

## Therapist Role and Techniques

To function most effectively, the TA group therapist must be authentic and genuine, and a skillful diagnostician and analyzer. Neither, by itself, is enough.

Even though TA is a therapist-centered approach, therapists' authenticity must communicate humility, equality, and openness. They should be able to model behavior that they expect of the members, such as a strong commitment and sense of responsibility to the group, and to any contracts that have been agreed upon. Within this basically democratic demeanor, therapists are free to be themselves. While certain techniques have been found to be especially useful to many TA therapists, they are in no way restricted from creating their own techniques as well.

In addition to the personal characteristics, therapists must be highly skilled in the collection and evaluation of group data; therefore, their powers of observation and interpretation must be well-developed. They must be astute and active listeners to the group's messages as well as skilled at analyzing ego states, transactions, games, and scripts; they must also be able to transmit those skills to group members so that the members can help each other, rather than rely solely on the therapist.

It is common for TA therapists to utilize a chalkboard as an aid in explaining the analytical concepts exhibited in group interactions. Using the chalkboard serves two purposes: it provides clarity to group transactions and it helps the group achieve the Adult state by enabling members to rationally scrutinize their transactions as they appear on the board.

In one of his essays on group treatment, Berne (1966) devoted an entire chapter to "The First Three Minutes" of the group encounter, indicating his emphasis on setting an appropriate climate and direction. Berne felt that this time was the most important in the therapy process. And, since TA is highly therapist-centered, it is the therapist's responsibility to develop a comfortable atmosphere and to determine a positive direction.

Berne wrote that, "for the group therapist to be the master of his own destiny requires a commitment which misses no opportunity to learn, uses every legitimate method to win, and permits no rest until every loss has been thoroughly analyzed so that no mistake will ever be repeated" (1966, 75).

## Interrogation

At times the group leader needs more information from a member in order to analyze the member's feelings or behavior. The therapist then merely asks a straightforward question of the member's Adult ego state, and hopes for a clear Adult response. Such questioning provides direction to the session, aids in data-collection, and models Adult behavior. However, it is important *neither* to get more information than is immediately needed, *nor* to use this technique if the member's Child or Parent is likely to respond. Otherwise, the member may seize the therapist's questioning as an opportunity to play games.

## Specification

The object of specification, Berne wrote, "is to fix certain information in his [the therapist's] mind and in the patient's mind, so that it can be referred to later in more decisive therapeutic operations" (1966, 234). In other words, when therapists seem reasonably confident that a member will accept their statements about demonstrated behavior, the therapist can then verbally clarify and formalize that finding, for later use. It is important not to engage in such specification if the member is likely to deny it later, or if it has not been sufficiently determined (in which case it might well lead to a sidetracking argument or to a psychoanalytic game).

## Confrontation

The therapist uses confrontation to point out inconsistencies between current behavior and behavior that has previously been analyzed and specified. Its objective is to stir the member and to gain a response from the uncontaminated Adult. If the confrontation has been well-timed and worded well, the result will usually be a thoughtful pause or an insightful laugh, both of which are deemed therapeutic.

## Explanation

Explanation by the therapist to a member represents an effort to interact with and strengthen a member's Adult ego state. Explanations should be brief and to the point; if previous transactions have properly prepared the members to accept the explanantion in their Adult ego states, then some significant cognitive learning can transpire.

## Illustration

The therapist uses illustration as a humorous follow-up to a successful confrontation in order to loosen up the members while still transmitting an important message. It is intended for the member's Adult consumption, while being certain that the Child is also listening and appreciative of the humor. In this process, it is necessary for the Parent to remain in the background and not interfere. The illustration can be a humorous anecdote dealing with issues external (but relevant) to the group, or it can be an internal focus of comparisons within the group. Illustrations can immediately follow a successful confrontation, or can be brought up several weeks later, depending on the nature of the situation.

## Confirmation

Even though a member's Adult ego state may have been strengthened and stabilized through confrontation and perhaps illustration, the Child does not give up inconsistent behavior and thoughts easily, and most will return at some point. When they do, they serve to confirm the therapist's earlier diagnosis, and should lead to a new confrontation that will further strengthen and reinforce the Adult's position.

## Interpretation

Up to this point, the therapist's strategy has been to stabilize, decontaminate, and strengthen the Adult ego states of the members. Now the therapist's Adult needs to team up with the member's Adult in order to gain control over the team composed of the member's Child plus the member's Parent—a team often torn by internal fighting as well. Interpretation is made with the member's Child state, looking for past reasons for inappropriate behavior, much in the same mode as traditional psychoanalysis. The goal is to deconfuse the Child, making a more total recovery or cure possible. However, if the Adult is strong enough to remain in control of this still-confused Child, and the member has gained enough symptomatic relief and social control to function quite well, this situation can be crystallized without going through the rigors of much interpretation.

## Crystallization

Crystallization is a therapist-to-member, Adult-to-Adult transaction in which the message is conveyed that the group members are perfectly capable of ending their psychological game playing if they wish. At this juncture, the process of transactional analysis is completed, for the therapist's job has been to bring the group members to the point of being able to choose between healthy and unhealthy behavior. Obviously, adequate preparation throughout the sessions has been necessary; the Adult has been strengthened, the Child has been modified, and hopefully the Parent's desires for control and dominance have been appropriately lessened.

# *Group Processes*

According to Berne (1966, 250), "the object for group treatment is to fight the past in the present in order to assure the future." The past is represented by the Child and Parent ego states, while the "present" focus is guarded by a strong Adult. Effective and appropriate relationships among the three ego states are essential for a productive future, and necessitate an Adult predominance. In order to reach that goal, certain group processes are advocated toward strengthening that Adult.

## Therapeutic Processes

Berne (1966) identified four therapeutic processes that are part of the group setting. Three of them are found in any social interaction—(1) the drive towards health, (2) the need for strokes, and (3) the corrective experiences found in all social relationships. The fourth process, however—the behaviors of the group leader—is different. Therapists are responsible for the preparation of the group members to engage productively in group processes through individual interviews or preparatory group meetings. The purpose for such screenings is to discuss commitment, communicate procedures, and establish minimal comfort levels, one with another, and not to exclude certain types from the group (Berne 1966).

The therapists' process objectives are primarily to focus on group work activities that involve Adult-to-Adult transactions. As the therapists listen to and observe group interactions, they become aware of games being played and can interrupt members with their diagnoses and analyses, thereby helping members with insight into their behavior and giving them permission not to play games. At times, therapists may need to give strong support and reassurance, or to persuade and demand, but these techniques should not be used frequently.

## Contractual Agreements

A well-known element in TA group therapy is the contractual agreement, usually made up of two parts. The first is the contract established between the therapist and member. This can be accomplished at preliminary individual interviews, where the potential members can explain their desires and the therapist can help in the clarification process. If members are too confused to contractualize such wishes, it may require numerous group sessions to specify the contract. Members may also change the contract one or more times upon discovering new aspects of their selves, and such changes, if based on significant learnings, are encouraged by the therapist.

The second kind of contract is a group contract, in which all members agree to offer samples of their behavior with and toward other people, regardless of what that behavior might be. In this contract, the therapist agrees to say anything that might be helpful to a group member and not to withhold information that is relevant to the purpose of the group. Both of these contractual agreements lend purpose and direction to the group process.

## Group Structure

The TA group structure is considered to have a very simple, two-pronged dimension. The *external* boundary separates the group from outside influences and varies according to the degree of cohesiveness found among members at any given time. The *internal* boundary is one that exists between the group therapist and the group members. According to TA, therapists cannot become "just another group member" without relinquishing important leadership responsibilities. TA therapists would neither desire such an outcome nor be able to function with it. Instead, they are primarily listeners, observers, diagnosticians, and analysts—and, secondarily, process facilitators.

## Analyses

The analyses in TA are geared to four different levels, which depend upon the nature and purpose of the group. In order to achieve the most complete treatment, all four need to be accomplished, and since each one is built upon the previous level, it is necessary that they be accomplished in order. However, some significant learning can accrue through understandings acquired at any of the levels without necessarily progressing through all four.

The first of these is *structural* analysis. At this level, group members examine the structure of their own ego states. The goal is to develop an increasing awareness within members of how their ego states function in reality, and to encourage decontamination of the past.

The second level, called *transactional* analysis, although also the name usually given to this whole approach to therapy, is here merely another level of analysis, and builds on structural analysis. At this level, the nature of both the major and minor transactions that occure within the group are analyzed. These transactions can be complementary, crossed, or ulterior. An understanding of the ego state from which an individual is communicating and the responses he or she receives from another member can provide enormous insights into the transactional patterns in which one engages throughout life.

The third level is *game* analysis, and necessitates knowledge of both ego states and transactions. A psychological game involves a series of ulterior transactions in which the players all gain the kinds of strokes they feel they need. The communication may appear vague or innocent at a superficial level, but at a deeper level, important messages are being given and received. The group therapists must carefully listen and observe to determine the games being played, and the payoffs being received. When they expose both the games and the players, they end the secrecy and thereby make the payoffs less lucrative. In addition, the therapist gives permission to the players not to play the games anymore, but rather to look for better and more meaningful ways to gain strokes and to structure their time.

The deepest level in TA is *script* analysis, which examines basic life plans, positions, and decisions, most of which individuals made as young children and are unconscious, though powerful, in the adult. Since these basic life plans are so deeply embedded in the adult, they are highly resistant to change—and any attempts require great leadership skills. The results of significant learning in this regard can be extremely disconcerting and depressing, especially in older adults who may feel they have little time to make changes. Obviously, script analysis represents a very difficult and demanding level of influence, and should be attempted only by the most skilled TA therapists.

## Summary

Infants are born with a positive view of themselves and their world, but need both physiological and psychological nurturing to preserve it. Such nurturing comes through transactions with other people—primarily adults, the most significant of whom are parents. Our innate psychological hunger for recognition and attention compels us to seek strokes, the nature of which (in later life) depends upon the kind we received and became accustomed to in early childhood; thus, strokes may be pleasant or unpleasant.

Much of our energy goes into structuring our time in order to get the strokes we believe we need. There are several ways of doing this, but the most significant, in terms of our psychological well-being, is by playing "games." By definition, games are always rewarding to the players in some way, or they would not continue to be played. Often, however, they are self-defeating in more significant ways.

These games are developed in response to a life position of "Okayness" that comes from our early contacts and transactions with parents and other authorities, and which determines the kinds of strokes we seek. This position is often solidified before the child begins school and leads to a premature life script that becomes more and more rigid in adulthood. When our transactions and life script become too unrewarding, group counseling may be sought. Such counseling may be at any of four levels, each one denoting greater depth and sophistication.

TA group therapists conceptualize their work by means of ego states. Each person is considered to have three such ego states (Child, Parent, Adult), only one of which can be in command of the personality at a given time. Depending upon the level of counseling that has been contracted, the group process may focus on the structure of one's personality, the nature of the transactions between group members, the analysis of psychological games being played by group members, and life script analysis. The basic goal of TA group therapy is to understand the ego states from which one is operating, and their most effective and appropriate use in life situations.

The personal qualities of TA group therapists are considered vital to the attainment of group goals. They must be ethical, responsible, purposeful, respectful and genuine, as well as intelligent enough to be able to use—and transmit to others—the conceptualizations of TA. Leaders must also be excellent listeners and observers, and astute diagnosticians and analyzers. Finally, they must have an adequate sense of timing, and the ability to use specific leadership techniques mentioned throughout this chapter.

# PART TWO

# *Theoretical Practitioners' Responses to Specific Critical Incidents*

## *Introduction*

Part I introduced the student to six selected theories of group therapy through presentations explaining how the theories developed, what constitutes their primary concepts, the techniques therapists utilize, and how the group therapy process is perceived in each. Now we are prepared to see how theoretical practitioners, representing each of the theories presented earlier, approach specific critical incidents that might occur in group therapy. Each of the following six chapters presents a critical incident, which is followed by the responses of each theoretical practitioner to the situation.

Students can be helped in developing their own rationale or theory of group therapy by first, selecting the theoretical orientation they feel they most likely would adopt; and, second, selecting the theoretical orientation they feel they least likely would adopt, and the reasons supporting both.

As the students approach each incident, we encourage them to read it first and, before reading how each of the theoretical practitioners responded to the incidents, answer the following questions:

1. How would you respond to the incident? Explain what thoughts you had as you determined your particular responses. Include what it is about the incident that prompted you to do what you did.
2. Explain why you chose the particular intervention you did, over any other you may have been considering.
3. Declare what consequences you anticipated from your action.
4. Explain which elements of your theory guided your interpretation of the incident and which subsequently led to your actions.

Finally, we have prepared a series of five questions which we feel will help you formalize your theory of group therapy. The questions comprise what we refer to as a *Theory Evaluation Form.* We suggest you try to respond to it after you complete reading each chapter in this part. After you finish reading all of the chapters, you can collate your responses to each of the questions, and thereby develop a *profile* that describes your theoretical approach to group therapy.

# CHAPTER SEVEN

# The Initial Session

The initial session often can have a significant effect upon the future of the group. How a group therapist chooses to deal with it is important. In this incident, our theoretical practitioners will be entering a group of nine members meeting for the first time.

## Incident #1

You are a counselor at a university counseling center. You have been acutely aware of the difficulty a number of freshmen students have been having in adjusting to college life. You offer to organize a counseling group to help students contend more effectively with their new environment.

Your group consists of nine volunteers (five men and four women), whom you have screened. Each has expressed a willingness to participate in the group you were forming. It is meeting today for the first time. All nine members are present as you enter the room and sit down. You introduce yourself, and the members introduce themselves. Then they each turn and look at you expectantly. There is an initial period of silence.

# Client-Centered Therapy

*Implemented by William R. Coulson*
Our La Jolla groups often begin in silence. We do not want anyone to take over and, consequently, offer no ground rules. We want a group experience that is not a repetition of what has happened before, including at La Jolla.

I do not want to know what is going to happen before we begin, or it would not be as good as it could be. If I guide the group, I bring it to premature focus, reducing the number of solutions generated within the group to deal with our common, immediate problems, such as: "Will I use my time well here? Will I get through this with integrity?" That problem, created by the act of bringing the group together, stands for and (if it is dealt with respectfully) includes the other problems that plague the members and the therapist in life. I hope for each individual to be stimulated to solve the group problem for him or herself, including elements that might lie so deep as to make a member unable to explicate them. I hope for a therapy group that will provide what Michael Polanyi calls a "heuristic experience"—a discovery, the full value of which will depend on maximum presence from us all and minimal cause to run through old routines, therapeutic or otherwise.

So there is often silence at the beginning. We do not yet know what we will do with ourselves. Finding solutions will be a struggle; one which, if we are honest, we often must return to waging in silence. In the early moments of the group, silence protects against takeover—by group members or the therapist. You might think it would *promote* takeover, by someone moving in to fill the vacuum. But that does not often happen. The therapist has a good deal of initial authority by virtue of title. If he or she does not take over in the silence, members seem unlikely to do it either. Once enough time has transpired for members to realize that therapists' best qualifications may be that they are persons like themselves, they will also know that no one need dominate the group.

In the initial awkward silence, I might say something like, "This silence isn't easy for me, either."

Another possibility in the initial silence is just to wait. I believe that is what I would do here. I will assume that silence provides the group with the opportunity to learn to tolerate ambiguity. That would not be my initial goal. But, since the silence arose anyway, I will tell myself (in order to keep quiet) there could be a good lesson in it—maybe about ambiguity or maybe that interactions can go well between people, even when they are awkward at first.

When I am tempted to intervene too soon in the silence, it is because I am asking myself such panicky questions as "What if nobody talks the whole hour?" The answer I remember having given myself is "Then at least it will be different." I have never been in a college counseling group where nobody talked for an hour—and I bet the members have not either. If this is the time it happens, it will surely have given us something to talk about later.

# Gestalt Therapy

*Implemented by Mirriam F. Polster*
The purpose in forming this group is to help entering college students to "contend more effectively with their new environment." It is not unreasonable to assume that since these young people have gotten this far, they have, for the most part, been doing okay in their lives and it is this particular situation that presents them with difficulties. While this is a reasonable assumption, there may be some more pervasive trouble for certain individuals and it will be wise to bear this in mind as the group starts.

I am guessing that one of the most prevalent characteristics of this group is that each member secretly suspects that the troubles he or she is having are unique and, in some vague way, reflect badly on him or herself. This uneasy suspicion is not uncommon at this age. Reinforcing this fear is everyone else's apparent success at dealing with this situation, making it too inconvenient or too risky to even air these doubts. It might mark them in the eyes of others and lead to a deeper sense of isolation.

Perls (1969) has defined growth as the movement from environmental support to self-support. This is a relative as well as gradual progression; we are never fully free of our reliance on some form of external support, but we do change our balance of dependency. This realignment of the balance between environmental support and self-support may well be an underlying question faced by the people in this group.

These young people are in transition; for some, this is the first dramatic turning point in their lives. They stand between what they have been and what they want to become, what they are and what they feel they should be. Their lives at home may have had many familiar comforts. There was a built-in society, familial, academic or religious, into which they were born and were gradually introduced with parental or sibling support. Here at the university, they have been dunked, all by themselves it must seem, into a fully functioning system with rules and customs already established (and in many cases unspecified) which they have to learn quickly. Everybody else, walking swiftly to classes with their friends, seems already to know the rules.

So here they are, their admonitions (to themselves) to keep quiet and not stand out are counterbalanced by the intensity of the stress they are experiencing. This is a common struggle and one which, when expressed and acknowledged, might serve as a unifying force in group formation. It is the dynamic of mutuality in the group that I, as leader, would foster at this stage. A common problem, expressed with feeling and seriously attended to, is probably the most potent basis for group cohesion. The uniquely individual form these problems may take for each of the young people can be revealed from this mutual source of support. The leader, in supporting this development and attending to the ways in which this expression can be made even more poignantly, is setting in motion the very force these students need eventually to move out of this group into independent action. They need to learn to support themselves better and to perceive more sensitively how others may be feeling so that they can identify people whom they might want for colleagues and friends.

So, after introductions are made, I will ask each of them to make a statement about their experiences as beginners in this new community. What pleased them? Dismayed them? Puzzled them? Confused them? What did they miss? Whom did they miss?

As the group continues, I will pay particular attention to how they listen to each other and how they express themselves. I will work at sharpening their language so that it better expresses what they want to communicate. They may be relying on familiar phrases or expressions, shorthand ways that communicated quickly and well at home but which do not mean the same things to the people here. They need to learn to make it with the people here and cannot afford merely to repeat old behaviors and habits. To do this, they have to be actively and energetically open to differences as well as commonalities with each other. Lively appreciation of differences is important because these can then be experienced as inviting and fascinating rather than discouraging or intimidating.

An appreciation of these differences can provide support because the group members will have devised various ways of coping with some of the specific problems that bother them. One person may have answers to another's questions, although still troubled by a problem that another has resolved, and so on. Articulating these differences becomes a way of getting unstuck, of supporting fertility of mind. The energy that these young people may be using to appear as if they fit in can be devoted instead to improvising behavior by taking examples from the group, trying them out elsewhere, and using the group to come back to and continue to work out what remains troublesome.

We can have role playing sessions where the group can enact either the circumstance or a situation with an individual that is giving them trouble. The change of perspective that may come from playing an aloof professor or an arrogant and harried graduate assistant may lead them either to view these characters in a different light or to find new sources of energy and support within themselves to cope more effectively with them. Experiments in direct speaking and clearly stating what they want can change the nature of their contacts with other people on campus. It is within this group, balancing individual venturesomeness against the need for group support, that creative solutions may be invented and tried out. What the group members do in the campus situation will not be a carbon copy of the experimental action they have tried out in the group; indeed it is better when it is not. The students need the experience of supported improvisation, which is, after all, what most actions are.

The group thus serves as the temporary environmental support that can bridge the gap, as accustomed support from a familiar environment diminishes, and support from the individual and a new group, grows.

# *I*ndividual Psychology

*Implemented by Guy J. Manaster*
The premise in this situation is that the university environment poses problems because it is different from, and larger than, the institutions the students have previously dealt with, *and* they do not know what to do. A therapist must be aware, in entering a group such as this, that one or some of the volunteer group members may have personal problems also. These problems may be felt for the first time with greater intensity in the new, different environment of the university. Not living at home may allow, if not force, freshman students to examine themselves and realize that some help is needed. So we begin this group as if its task was evident—to assist in adjustment to a new environment—while staying sensitive to the possibility of more severe personal problems needing remediation within, or outside of, the group.

At the critical, first moment in this situation, I will set the task-specific tone for the group with an introductory message such as: "I offered to organize this group because I know how difficult it can be to get it together and get going in college. There are three basic life tasks—work and school, friends and community, and loved ones. When you come to college you want to make it in school and come out prepared to appreciate life and to get a fulfilling job you both enjoy and do well. You probably don't know many people here, if you know anyone. You want to make friends and have a good time. This may be the first time you have lived away from your family, and you may be lonesome. You may have been going with someone at home but you probably want to go out with someone here. What you want really is to belong, and to feel that you belong. Everyone wants to belong.

"However, there are things you don't know, or think you don't know, or can't do. Some concerns may seem trivial. I once knew a guy who left college when his clean clothes ran out. He was embarrassed to go to the laundry with them. Some concerns seem crucial, important, and immediate, but are they? Do you have an academic major area? Do you need one now? I think our job here is to find out what concerns we have, what we don't know or feel we can't do. I think between all of us we can figure this place out. Maybe we can start out by each of us telling the others what is bothering us most. ———, would you tell us what's bugging or worrying you, what you want? Then we will go around the group, and figure out how we want to proceed."

My intentions with this opening are very direct and are based in Adlerian theory. First, I want us to get going in the group and want to get all of the group members working out specific adjustment problems. The sooner they meet a challenge and deal with it successfully, the sooner they will feel confidence to go on to conquer other challenges.

Next, I want the group to share concerns as quickly as possible. Each member will, in his or her own way, have notions of inferiority based at least in part on the idea that he or she is the only one with these kinds of concerns. In a homogeneous group such as this one, considerable commonality of concerns will, no doubt, be presented. If the problem areas are not clearly the same, the reasons for their being concerns may be similar among the group. I will try to show the similarities, such as the members' attempts to remain different, avoid failure no matter how inconsequential, buoy themselves up by feeling homesick, dwelling on "back home" where they were loved and appreciated. Both group comradery and a greater feeling of commonness with other freshmen will, I hope, come from this sharing and interpreting.

After listening to everyone in the group, we will have a slate of problems, which together we will organize in order to solve. This might entail, over ensuing weeks, skill-building in problem solving and information gathering, and development of social skills through role playing or psychodrama. A good deal of value clarification may be needed, and some instance of specifically focused, mutually agreed on behavioral goal setting will be valuable. The tools used, the counseling techniques, may not be Adlerian (that is, introduced and developed by Adler or his followers), but they will be used within the Adlerian framework of understanding the individual and group process.

# *R*ational-Emotive Therapy

*Implemented by Albert Ellis*

This is an ideal situation for the use of Rational-Emotive group therapy, since the group starts off from scratch and has not been allowed or encouraged to flounder in any nondirective manner, nor to acquire a prejudice in favor of becoming absorbed in its members' early history, in their "family" relationship to each other, in their attachment to the group leader, in their obsessive-compulsive interest in the group process itself, or in various other kinds of theories that are dear to the heart of most leaders and which are therefore willy-nilly crammed down the gullible gullets of most therapy group members. For a change, the prejudices of RET will be able to prevail! In my thinking about the group and what form I would like to see it take before I actually begin working with it, I will examine the general and specific goals of Rational-Emotive Therapy and how they might best be implemented in this particular group.

Doing so, I see RET as designed to help virtually all humans, and particularly intelligent ones, cope with their regular life problems and with their own tendencies to disturb themselves. I assume that virtually all college freshmen, in particular, are born and reared with a huge propensity to cause themselves needless emotional pain and turmoil; but that they also have several significant innate healthy or rational tendencies, including the tendency to think, to think about their thinking, to be curious, to learn, to become aware of their own emotional disturbances, to desire to change and actualize themselves, and to be able to choose much of their future emotional and behavioral destiny. I therefore assume that just about all the members of the present group will be able to benefit from RET; and that some of them can be shown how to make profound changes in their thinking, emoting, and behaving by learning and practicing its principles.

I will open the first session of the group by stating my goals in forming the group, and will try to discover whether all or most of the members are willing to go along with these goals. I will say something like: "Let me explain my main motives in forming this group. I think that all of you, as you have told me already in my individual talks with you, would like to contend more effectively with your new college environment and that you have the ability to learn to do so. As humans, you have some degree of free will or choice in the things you do—though let's not run this idea into the ground and piously claim that you are totally free. Bullshit! You, as humans, are somewhat limited by your heredity and by your environment. You can't do anything you wish to do—even though you can do much of what you would like to carry out.

"One of your important limitations is that in many ways you tend to think crookedly and to behave dysfunctionally; and you do so mainly because that's the kind of creature you are—limited. In spite of your intelligence and education, you still often tend to think irrationally: to use absolutistic modes of thought; to believe in nonexistent magic; to observe poorly and often to make antiempirical conclusions about your observations; to make fairly frequent use of illogical forms, such as nonsequiturs, arbitrary inference, and circular thinking; to defy and to devil-ify yourself and other humans; and often to override your straight thinking with dogmas, overgeneralizations, bigotries, prejudices, and superstitions.

"In terms of the form of psychotherapy and group therapy that I am going to employ with you in our subsequent sessions, all of you, like virtually all the rest of the human race, strongly tend to be intense *mus*turbators. You mistakenly—and quite self-defeatingly—often think that you absolutely *must* do well and be approved by others; second, that you *should* and *must* be dealt with considerately and fairly by the other people with whom you closely associate; and third, that the world *ought to* and *must* provide you with conditions that give you, fairly easily and quickly, whatever you dearly want and refrain from giving you the things and situations that you consider highly obnoxious.

"Perhaps you can manage, since some of you are talented in this respect, to upset yourself emotionally without any use of imperatives like *must, should, ought, got to, have to,* and *need.* Perhaps, but I doubt it. So far, whenever I have come across a disturbed person during the last quarter of a century, I have immediately been able to spot his or her *musts* that largely lead to this person's disturbance. And I have also found that the three main derivatives that people have as irrational ideas actually seem to stem from their basic *musts.* These derivatives are:

1. Since I *must* do well and be approved of by all the people I consider significant, it's *awful* if and when I don't!
2. I *can't stand* failing and being disapproved of by others, as I *must* not fail and *must* not be disapproved of!
3. Because I have failed and been disapproved of by my significant others, as I *must* not be, I am a *rotten person* who is not likely to do well at anything in the future and who really does not deserve good things.

"Now what we are going to do, in the course of these group therapy sessions, is to zero in on any or all of the things that bother you—or, in RET terms, about which you choose to bother yourself. If you have problems in school, in your social affairs, in your love life, with your parents, or in any other area, I want you to bring them in—and we will work on them together. But, even more importantly, we shall be interested in your problems *about* your problems. Thus, if you are doing poorly in your school work, we shall not only concern ourselves with ways in which you can do better, we shall also look at your feelings about this school work—especially feelings of anxiety, depression, inadequacy, hostility, or apathy. In RET we define such feelings as inappropriate—meaning they do not help you to live happily and get more of what you want and less of what you don't want.

"This doesn't mean that we want you to be unfeeling and unemotional. Rational, in RET, doesn't mean unemotional, calm, indifferent, or passive. It means, usually, quite emotional: that is, vitally concerned with your own and others' well-being and keenly sorry, regretful, disappointed, annoyed, and irritated when things are not going well for you and those for whom you care. Rational also means strongly determined to change what you don't like in the world, including your own self-defeating feelings and acts; and it means willing to *work* for a happier, more fulfilled kind of existence."

I will stop at this point and give the group members a chance to speak up and express themselves: to argue with me, to bring up other ideas, and especially to say what they would like to get out of the group sessions. I would have all of them try to bring up at least one problem that seems to be bothering them most at the present time: something that they would like to work on. I would have them briefly tell something about themselves—where they are from, why they came to college, what some of their main goals in life are, and the like.

I will then ask a member who is particularly bothered about something now—such as the problem of being relatively alone and friendless in this new college situation—to bring this up for discussion. I will also ask how many of the others felt similarly bothered. I can illustrate RET to the group members, largely using this first individual's problem: showing her, for example, that she felt lonely at point C (emotional and behavioral Consequence) after being in a situation at point A (Activating Experience); and that her new college situation, A, did not *make her* feel lonely, although it may have *contributed* to this feeling. I would try to show her (and the other group members) that she mainly chooses to upset herself, at point B (her Belief System about what is happening at A), by *demanding* and *commanding* that a better situation exists rather than merely *preferring* and *wishing* that it be better.

As I revealed to this group her own irrational Beliefs (at point B) with which she was creating her inappropriate feelings (of self-downing, hostility, and self-pity) at point C (Consequence), I would also quickly start challenging these ideas and Disputing them, at point D. Thus, I might show her that she was telling herself, at B: "People *should* be more friendly to me in this new college environment! I *can't bear* their curtness and indifference! What a *terrible place* this is compared to the way things are at home!" I would try to get her to Dispute these irrational Beliefs by asking her, "Where is the evidence that people *should be* as friendly as you'd *like* them to be? In what way can't you *bear* their curtness and indifference? Assuming that things really are more difficult here than at home, how does that difficulty make this a *terrible place?"* And I would try to get her, at least temporarily, to give up these self-defeating, groundless ideas.

While doing this, I will try to involve the other group members in Disputing and challenging the member who brought up a specific problem. In other words, I will get the group members immediately started on RET problem solving, discussing both of its aspects. First, discussing one's problem *about* a problem, or one's feelings of emotional upset when one experiences this problem; and trying to see how they arise from one's own thinking or attitude toward the problem; then making some concerted attempt to change that attitude and to eliminate or minimize the emotional disturbance. Second, as the disturbance seems to be getting under one's control, going back to the original practical problem and trying to see how it can be solved. Thus, in the young woman's case, once she began to stop hating herself, hating others, and thinking of the school as a terrible place, the group would discuss with her what she could do about making more friends and being alone less. For example, she could speak more to the other students in her dormitory, get together with some of those in her class to study together, join some of the college clubs, and the like.

Before the first session ended, I would hope that I had presented the main elements of RET, and some of its usual goals, and illustrated some of its techniques by applying them to at least one major problem brought up in the group. I would also give an activity-oriented homework assignment to the member(s) whose problems we are trying to resolve. Thus, our lonely members might be given the homework assignment of opening a conversation with at least three new people in the course of the next week. All the members of the group might also be given a shame-attacking assignment, such as doing something they consider foolish, shameful, or embarrassing, and working on their Belief System so that they would not feel the usual degree of shame that they normally feel when doing this "embarrassing" thing.

In this manner, I will be setting the stage for the group to have an ongoing experience of Rational-Emotive Therapy. I will suggest that the members give it a chance for at least four or five sessions, to see what they could learn from it, but that if any members objected seriously to the procedures that are going to be used, they could discuss these objections from time to time, and also choose to quit the group. If several of the group members want a quite different kind of group experience—such as a psychoanalytically oriented or encounter-type of experience—I will suggest that they still try this RET group for awhile, and if they are still dissatisfied, that they then try to find a group more amenable to their desires. I would not fall into the trap of seriously modifying the procedure that I usually follow in an RET group, since I personally believe in the effectiveness of that procedure. And if several or most of the group members really want to do something else, I think they should do it with a leader who believes in that alternate kind of procedure.

## Reality Therapy

*Implemented by Thomas E. Bratter*
When the group would convene for the first time, I would attempt to arrive before the session is scheduled to begin so I could greet the members individually and introduce them to one another. I would start precisely at the agreed upon time by suggesting that each take a few minutes to share with the group whatever he or she wished and briefly state some of the prominent reasons for wanting to join. In all probability, after the introductions are concluded, there would be an initial silence. I would welcome the opportunity to break the silence and set the ground rules.

   "I'm pleased you decided to come because I've heard much sensitivity and intelligence in this room. It's funny, because listening to you describe yourselves and concerns remind me of when I went away to college. Even though I was only twenty miles away from my family, the first night I can recall crying. I was frightened that I wouldn't make any friends...and that I wasn't as bright as everyone else. But, I guess my big fear was that I was different...strange...crazy. I wish I had the opportunity to meet with some people to discuss my fears because I think that would have helped. Actually, I think that is all we can do here.... To share experiences...the good...the bad...the pleasant...the painful. I envy you, because you are lucky that here you can be real...you can tell it like it is. But I do not expect you to begin to 'bare your heart and soul' because it will take some time before we begin to trust each other. I sincerely hope that whatever is said in here remains in here. Confidentiality is important because no one will want to talk. Hell, I wouldn't. I do not know what we can do if someone decides to publish what we say in the newspaper, but I hope this is not something which will occupy group time. The only thing which would insult me enormously is if anyone should come here 'high.' Again, that would be a group decision, but it would really annoy me because we are adults and here to relate honestly and openly. Obviously, when someone is talking, we can show them the respect they deserve and not interrupt them. The final rule is, of course, no violence or threats of violence. We can become angry and show our rage but we do not need to revert back to animals and threaten. Hell, I've spoken too long. Does anyone have any questions or comments?"

# *Transactional Analysis*

### *Implemented by Herbert Hampshire*

A Transactional Analysis (TA) group would be likely to start out with each member having established a contract in a preliminary meeting with the therapist. There are occasions, however, when the therapist meets the clients for the first time at the initial session of the group. This is probable in university clinics or community centers where intake interviews are conducted by another clinician and an assignment to a group is made.

In this situation, it is important to focus the group of students on establishing individual goals and articulation purposes at the outset. If the procedure is not followed, a group process is initiated that leaves members' individual dynamics in a position of lower priority than would naturally be the case. The task in a TA group is to effect a cure for the specific problem(s) identified by the individual so that he or she may move to another concern or leave the group until or unless some other problem is identified that prompts them to re-enter treatment.

If I have met the group members previously, I will start the group by identifying a nonverbal response or by asking who wants to work on something. Introductions are then handled in whatever way they come up in the group. This allows individuals to experience and demonstrate how they react to an absence of clear "rules"and how they solve the "problem" of not knowing each other's names. Very often, the way this procedure is handled reveals a great deal about group members' programming. One person will experience anxiety at the absence of directive leadership and resolve the conflict by "taking over," announcing that "we ought to start by introducing ourselves." Others will reveal their level of adaption by inquiring whether they "should" or whether they "can" introduce themselves. Often individuals will avoid the issue of names if the therapist does not focus on it and then insert it later in some parenthetical way that makes it appear to have little significance. No matter what form the transactions around introductions takes, it is useful for diagnostic as well as therpeutic purposes to let the process play itself out with as little structure being introduced by the therapist as possible.

If I have not met the group members previously, I will tell them my name and then "get to work." I might identify someone's apparent discomfort or agitation by inviting them to verbalize their feelings. The direction this interaction takes is toward establishing a contract. I will explain, essentially didactically, the importance of each person identifying which aspect of their functioning they want to change. The formation of effective contracts can often take a good deal of therapy and is a process that is continually sharpened and refined. It is important that patients be clear at all times about what they are seeking from the treatment.

The process of "contract negotiations" is also therapeutic. Frequently people come into therapy for reasons that are programmatic. They think "something is wrong" with them, or they have been pressured by others into concluding they "ought to" change. Students, for example, seek therapy for such problems as being "unable to study." The most obvious example of this pattern in other settings is the alcoholic who is trapped into treatment by a spouse who threatens to leave or a boss who threatens the loss of their job. The first task of treatment with these patients is to assist them in recognizing they are not in group treatment because *they* want something and that they are defining their problem in a way that makes them their own enemy. Students who enter therapy because they "ought to" study more are essentially attacking themselves for their own behavior. In the process of establishing a contract, it may become clear that members want to disconnect from Parental pressure to a degree that allows them to determine whether they even want to be in school. The student who "wants to change" very often has no sense that he or she can deal with their feelings and other people's in any way other than to adapt to external pressures.

It is a repeated clinical observation that treatment is not effective when a contract is made with a Parent and/or in opposition to a Natural Child. Contracts opposing the child are matters requiring control and not treatment. An effective therapeutic contract requires a goal that is defined by the person and which can be observably reached. The rule of thumb I suggest to patients is to define their purpose for being in treatment so it is apparent *to someone else* when achieved. The contract must be a genuine contract in the sense that it also must include a recognition of what the "goal" is and what the therapist can contribute to the attainment of the goal.

Particularly at the outset of this group, but at other times as well, I will periodically "digress" from what someone is working on to do some didactic intervention. If the group is unfamiliar with TA, I will briefly explain the concepts of ego states and transactions. This is likely to be one of the few times I will rely heavily on the language of TA. There is strikingly little use in my groups of "TA jargon" for precisely the reason that it is so easy to convert it into a jargon. The concepts are extraordinarily useful in producing clarity for both therapist and patient, but what needs to be talked about are feelings, problems, and people; not ego state, game diagnoses, and the like. I am more likely to ask someone how they think someone is likely to respond to what they just said than to identify that they are playing a game of "Now I Got You, You Son-of-a-Bitch." The purpose of TA treatment is to cure people and empower them to be autonomous and effective, not to prove how clever the therapist is at being incisively analytical. Patients in TA often read books on the subject and take workshops. This is encouraged since it provides them with the same tools for producing clarity and conciousness available to the therapist. It is not supported, however, when the language becomes something to hide behind while they are resisting change.

## Theory Evaluation Form

1. Which theoretical practitioner did you most resemble? Why?

2. Which theoretical practitioner did you least resemble? Why?

3. What does your response to *Question 1* tell you about yourself and your leadership styles as a potential or present group therapist?

4. What does your response to *Question 2* tell you about yourself and your leadership style as a potential or present group therapist?

5. After rereading how the theoretical practitioner of your choice responded to the incident, how would you modify or change your response?

# CHAPTER EIGHT

# Group Attack of the Therapist

The following incident is one most therapists face in the life of a group. Sometime into the third session, the group turns and attacks you, the therapist.

## Incident #2

The group is made up of five couples. Initially each couple had been seeing you separately. However, as you came to realize that their areas of concern had much in common, you asked each couple if they would be interested in joining a group of couples. You explained the rationale supporting your consideration for establishing the group, including the added value and benefits for recognizing behavior(s) that groups provide beyond meeting individually. They all volunteered to give it a try.

Briefly, the members are described as follows:

Couple #1: Nicholas and Laurie have been married for 15 years. They have two children, ages 10 and 13. Nicholas is 35, has a degree in engineering and is employed as a design engineer. Peggy is 33. She has been a homemaker since they were married after graduating from high school. Peggy has expressed a desire to go to college and has stated that she is not sure she wants to remain being just a housewife. Nicholas is confused over this sudden turn in events.

Couple #2: Larry and Pamela have been married for two years. They have no children. Larry is 26, has an associate degree and is an associate with an ophthalmologist. Pamela is 25 and is employed as a registered nurse at the local hospital. When they first came to you, they stated that they were unhappy with their marriage but were not sure why.

Couple #3: Paul and Joan have been married for eight years. They have three children, ages 4, 6, and 7. Paul is 34, a high school graduate and a self-employed plumber. Joan is 33, holds an M.A. in education and is teaching fourth grade at a local elementary school. Joan initiated their contact with you. When you first met them, the presenting issue was Joan's concern that Paul seemed to be avoiding her and Paul had expressed that he was not happy.

Couple #4: John and Helen have been married for 10 years. This is Helen's second marriage. They have two children, ages 11 and 13, both of whom are from Helen's first marriage. John is 40, and had attended college for three years and now operates a printing company. Helen is 39, a high school graduate, and is employed as a teacher's aide. She has stated that she wants to go to college. John has voiced opposition to this and they have reached an impasse.

Couple #5: Peter and Doris have lived together for 10 years. They have two children, ages 4 and 6. Peter is 31 and owns a florist shop. Doris is 31. She is a cosmetologist and is employed by a department store. They came to you because they felt their marriage was not the same as it used to be.

The first two sessions had a great deal of activity. Member-to-member interaction seemed to develop easily. Early in the second session, the members engaged in a significant amount of disclosure and confrontation. It came about as a result of Nicholas's disclosure of his confusion about why his wife should want to go to school. He stated he felt that once she got a taste of it, she might want to go to work, and he questioned where this would all lead. As far as he was concerned, he felt their marriage was just fine the way it was and he could not understand why it should change. As you listened to him, you observed how his wife was responding. She was sitting with her feet crossed in front of her and her arms and hands resting on her lap; eyes looking toward her hands. Her face was expressionless. Your eyes shifted to the rest of the members. You could see John nodding as though he was agreeing with or understood Nicholas's comments. His wife was looking at Laurie. Larry, Pamela, Paul, and Joan were listening intently to Nicholas. He no sooner had completed his statement, when Doris, with her voice sounding tense, stated, "That sounded just like a man! All they ever think about is that because their wives are working, they might end up running around!" Before she was able to continue, her statement drew responses from the rest of the group. You observed (to yourself) that Laurie had not participated in the ensuing interaction. You determined it was perhaps too early to make this observation known and that perhaps Laurie would, in her own time, present herself. The emotional level of the group was still relatively high as you moved the session to termination.

At the third session, you noticed that the members were very jovial and quite verbal as they entered the room. As a matter of fact, they continued to discuss a number of issues such as dieting, politics, and sports throughout the first 15 minutes of the session. You finally offered that you thought this level of discussion was not dealing with the issues or purposes of the group and asked the members if they were aware of the direction their discussion had undergone. There was a brief silence in the group. Then one of the members attacked you for seeming to appear cool, distant, and uncaring. With that, another stated she was beginning to question your qualifications as a therapist. The others joined in the attack, each in turn questioning, in one form or another, your credibility as a therapist.

## Client-Centered Therapy

*Implemented by William R. Coulson*

As a group begins, members grant the leader expertise, but I do not want it. My task, as I define it, is to work gradually into membership, to the point that I am not special. A major criterion of leadership will have been met when other members see me as a person like themselves.

I do not mean to be self-effacing. I also want members to see themselves as persons, having all the power that comes with being the leader. When I am group leader, I feel like Superperson. The title does it for me. It permits me to be as sharp and attentive as I would like always to be—whether member or leader—but which as member, ordinarily embarrasses me, lest someone accuse me of trying to be leader. I doubt that anyone would actually make such an accusation. Nonetheless, I often seem to need an initial role in order to drop my reserve and be as powerful as a person. I do not want to give up this power. I want to distribute it. Then all of us will be Superpersons.

As such, each of us will be different. Being persons includes our various backgrounds, the particular persons we have become. I do not want to pretend, for example, that I am not a professional psychologist.

But I do not want special respect since group members have their own backgrounds, helping qualify them to contribute uniquely to the others. It is this distribution of unique perspectives within the group, which I believe defines the power of group over individual therapy. The necessary resources are among us, not in only one. This is the Client-Centered hypotheses as applied to group work.

The present trouble in this group arose because the therapist failed to provide a personal perspective at a time when it was needed, and he or she now is being punished for it. One member calls the therapist detached ("cool, distant, and uncaring"). I doubt that the therapist is that way as a person. Yet one can see where the judgment of detachment originates. The leader seemingly has not participated except with unspoken or professional observations. My concern as the therapist now is that I not maintain this stance—in order to avoid a defense against the group's attack.

The incident offers an opportunity for rich personal learning, if the therapist will only take it. It requires the therapist to remain alert. For myself, I cannot envision a discrete picture of learning in this incident that could equal the latent possibilities in the actual interaction. The best of these possibilities will be quite unknown until the moment of their arrival at the next turn of the conversation. To take advantage of this opportunity, the therapist only need avoid shutting down.

The greatest danger in being under attack is to become psychological, seeing the group's aggression as *solely* the sign of members' own minor (and major) pathologies. Granted therapists must not wilt under the attack by taking it too personally; they must, therefore, maintain an ability to see the attack as having as much to do with the group as with the therapist. But, to get full benefit from the criticism, they must listen to it openly. When it is offered, they cannot be thinking, "I know where *that* comes from." They have to acknowledge that others can tell them important things about themselves that they cannot know of their own. In the simplest terms, group members can *see* them; that's something they cannot do for themselves. The final decision about the importance of what group members tell therapists about themselves will and must remain with them. But they must not censor it through psychologizing about their critics. There is more than one kind of defensiveness. Therapists are unlikely to display the blatant, argumentative kind. If they become defensive under the pressure they now receive from the group, it is likely to be in an unwarranted extension of professional form, namely psychologism (Buber 1967).

I see the therapist as having made two errors in this situation. One occurred at the end of the last session, and the other just preceded the group's criticism.

1. There was trauma in the second session. Doris rebuked Nicholas, seemingly out of the blue. She made an outrageous generalization

about the husbands of working women. She must have been talking about her own marriage, but she did not get to finish. The group took off like a covey of quail, beating wings, banging against the ceiling, bouncing off the walls. That's how the second session ended, "the emotional level of the group still relatively high." Fright continued to affect the group at the next session. Members gravitated to small talk to protect themselves against the possible further trauma of examining or even acknowledging what had happened the last time.

Any trauma will cause a hole in the group unless someone has the nerve to point to it. As therapist, I would have done so myself if no one else had, just out of self-protection. I know that if the disruption of the second session was not explicitly noted in the group, it would have come back to haunt us later. Each person would carry a private opinion about what had happened. But there would be no common acceptance and readiness to move to a deeper level unless the incident was discussed in the group.

It is safe to guess that the individual couples talked about the incident when they got home after the second session—and that they talked about the therapist. I have sensitivity for the therapist being involved in a couples group without being part of a couple. One knows that husbands and wives are going to talk about the session as they drive home. That is one of the benefits of couples groups: therapy goes on into the night. The therapist who works alone runs the risk of becoming a handy target when things become difficult for the group. So I bring protection with me when I do couples groups: my wife becomes a member with me.

I hope she doesn't tell on me, tell the group the bad things I do at home. But I hope for the same direction (and intuitive sense of what is truly helpful in therapy) among the other couples, too. It is a waste of time when they bring stories of home life with them. There is little one can do to help. They have all the data. Someone will make a suggestion for improvement, and they will say, "We've tried that." There is little virtue in exchanging suggestions in therapy groups of any kind. It is far more interesting and effective when members react to one another as persons in the moment. Couples have the advantage in therapy of living together and being able to take the session home with them if they wish. But they cannot constructively bring home life to the group. They make themselves experts when they do, but experts only on their private histories. We need no experts. We do far better dealing with what we all can see, and that means what is happening in the group itself.

There was a big happening in this group and nobody mentioned it. That's too much like life to suit me. The therapist should have said something at the end of the second session, even at the risk of running overtime.

2. The second mistake was scolding the group for making small talk at the start of the third session. *Of course* they made small talk. The group had ended in an uproar the last time they met, and they were afraid to go near it again. The therapist must have known what they were avoiding. Rather than accuse them of "not dealing with the issues or purposes of the group" (a phrase that, if actually used in group, surely would sound superior and coldly professional), the therapist should have admitted knowing there was a hole in the group or even confess—if it were so—a personal desire to avoid it, too.

The therapist should now suffer the consequences in this instance and listen to what the group has to say. The therapist should realize that some of the group's criticism will be overdetermined (we would not be far off to say that they are scapegoating the therapist), but to learn from it, too. Hearing criticism directly (rather than hearing of it having been spoken behind one's back) is a rare enough opportunity that one ought to get all he or she can out of it.

For myself, I would probably blow the opportunity to learn from criticism, particularly if the group were unanimous in condemning me. But I would *want* to learn from it. Somewhere at the back of my mind, so far back that it might be unreachable when I was under pressure, I would have the idea that I needed to hear from people about myself, including, and especially, my mistakes. I would really *want* to treat these people as colleagues who, if I could listen to them (and perhaps if they could speak a little more gently) would help me gain perspective. Our therapist has been "observing" his or her "subjects" and, indeed, has been "critical." But the tables have turned; the subjects have now become critical themselves. We should have expected it. Any attempt to limit therapeutic judgment to the therapist alone would distort the obvious: that human intelligence, experience, and insight are widely distributed. The therapist has no corner on wisdom. Not only will group members exercise judgment of their own, they will surpass the therapist.

# Gestalt Therapy

*Implemented by Mirriam F. Polster*

This scene does not sound like one I would have gotten into. I do not mean that I might never be attacked or criticized. Rather, I would have behaved differently both at the end of the previous session and at the beginning of this one.

Doris's denunciation of men occurs in stereotypical terms near the end of the second session and gets lost in what the rest of the group says afterwards. An opportunity for dialogue has been missed. Her statement is an abstraction, dealing only in generalities. It would have been important in the second session to bring it into the present circumstances by attaching it to the specifics of what Nicholas has just said. As it did end, Doris's energy is left constricted, tense, and deflected (Polster & Polster 1973), and a chance for vital confrontation and contact is not supported. I would ask Doris to tell Nicholas more about her experience with "all men" and what it is in particular that she finds objectionable in what he has just said. Is she saying he is like all the rest? How? What does she know about him that suggested this? How does she want to respond to what the other group members have said?

Nicholas, too, has been vague and general. His statement requires more time to develop into specific revelations about his fears. What is it about Laurie's return to school that makes him apprehensive? If he is confused about why she wants to go back, why doesn't he ask her? If he is fearful about the consequences of her returning to school, what prevents him from telling her of his worries in a way that respects her needs and still honors his own uncertainty? What actual experiences has Nicholas had when this subject has come up between him and Laurie? Has he felt that there were things he had not told her, that remained unsaid and unfinished between them? Our situation presents an opportunity for the dialogue that is essential between them. Instead, Nicholas is allowed to remain vague and Laurie sits there, staring at her hands, saying nothing. Is this a reenactment of how things go at home when this subject is broached, or has it previously led to such painful or unresolved feelings that a fresh discussion is to be avoided at all costs?

In responding to these events in the second session, I will try to heighten the possibilities for dialogue by sharpening the participants' awareness of particular feelings and complaints, and also by body postures. The way Laurie is sitting, even though silent, is saying something. Can she put this into words? Would it then express hopelessness or resentment? How does Nicholas feel about her silence? How do the others respond to it? Addressing each other directly is a step toward resolution. How well Nicholas, Doris, Laurie, and the others can support strong contact, or flee from it, can then become more apparent and more workable. Right now, much of their energy goes into deflection; Nicholas gets confused and does not know how to ask the questions dealing specifically with his fears; Doris's complaints are off-target and stereotypically bitter; Laurie remains silent; and the group focus is allowed to dissolve into diffuse comment with little follow-up.

At the beginning of the third session, I would not have done what the group leader did—I would not have interpreted the group's behavior as avoidant. The traditional definition of resistance ignores the energy and creativity that may be expressed, in this case, the small talk, and moves instead to what is *not* being expressed, the last session's confrontation. While this is a valid perspective, it emphasizes the opinion of the group leader, who decides what is important and tells everybody else that *they* are resisting. We could say that the group leader is resisting also—resisting the joviality and talkativeness of the group and taking a stand slightly lower than the angels, telling the mortals to get down to business. To regard the group's behavior as merely resistant is to disrespect their self-regulatory capacity to learn how to pace themselves. If I were interested in some other topic, I would simply put it out. I might say that I am eager to pick up where we left off last time—are they?

If we view what is happening at the beginning of the third session as expressive rather than resistant behavior (Polster & Polster 1973), we see different results. The group is interacting with energy and excitement. The members are talking about something other than their marital difficulties, it is true, but I will observe to see if they are listening to each other more attentively and taking each other's reactions and opinions more seriously than before. Perhaps learning how someone else goes about dieting is a preface to getting back to a deeper issue where that person's opinion will also be taken more seriously. Perhaps the group is warming up to get back to the loaded discussion of the previous session and is testing the atmosphere to see if grudges or sore feelings remain. Their self-regulation needs room to operate; if they feel driven back into confronting an issue, then I have changed the issue; they are no longer responding to Nicholas, Doris, and Laurie but also to me *compelling* them to respond. In a way, I have deflected them from the topic.

People in a group often need to determine the stability and trustworthiness of the group response. While they can be overly careful about this on occasion, this is neverthless a self-supportive action before heading into new emotional territory. They are exploring the balance between discretion, wariness, passion, bitterness, apprehension, directness, hopelessness, and the whole spectrum of feelings that can either muddy up or enliven the interaction of people, married to each other or not.

So I might wait out what appears to be small talk and look for an opening to bring it around to more familiarly therapeutic concerns. I avoided using the word more *serious* concerns. Humor and joviality *are* often deflections, but deflection can sometimes serve a useful purpose. People may need to skirt an issue, to buy time and perspective in a situation in which they might otherwise feel pushed beyond their present capacity to support themselves. Gradual descent into hot water is important for more than getting into bathtubs.

The opening could come directly from what one person may say or from another's response. For example, Doris, in talking about dieting, might say something about how unfair it is that women have to worry more about their appearance than men; someone talking about politics might express an opinion about the feminist movement, and so on. I could, instead of this approach, raise the issue directly by saying, "When we stopped last time we were in the middle of a hot discussion. Does anyone have some unfinished business left from that time?" Or I could ask some of the more vocal people from last time if there was something more they wanted to say now. Had they gotten their views across or did they feel misunderstood and want to add something? I would make sure this time that Laurie did not remain a cipher. This was her husband talking, what were her reactions to his position? I might also ask John how he felt about Nicholas's speech. And certainly Helen.

Most important, though, I am responding to the energy level and excitement of the group. These assets are too valuable to be scolded out of existence because at the moment they are not being applied to what I consider to be the central focus.

This is a group of people whose excitement customarily does not work *for* them. They convert it into anxiety, watchfulness, and confusion. These individuals need to experience trusting their excitement and learning how to support clarity and enthusiasm in their relationships. By staying aware of the specifics of their experience, as it is occurring, and not complying with someone else's "shoulds" (even the therapist's), they will learn to support their actions in the present moment. Their sensations and feelings can then become orienting and arousing rather than distracting. Their experience of themselves can root them in the present instead of catapulting them into a future made scary, perpetually vaguely worded in impersonal clichés where they have all the painful sensations of arousal without the opportunity for interaction and resolution that exist only in the present.

## Individual Psychology

### Implemented by Guy J. Manaster

This situation is a beauty. It holds great potential for development of the group as a whole and of individuals. This presents an opportunity for group members to reveal themselves and their goals in interpersonal interaction, and for interpretation of their goals in the group. It also gives me a chance to learn about myself and how I come across as group leader.

My previous tendency in this type of situation was to feel defensive; I had to fight my inclination to defend myself and do battle. I cannot remember ever giving in to that inclination but I surely remember feeling like doing so. Maybe it is just maturity, but I prefer to think that I have internalized Adlerian theory over the years and gained both confidence in my adequacy and awareness of my imperfections. Openness to new options for thinking and behaving are the result. The response that immediately comes to mind in this situation is, "You may be right. What do you think I should be doing? What would a *real* therapist be doing?"

This response, I hope, first makes the point that I do not always have to be right, all-knowing, supremely confident, but rather that I am interested in learning and growing while still feeling adequate. This point is particularly important for Nicholas and John, and probably Doris, all of whom appear to want things to be and therefore see things as, clear, black or white, and definite.

My response also is intended to indicate respect for the group's opinion. The group leader's interjection in the third session that led to this attack can be read as, and may well have been taken by the group as, a put-down. If the group reaction has arisen because the leader conveyed an attitude of "enough of this silly talk—let's get down to business—don't you know that you've been avoiding the issues," then an indirect, if not a direct, apology by the leader is called for. The leader may have inadvertently given that impression and should try to counter it. As leader, even if I had not transmitted this holier-than-thou attitude, which I know I would not have felt, I want to show my respect for the group members as worthy people. Central to positive mental health in Adlerian theory is the feeling of equality with others. Equality and mutual respect are important in this group, where the difficulty inherent in marriage partners living as equals is compounded by traditional notions of differential status and value accorded by sex and credentials.

It is presumptuous to suppose that "You may be right" actually communicates all of these meanings, but from our previous contact and with follow-up, I would try to convey these points.

What was the purpose of the rest of my response? First I want to know what they want. Second, I have set up a straw-man, "a *real* therapist," the perfect therapist, in order to again present opportunities to emphasize personal and general fallibility, equality, and a spirit of working together.

I have two hunches. The first, mentioned above, is that I started this by putting the group down and they are saying "It's your fault we are off the mark. If you were a good therapist we would be a good group." I have stated how and why I would try to counter and make use of this theme.

My second hunch is that many in the group want *the answer* to their problems. By asking what they want of me, or someone competent in another therapeutic approach, I can find out if this is true. If they answer that a *real* therapist would give more direction, tell them who is right, what to do, and the like, then my hunch would be confirmed. The discussion to follow would then have to turn to questions of values— what Adler called "the common sense of social living"—is there a right way, *an answer?* And I would have to confess that I do not know the answer. My task, as I see it and would explain it, is to assist in the development of processes based on social interest that foster equality of responsibility and satisfaction within the couple.

My hunches may be wrong. If they are, my response should, in any event, open the way for a new level of group process with some improvement in the ability of the group leader.

# ℛ*ational-Emotive Therapy*

### Implemented by Albert Ellis

In terms of Rational-Emotive Therapy (RET), the situation is partly that of a cop-out: the members of the group are probably doing what they most naturally and easily do—avoiding difficult problems and avoiding the issues or purposes of the group because it takes less effort on their part and because it is easier for them to discuss whatever comes up and not to get down to brass tacks. RET sees this as the normal tendency of humans to have low frustration tolerance and to go for immediate satisfactions rather then long-range gains.

As a group leader, therefore, I expect this kind of thing to occur and to keep occurring. By luck, and probably not because I was doing very well myself as a leader during the first two sessions, Nicholas got to something important in his relations with his wife and showed that he was confused; and by luck, Doris reacted emotionally to Nicholas and showed her strong feeling about men dominating women in marriage and being overconcerned about their wives running around, rather than concerned about what their wives really want to do in life. But this issue was not fully discussed, because time ran out, so I would raise it again at the third session. More than one couple expressed a problem with the wife's career goals conflicting with the husband's desire for the woman to return to the old ways.

By this third session, I would realize that I had not structured the group process sufficiently and explained to the members that we are neither merely interested in their expression of feelings nor are we too interested in their discussing unimportant topics or questions irrelevant to therapy, such as politics and sports. I would therefore explain to the members the basic purposes of an RET therapy group: that the group is here to bring out practical problems and emotional problems about these practical problems. I would also explain that the goal is to understand and resolve the emotional problems first, and then to work, simultaneously, on the resolution of the practical marital and personal problems of the participants.

I would emphasize that one of the main purposes of the group is to help the members solve their marital difficulties as well as their personal difficulties; and that since they all have somewhat similar problems in this respect, we shall try to explore those difficulties that are common to most of them and see what general, as well as individual, solutions can be arrived at. I would emphasize that this is a RET-oriented therapy group; and that, as leader, I expect to help all the group members see that when they have practical marital problems, they almost always have an emotional problem or problem *about* the practical problem. The goal of RET group therapy is to help them see that they have some basic irrational beliefs that directly cause or create their disturbed emotional reactions. I hope, therefore, that they will disclose their emotional problems, and when they do, to look for the irrational beliefs that lie behind these problems and to get them to dispute and surrender these beliefs.

I will then address the specific member who has attacked me for appearing cool, distant, and uncaring in the following manner: "Yes, John, you may well be right in accusing me of appearing cool, distant, and uncaring. I think that I definitely care about your, and the other group members' problems and disturbances, and am very concerned about helping you with these difficulties. But that doesn't mean that I care, personally, about *you*—that I like you or love you, or would want to have you as one of my close friends. Actually, with some of your pretty abominable behavior—such as your hostility toward your wife and your business associates, which you have already spoken about— I'm not sure that I would want to be friendly with you at all, if I met you under social circumstances. I think I would find you bright and interesting, and might well want to discuss certain issues with you—but, I doubt if I would find you very friendly! If you worked on and got rid of that hostility of yours—yes, perhaps then I would. But right now, with the hostility you show toward others; and even with the tone of voice you are now displaying toward me, about my supposed coolness—no, I don't think I would feel very friendly toward you.

"Besides, the purpose of RET therapy groups is not to display friendship, love, or warmth from the therapist to the group members, nor even from the group members to each other. If such warmth arises, as it sometimes does, fine. But love and warmth is not exactly group therapy; and, in fact, it is often the reverse. One of the main things that people think they need—and I believe you are well in this class right now—is the undying and near-perfect approval of others. Well, they don't—they only *think* they do. Not that love and approval aren't nice; they definitely are! But *nice* doesn't mean *necessary!* If you want approval and you get it from others, great! That adds to your life. But if you think you *need*, you absolutely *must* have it, you are really in trouble. You feel marvelous, of course, when you do get it; and very upset and angry—as you and the group members seem to be showing right now—when you don't.

"One of the fundamental propositions of RET is that people do not *need* what they *want.* Almost all of their desires and preferences, however great, are legitimate; and almost all their *needs* and *necessities* are quite illegitimate. For if you want something very much and don't get it, you are merely keenly disappointed and sorry. But if you think you absolutely need it and don't get it, you are destroyed: depressed, anxious, self-hating. So in RET, we deliberately don't give therapeutic love; for that might encourage you to become a bigger baby than you already are! Unconditional acceptance; full respect for you as an individual, no matter how badly you may perform, is what we do try to give in RET; and also what we try to help individuals to give themselves and to all other humans.

"I am trying to get you—and all the other group members—to unconditionally, fully accept and respect *yourself.* And if I succeed, in spite of, or even because of, my 'coolness,' I shall help you accept yourself *whether or not* I approve of you and *whether or not* you act very competently during your life. If I can help you see things that way, you'll really have it made! And the question of whether or not I approve of you or like you will be important, perhaps, but hardly vital."

If John wanted to talk more about this, I would welcome his doing so. I would try to show him that his anger at me comes not from his desire for me to be a better therapist, and not from his feeling sorry and frustrated that I am not—but from his demanding and commanding that I *must* be the kind of good therapist that he wants and that it is *terrible* and I am a *rotten person* if I am not.

At the same time, I would try to draw the other members of the group into his discussion, and would attempt to show all of them: (1) that I might well be right about my leadership of the group, because I have been following, quite deliberately, a RET pattern of group therapy that usually brings about excellent results with most group members; (2) that I might be wrong about my leadership, because I really am an uncaring person and have been missing the boat in several important respects; (3) that even if I am wrong and uncaring, they do not have to put themselves down and make themselves panicked and depressed about my shortcomings as a group leader; and (4) that even if I am wrong and inept, they do not have to anger themselves at me for having these failings; but can, instead, regretfully decide that I am not the kind of leader they want and look elsewhere for another type of therapy or another type of RET leader.

I might possibly, in the course of my talking to the members of the group, deliberately feign anger at and strongly criticize one of them for "wrongly" being opposed to me. Then I would suddenly stop my verbal attack, especially if the person I picked on became upset and started to attack me back, and show that I had feigned anger as an emotive exercise, to draw out the attacked person's (and the other group members') reactions. We would then explore some of these reactions in detail, see whether various members had felt very hurt or angry at my tirade, show them exactly what they had been telling themselves to create these disturbed feelings, and indicate what they could do to dispute and challenge their irrational beliefs and to rid themselves of these feelings.

I would also try to give some or all of the group members a homework assignment—perhaps one in which they deliberately courted the companionship of a cold, distant, uncaring person, letting themselves feel anxious, depressed, self-pitying, or angry when in this person's presence, and then work on these disturbed feelings and try to change them into more appropriate feelings of sorrow, disappointment, frustration, and annoyance.

In the above way, I would try to show the group what the RET version of group therapy is, and how it differs radically from some other forms of treatment. I would try to show them that, as RET firmly posits, A (Activating Experiences) does not directly lead to or cause C (disturbed emotional Consequences). The more direct and important cause or contribution to C is B (people's Belief Systems about what is happening to them at A).

I would illustrate to them, moreover, in general, and from the events and feelings occurring to them in the group, that their Beliefs, at B, almost invariably are of two kinds when they feel disturbed at C. First, they have a set of rational Beliefs (rB's), which consists of preferences or desires. For example: "I don't like the leader's behavior! I wish he didn't act that way! What a pain in the ass!" These rB's tend to lead them to feel appropriate Consequences (aC's), such as feelings of sorrow, regret, disappointment, and annoyance. Second, they have a set of irrational Beliefs (iB's), which consists of commands or demands. For example: "The leader *must* not behave the way that he does! How *awful!* I *can't stand* his behaving in that manner! What a horrible leader and a *terrible person* he is!" These iB's tend to lead them to feel inappropriate Consequences (iC's), such as hurt, self-downing, hostility, or self-pity.

I would then show the group members what I had neglected to show them previously: that all their irrational, self-defeating Beliefs are only hypotheses and not facts; and that they can actively and vigorously Dispute these hypotheses at point D. D, or Disputing of irrational Beliefs, is the scientific method of asking themselves such questions as: "Where is the evidence that the leader *must* not behave the way he does? Prove that it is *awful* if he acts badly or inefficiently. In what way can't I *stand* his behaving poorly, against my and the group's interest? Where is it written that he, because he acts badly, is a *terrible person?*"

Asking these questions, they would then arrive at E, a new Effect or new philosophy of life. E is a realistic acceptance of the way the world (or at least, the group member's world) is. If they would correctly answer their own Disputational questions at D, they would usually arrive at E, along these lines: "Yes, the leader of this group has probably behaved in an ineffectual, incorrect manner—as fallible humans often behave; consequently, he will sometimes continue to act that badly and to lead the group that poorly in the future. Too damned bad! Although I'll never like being inconvenienced by him and his activity in this manner, I definitely can stand it, and can continue to live and to be relatively happy in spite of his incompetent performances.

Notice that the RET assumptions—like those of most other psychotherapies, but perhaps a little more honestly and openly—is that no matter what goes on in the group (or in the lives of the members when they are outside the group), and no matter how poorly and foolishly the leader acts in the course of the group process, the members still *upset themselves* not by taking something seriously or making it important but by taking it *too* seriously and making it *all*-important or *sacred*. Virtually everything, therefore, that happens inside or outside the group can be used as a focal point to show any individual member, or all the members combined, that they are irrationally creating their own feelings of anxiety, depression, hostility, worthlessness, apathy, and self-pity, and that they can choose to think, feel, and behave much more effectively, in accordance with their own personal goals and values.

Once this idea of people's *self*-conditioning and the *self*-choosing of the way they react to "obnoxious" stimuli is accepted by the group members, they can then be helped to go back to A, their Activating Experiences, and either see them differently (with less prejudice) or try to change them. In this present instance, once I help John and the others to see that however badly I behaved, they do not have to upset themselves about it, they will be in a position to see more accurately whether I really did behave that poorly. If I had not, then they could look into their own hearts and change their own feelings about my "bad" leadership. And if I had, they could much more determinedly and undisturbedly try to show me the error of my ways, and to get me to change. Or, finally, they could decide that staying in the group was hardly worth their while, and could individually or collectively quit.

RET, then, attempts to help the group members identify their own disturbed thoughts, emotions, and behaviors and to change them; and *then* to consider changing the situation which they are in. It does not *merely* focus on one of these two goals but on both of them.

## Reality Therapy

*Implemented by Thomas E. Bratter*
The group leader in this situation appears to have assumed a more traditional analytical-passive orientation. Not surprisingly, because of their own fears and resistance, the group members have decided to challenge the leader and his or her qualifications.

I believe those people with whom I work certainly are entitled to ask questions about my values and credentials. Rather than play therapeutic games, I would respond to such a request forthrightly and outline my professional credentials and experience in counseling.

In the group situation described, however, the timing of the disclosure reveals that the group has been frustrated and angered by the "cool, distant, and uncaring" therapeutic stance of the psychotherapist. Most assuredly, believing as I do, I would have avoided placing myself in a position where either my credentials or the therapeutic distance would have become legitimate issues. Let us assume, however, that I acted as the group leader has, and now the group has begun to demand some sort of explanation.

I would begin by saying: "I hear your anger and criticism, which I admit, in part, is valid. I can contribute more. I will make a commitment to do so. Yet, I am curious why the group wants me to run the show. I am impressed with the energy and intelligence in this room. No one has risked much by talking about themselves. There have been times when I hoped that someone would have related to what was being said, but for whatever reason, it failed to materialize. Perhaps this would be a good time for us to reevaluate what we want from the group experience. I would appreciate learning why no one has wanted to discuss a personal issue for the first fifteen minutes." In so doing, I would accept some of the responsibility for the slow start, but then subtly suggest that everyone could have assumed a more active role and risked more personally. By heeding the criticism and then changing my behavior, I would have become a responsible role model. It is important to note that I would have agreed to change my behavior, because I believe the comments are valid. If I disagreed with the suggestion, I would explain my rationale and would not change.

## Transactional Analysis

*Implemented by Herbert Hampshire*
Working with couples is distinctly challenging as well as gratifying since one can examine not only individual scripts but the interlocking script that provides constant reinforcement and validation. Working with couples in groups has the added dimension of the group process. Members come into therapy for the paradoxical purposes of both changing the ways they function and maintaining their system against all assaults. This becomes especially apparent when working with couples since it is clear the direction that the investment of energy often takes is toward changing the spouse rather than oneself.

The task with couples is always, to one degree or another, to undermine the existing symbiotic relationship and to produce what Murray Bowen calls "individuation" and Eric Berne calls "autonomy." In light of this goal, I place emphasis at the outset on establishing a contract with *each* marital partner. Much of the "wheel-spinning" in marital therapy occurs out of the omission of this stage. Nicholas and Laurie exemplify this point dramatically. When Nicholas says that "their marriage was just fine the way it was, and he can't understand why it should change," he demonstrates the fusion of the couple. Anything Laurie seeks to do in relation to herself is, within the context of the couple, perceived as something being done to the relationship. There is an illusion of shared purpose, with both of them "working on the marriage," while in fact, Laurie's purpose is to move away from allowing the context of the marriage to define her functioning and limit her behavior, while Nicholas is seeking to maintain the primacy of their original contract. Since they were married at relatively young ages and had a child after only one year, it is likely that Laurie now sees herself as having "sold out on herself" and as having "missed options" that she did not even recognize at the time. Within her programming, she has no apparent way to relate to her anger and resentment as well as to her sadness. If her contract in therapy were related to developing the capacity to relate effectively to her own feelings, it would be possible for her movement in that direction to take place with Nicholas's growing cooperative participation. If her purpose is kept at "something for herself," that is, defined as outside the structure of their marriage relationship, it is unlikely that therapy will proceed in any direction other than the escalation of antagonistic functioning.

Nicholas and Laurie are also classically illustrative of the game Berne saw as most often played out maritally—the game of "If It Weren't For You." The basic dynamics of the game revolve around a spouse, in this case, the wife, who is phobic in some way and the other spouse whose personal insecurity results in a "need to be needed" which takes the form of controlling rigidity. Thus, at the social level, Laurie wants to do something that Nicholas restricts her from doing. At the psychological level, she is afraid to do it and he is afraid of having minimal worth or power. This example provides an illustration of the use of games in therapy. The value at the outset is to provide a direct and straightforward method of assessing the consequences of accepting at face value the stated motivation of the patient. The therapist who agrees, simplistically, that Laurie's purpose is "merely" to get free of her husband's domination and to go to college runs the risk of using the power of his or her position to override Nicholas's very critical psychological value to her and to leave Laurie with little preparation in dealing with either her anxiety or her potential "failure." Game analysis also provides direct insight into the pattern of childhood, family, and functioning that existed for both partners, allowing one to know the directions to move in elucidating for each partner the roots of their unconscious functioning.

It is always therapeutically dangerous to discount an emotional reaction as intense as Laurie's was in the second session. Her failure to verbalize her feelings merely serves to underscore the degree of conflict that has been engaged. In one sense, the pattern of interaction between Nicholas and Laurie is representative of their relationship. Ostensibly, he is in total control of what is taking place and she is passively adapting—an indication of what has been going on throughout their marriage. Inevitably, when the submissive partner either has built up sufficient resentment or has become less phobic about responding, the system will be disturbed by a more active attempt to reorganize the balance of power.

The Child ego state's emotional reactions are noticeable even when there appears to be a covert agreement to pretend it does not exist. Thus, all members of the group, even Nicholas, are responsive in some way to Laurie's communication of being the "victim." If the therapist allows that to go unnoticed, the entire group may perceive it unsafe to be weak or tentative, and believe that the therapist is unable to cope with or override the power of the programmatic responses of group members. This will typically lead to a retreat into a Parent ego state that will critically attack the therapist or withdraw from the group.

The most important aspect of intervening with Laurie would be to eliminate the pattern of ignoring her responses. It would be sufficient to comment, "Laurie, I notice your discomfort: it would be good to put your reactions and feelings into words." It would matter less whether she accepted the invitation than that her difficulty in speaking had been acknowledged. Optimally, interventions would have shifted the pattern of the group to a more dynamically effective level.

When there is a great deal of interaction from the outset, it often indicates that individuals are able to "hide-out" and avoid a level of self-revelation that would be anxiety-provoking. Couples feel less vulnerable because they are not there as themselves at the outset but as a duo—which covers individual anxieties. All homogeneous groups have the potential for falling into patterns of pastiming that *appear* to be interactive but which are, in fact, little different from what is engaged in at cocktail parties or bridge clubs.

From the beginning, it is important to reframe interactions so they may become more authentic. When Doris responds with "that sounds just like a man," I would be likely to ask her to speak directly to Nicholas and tell him how she felt about what he had been saying. Or I would ask her if she thought *her* husband had concerns about her "running around," and, if so, to talk directly about how she reacted to this. Or, I would point out that it sounded as if she were empathizing with Laurie and invite her to communicate that message directly to Laurie.

Moving interactions to a more authentic level becomes especially important when individuals in the group share dynamic issues and therefore have a tendency unconsciously to "protect" each other.

There is much overlap among the couples in the group. Nicholas and Laurie as well as John and Helen are contending with the woman's redefinition of self and a desire to extend herself outside the home. Implicit are issues of control, domination, and submission. In some ways, Paul and Joan share the dynamic with a sex-role reversal. Joan is more educated and initiated the therapy contact while Paul was apparently resisting being controlled by "avoiding her." Both Larry and Pamela, and Peter and Doris are vague about what they want and what is "wrong" with their marriages. There is an underlying thread of helplessness and inability to achieve clarity and to obtain gratification. In each of these couples, one would expect a strong pull toward relating to the therapist Parentally—as judge, decision-maker, rescuer, and protector.

The continuation of pastiming when the therapist begins the group, is a communication of anger at a therapist for "failing" in some way. It is as if the therapist has not demonstrated that he or she is "in charge of" the group, and therefore, the group need not recognize any leadership. When this becomes explicit, as in this case where the group members are openly attacking the therapist, it is easier to relate to. (To some degree, the group's response in this instance is provoked by the Parental observation of the therapist that was probably experienced as critical and accusatory.)

One of the first concerns in the therapist's response to the expression of anger is to assess the degree to which there is Adult input contained in the members' reactions. Neglecting this assessment runs the risk of being hooked into a defensive, Parental reaction based on blaming the group members in some way. When a therapist does react in this way, it effectively undermines any potential therapeutic benefit for the group.

The key in responding to this situation is to allow the interaction to continue the process of revealing members' programming. I would be likely to move in the direction of getting people to define what it was they saw as "cool, distant, and uncaring." This would lead to their identification that they were unwittingly seeking Parental rescuing—as they were accustomed to elicit in stress situations—or that they were protecting an internal Parent by not getting from others in the group what they saw the therapist failing to provide. As always, I would pursue the programming in the form of transactions with specific group members rather than talking to "the group" as a whole. In selecting the person to relate to directly, I would choose those with the greatest degree of affect associated with the conflict or those in whose scripts the issues were most salient. Since a great deal of the affect was generated from the previous session, I might ask Laurie to verbalize how she had felt about the therapist not rescuing or assisting her. For the same reason, I might work with Nicholas to get him to see that he, in fact, did not want Laurie "picked on" or discounted the previous week.

## *Theory Evaluation Form*

1. Which theoretical practitioner did you most resemble? Why?

2. Which theoretical practitioner did you least resemble? Why?

3. What does your response to *Question 1* tell you about yourself and your leadership style as a potential or present group therapist?

4. What does your response to *Question 2* tell you about yourself and your leadership style as a potential or present group therapist?

5. After rereading how the theoretical practitioner of your choice responded to the incident, how would you modify or change your response?

# CHAPTER NINE

# *M*ass Group Denial

In this incident, the group faces a very significant moment and it appears the members are engaged in mass denial. How the therapist chooses to interpret this incident will affect the way he or she intervenes and, ultimately, may have a direct bearing upon the direction the group moves throughout the remainder of therapy.

## *I*ncident #3

One of the head nurses from a large hospital in your community has contacted you. She informs you that a group of 10 student nurses for whom she is responsible has expressed concern over personal difficulties in dealing with terminally ill patients and their families. She asks you to help. You agree to meet with the nurses as a group over a period of time.

This is the fourth session. Until now, the group has been dealing with a variety of issues that were not directly related to the primary purpose for coming together. Topics ranged from how they chose nursing as a career, complaints about the training schedule, insensitivity of some senior nurses, the rewarding experiences they had in the maternity wing, and the like. You observed that today Jean had been rather silent, and that when she did speak, it was usually to agree with something one of the others said. This was not her usual way of behaving; typically, she had been an initiator and very active contributor in group discussions. Suddenly without warning, she blurted out that she did not think the group was truly aware of what nursing was really about, and that what they had been dealing with was very safe and neat stuff. The other side, the real side, had a lot of sadness. Her voice was quivering and she was shaking as she continued to relate to the group the incident she had faced today. A 10-year-old boy to whom she had been assigned, and for whom she had developed a great fondness, died from leukemia shortly before the meeting. Part of her responsibility was to report the youth's death and to be with the attending physician when he or she informed the child's parents. The group fell silent. This was the first time any of them had directly approached the topic of death.

As you observed the silence, your eyes searched out each of the members. You could see that Jean's outpouring apparently had the effect of immobilizing the group. You were about to intervene with a comment about what you had just been observing, when Diane said that the doctor of one of her patients had informed her that the patient had been responding very positively to new treatment. With that, Tom said that he was glad he was having this experience because it helped him to realize he wanted to specialize in pediatrics. Julie nodded her head as though she were in agreement with Tom. It was not long before the group's discussion seemed to be moving away from Jean's disclosure. It was obvious to you that Jean's statement presented an issue that posed a threat to them. You knew it was an important topic that needed to be dealt with; but it was clear that the group was avoiding it.

# *C*lient-Centered Therapy

*Implemented by William R. Coulson*
I would be hopeful for this group. Ten nursing students who want to get together to deal with their feelings is a group with a lot of potential.

Maybe what they are facing now, however, is the sense that if they follow Jean's lead and move into their feelings, it will be artificial. When people are not used to speaking personally, they feel self-conscious about verbalizing feelings. Jean has had such a sad experience with the passing of her young friend that she cannot ignore her feelings; they are going to surface, if anyone will give them the slightest assistance. But the others, although they have talked initially of wanting to deal with feelings, now back away. I suspect they fear that if they let themselves feel Jean's sadness, and then express their fears, they will have been had—as with a brainwashing group when you give in to the conditioning regimen and start doing things unnatural for you.

One of the criticisms of feeling and expression groups like this one is that they are artificial. Members achieve a level of depth that is unreal, a level they can neither replicate in life nor even maintain with one another outside the group.

In order for the filtering process to occur from group to life outside the group, something worthwhile has to happen in the group. To have impact, it must be different than life. Usually it has to do with feelings, the part of ourselves that ordinarily is withheld. In the group we *move into feelings* and thus, create trauma. It is not real trauma. Nobody is even bruised. But members anticipate it as traumatic, and the nursing students' reaction to Jean's expression of feelings is to back away from it. They do not want to touch it. By experiencing a traumatic event together, members of a therapy group become close and begin to trust one another. If the nursing students continue to scatter because of Jean's expression of feelings, there will be no common experience. Jean's feelings will have divided them. If they are to succeed in pulling together in this crisis, they will have to talk about what they are now inclined to avoid.

In lieu of facing deeper feelings, members are acting as though the group experience is just another slice of life. Maybe they are protecting against the potential charge of artificiality ("She wouldn't say these things if it weren't for this meeting"). To help overcome this perception, I would move into Jean's feelings. I want to help members now reach that level of depth with one another that a critic might call unreal.

How would I proceed? First, I would realize that other members' lack of expression of their feelings does not mean they are not having them. If I am touched by Jean's account of the death of a little boy, that is a legitimate clue to the possibility that others are touched, too. Empathy works through identification.

Second, if I am going to be alert to my own reactions and listen attentively to Jean, I doubt I can be doing a third thing, looking around the room, observing the reactions of the members to what Jean is saying. I want to pay attention to Jean because I will not be able to feel with her if I am concentrating on the others. I disagree with the principle that the therapist is supposed to be alert to the behavioral clues his or her members provide: what they do with their hands, their eyes, and the like, and believe that only in feeling *with* her can I know, except from memory, what sort of human experience this is.

Third, let us assume that I have been so absorbed in Jean's report that I start to cry. This could happen. The death of a small child is a sad thing.

Then what should we do? Well, we'd have our trauma all right ("The therapist is crying. Now what?"). What if it turned out that Jean, or I, were the only ones who felt that badly about what she had experienced? Then, again, we would have something vital and immediate to talk about: how come we're so different? Maybe they would say, "Doc, you can't take these things so personally. You'd never survive in hospital work." They would say it with the intention of helping me; as I pointed out in the first incident, it could be helpful to them to help me. Then, too, we would at last be dealing with the subject we thought we wanted to talk about in the first place: our personal reactions to death.

So it might not be such a bad thing if I were moved to tears by Jean's story. I would not cry *in order to* let them help me or in order to finally get to the topic. But if the sadness arose, I would not resist it.

Fourth, let us say I have a cooler head and am not so deeply moved by Jean's account that I become emotional and miss the fact that others want to change the subject. Would I point out to them that they are avoiding Jean's theme? No. The most important thing to do is talk to Jean. If group members could not do it, I would begin myself, hoping they would take over, or at least join in, when they saw that Jean's sadness was not going to destroy them. I would ask her if she could say more. I would try to accompany her into her feelings and hope to bring the group along. I take it on faith that to be alive is to have deep feelings. Many people have trouble letting feelings out and, consequently, those feelings become barriers to personal development. I would now pursue the feelings, convinced that afterward someone would say, or want to say, "Thanks, I needed that."

Fifth, what if I noticed that although he was making brave noises, Tom's chin was trembling, too? Would I say, "I notice your chin is trembling, Tom"? No. I find it distracts people to describe their behavior. What needs to be highlighted is the *meaning* a person intends to express, not the clues by which you read it.

The purpose of sharing what I would and would not do is to help the group move toward a deep and feeling-centered experience. Too often, people express their feelings only in the closet. Group therapy brings them into the open. Openness about previously private matters gives group work its potential to help a person start growing again— especially in the professions related to medicine, where people have learned to keep their feelings under wraps.

The problem posed for members of the nurses' group (or by any other therapy group) is an existential one: "How to find our way through our hours together without an agenda." The solution is not a technical or expert one, or one known in advance. It is, I believe, an artistic one. In the process of creating it—and in many cases finding the process more satisfying than if the problem and its solution were more focused—members gain confidence about developing the same kind of artistic mastery in their own lives.

My guess is that Diane, Tom, Julie, and the others are backing away from Jean's approach to her sorrow because they feel like they are still in public. Her story invites them to yield to their feelings. Quite possibly, this is frightening to them, as the prospect of any important new behavior might be frightening. A sense of the isolation of the group experience from daily life can make letting go more possible, but this psychological isolation is probably what has not yet developed in the nurses' group.

As a group leader, I try to make success more likely by not giving guidance, a situation that by itself sets up a sharp difference between the group and the many settings in which members are expected to follow instructions. They may want instructions now. But I would rather see the group as a struggle, in which all of us will have to work hard, and maybe even be wildly inventive at times in order to find what we need.

Finding one's way successfully through the near-cultivated diffuseness of a good therapy group can lead to a real sense of achievement— and a confidence that a similar kind of artistic power is possible in life and work.

## Gestalt Therapy

*Implemented by Mirriam F. Polster*
This situation dramatizes one of the functions of a group leader. Here is the first statement in four weeks of a concern that I know all the group members share. And yet, when one of them begins to address this problem directly, the others deflect and miss making contact either with Jean or with each other by confronting their own difficulties about the death of a patient.

The ability to confront pain either in oneself or in another often rests on a sense of self-support. When I feel extended beyond my customary boundaries, I am experiencing a loss of the support systems that usually provide me with orientation, vitality, and the belief that I am in control of my own actions and competent to meet the requirements of the circumstances in which I find myself. These I-boundaries (Polster & Polster 1973) are the flexible, permeable demarcations between what I have been thus far in my life and what I am willing to become, what risks I am willing to take, what new and intense experience I am ready to move into, and my willingness to assimilate the unfamiliar excitement this experience may generate.

These student nurses are moving into uncharted territory. They may have confronted death before, but they were not then professionals. Their sense of participation in those deaths must have been more marginal. Surely they had little or no sense of responsibility or participation in the decisions about the actual care and treatment of the person who died.

Jean has been the initiator in previous sessions and she is again this time. Perhaps she is more open to her feelings and therefore is often the first one to venture into new developmental areas. Her sense of self-support has enabled her to move into her experience many times before and has served her well previously. But now she confronts a situation where her self-support system is temporarily insufficient. She takes the logical and appropriate next step—she looks for what support she can get from her environment, her fellow students.

But her colleagues seem unavailable. Diane continues as if nothing had happened. She changes the subject—to a brighter topic—as if Jean had not spoken or as if Jean had committed a social error that she was politely ignoring. Tom and Julie are happy to collude in the deflection (Polster & Polster 1973). Their self-support systems may well be more primitive than Jean's. Unwilling to confront the pain she has expressed, they try to deny it altogether, to make it go away. This is not only a more primitive stance, it is also more precarious (demanding more denial and deflection to sustain) and more self-limiting. Jean moves with intensity and feeling into her evolution as a professional. They hope to become professionals, but may be less willing than she to accept the personal changes that are inevitable.

I must return to Jean at this moment and ask how she feels about the lack of response to her expression of sadness. I might tell her what feelings she has aroused in me and ask if anyone else was also moved. I am interested in Jean obtaining the support she seeks now from the community and in mobilizing her own self-support as she continues to explore the sadness she is feeling. She has said that she believes this occurs often in nursing—and she is right. It is important, too, for her fellow students not to pass over this moment and treat it anticeptically. They may learn from Jean's courage and find ways to face up to the sadness that will (if it has not yet) rise before them, too.

I might ask Jean to visualize the young boy and to speak to him in fantasy, to tell him about what she might have liked to say to him while he was alive and that she left unsaid. I would ask her to imagine his response. How might he reply? Speaking through Jean, he might respond with blame or understanding or confusion or gratitude or a whole range of feelings, all of which might be what Jean herself is struggling with and is dreading that the boy's parents, too, might think or feel.

As she does this, I watch to see how Jean supports herself, whether she sits in a way that is upright, flexible, and supported or whether she slouches down and slumps defeatedly in her chair; whether her breathing is adequate to the words she is saying or if she is breathing shallowly and runs out of her vital supply of air just when she is confronting sorrow and needs more of it. I want the dialogue to continue until there is a sense of meeting between Jean and the fantasied dead boy and then perhaps ask Jean what she might like to say to the boy's parents, encouraging here, too, the establishment of dialogue that could lead to an eventual sense of completion and rest. Sadness cannot be avoided in Jean's profession. She knows this. But missed communication can add more pain to already existing pain.

By fully going with Jean in this deep experience, and seeing it through to a fruitful sense of closure, the stage is set for other nurses to explore their own feelings in depth. It adds momentum and support and gives form to what may have been, up to now, feelings that the other student nurses believed they had no way into. To see someone come through a painful experience is inspirational.

## *Individual Psychology*

*Implemented by Guy J. Manaster*

Among Adler's early recollections (used as a projective device by Individual Psychologists) was one about death. He felt that concern about death was a primary motivation in his and others' decision to become doctors. Stories are told about Adler lecturing to medical students and asking them to think of the earliest incident or scene they could remember. Usually more than 60 percent of the students' earliest memories dealt with death. This is only to point out that Adlerian psychology has long been aware of death as an issue that must be faced intellectually and emotionally by members of the medical profession.

In this situation, I am aware of the importance of the issue of death for the group. The group is equally aware of the need to face the issue. Jean raised it, is distraught, and the group has rushed on. Adlerian therapy is noted as one of the earliest directive therapies and users of the paradox. I think this an appropriate moment for a paradoxical intervention into the group process.

I would say something like: "Excuse me, but the discussion so far today seems to be moving in a definite direction that illuminates our task. The death of a young patient today has really upset Jean. Diane, Tom, and Julie seem very positive about working with new successful treatments and usual childhood diseases. Why don't we get to work figuring out how we can be nurses who work only with well people."

Should the group somehow not pick up on this idea, I would continue with it until someone noted the paradox and its absurdity. I doubt it would take long. Probably someone would reply immediately to my statement with something like, "How can one be a nurse and only work with well people? That isn't nursing."

I might answer with a variation on the old story about the mother who wanted her son to be a dermatologist. "Maybe you could be dermatological nurses. It's a good business. Your patients never die and never get better."

Pause. Silence. Wait.

"I mean no one wants their patients to die. And no one here wants to talk about death or dying, or even talk to Jean who tried to get us to talk about it and went through a lot to bring it up."

Pause. Silence. Wait.

It is inconceivable to me that by this point the group would not have faced the issue, begun to discuss it, and particularly come back to Jean. Yet it is possible. For the sake of illustrating how directive an Adlerian therapist can be, I will continue as if this last silence was not broken. After a prolonged and, I assume, uncomfortable period of silence, I would go on:

"If you are to be nurses, you are going to treat the critically ill. Some of them will die. It will be rough. It will be less rough if you understand how you think and feel about death, dealing with dying people and their families. But this will be something you will have to work on now, and periodically throughout your career—if you intend to be a nurse. And if you now choose not to become nurses, *you* will still die—maybe you can put off thinking about it longer if you are not in a health profession, but you will die and will in all likelihood have to consider it later if not sooner.

"If we cannot talk about death and dying, here, now, I suggest we break and meet next week to talk about new careers." I would ask Jean to stay and talk with me about her concerns.

Even after this terminating statement, I would be more than willing to begin the pertinent discussion if the group wanted to do so. However, if there was no dissent, I would get up and take Jean to another office to talk.

This may seem harsh and heavy, but Adlerian theory credits people with great strength and resiliency. It also clearly implies that all decisions are individual decisions, that individuals bear the burden and responsibility for their decisions and lives. I believe that I am merely throwing the burden where it belongs—on each of the group members.

During the week, all members may struggle with the issue. Although I would hope to speak individually with any who decide they would rather not confront the death and dying issue and want to change careers, it seems a good time to make the decision—and it is their own decision to make individually. Reality may be harsh, and they are facing the reality of their chosen career. Most will be back, probably all, and we can then discuss the issue in the face of reality and their resolve.

Throughout my elaboration of these critical incidents from *my* Adlerian, not *the* Adlerian, perspective, I have had to make guesses and intuit persons from very limited material. Adlerians generally make guesses from little information within the framework of the theory, but with the patient there to verify or disregard the therapist's interpretation. Therefore, as a bit of a hedge, I will end with Adler's line: "Everything can be different."

## *Rational-Emotive Therapy*

### Implemented by Albert Ellis

I would assume, on the basis of Rational-Emotive Therapy theory and group therapy in general, that the members of this group are unwilling to deal with the serious issue raised by Jean, but that it probably would be better for them to face it and thereby help themselves and each other come to some kind of resolution about it. The main RET assumption I would have is that people shy away from discussions of death, their own and others, largely because they have low frustration tolerance. Individuals do not want to accept the fact that in order to be afforded the boon of living we also have to die; and that it is sad and deplorable but not "horrible," "awful," or "depressing." Humans naturally and easily tend to believe that it is: first, because they are born with a tendency to whine about and refuse to accept some of the grimmest realities of their lives; and second, because they are reinforced in these irrational beliefs and reactions by cultural phenomena, such as the teachings of their family, church, mass media, teachers, and the like.

The assumption of RET, on the contrary, is that humans are almost all capable of accepting what they do not like: of facing the harshness and hassles of their existence and gracefully lumping them. They are "existentially anxious" in the face of dying and death, in the sense that they are virtually all seriously *concerned* about these phenomena and want to do their best to ward them off as long as they can. They have self-preservation drives, partly of a biological nature and partly taught, that motivate them to take death quite seriously and to take precautions against its early occurrence. But their "anxiety" about it is only existential in the sense that they virtually all feel it. It is not self-preservation, as is deep concern. And it can largely be minimized or eliminated. For "anxiety," in RET terms, is *over*concern or *needless* concern: namely, the idea that unusual hassles or death *should* not, *must* not exist; that it is *awful* when it does; that people cannot *stand* the thought of it; and that the world is a *horrible place* when it inevitably presents obstacles and difficulties of this sort to humans.

While RET, therefore, does not try to interfere with concern, cautiousness, or vigilance, it does try to separate these feelings and actions from those of anxiety, obsessiveness with life and safety, and panic. In the group in question, my assumption would be that the members are largely panicked about the thought of (1) dying themselves and (2) the death of their loved ones or their patients. They therefore submerge or squelch this state of panic by refusing to look at the problems that Jean is presenting; and they go back to the same kinds of relatively trivial issues being discussed before Jean "uncomfortably" raised the topic of death. Although they are quite entitled to do this and to avoid thinking about death if that is what they really want to do, a healthier reaction would be for them to face this issue, deal with Jean's concerns and their own problems regarding it, and then "drop" it largely *because* they have dealt with it and not because they have swept it under the rug.

In an instance like this, where some would say that the group members have "unconsciously" copped out and avoided the issue of dying, the RET therapy would agree that this is probably true, but would not see their "unconscious" reaction as one that is exceptionally deepseated or unavailable to consciousness. Instead, RET would assume (as I would) that they have semiconsciously (or what Freud originally called preconsciously) squelched this issue, and that they could fairly easily look at it again and bring it to their consciousness. So I would make an attempt to get them to do this: to bring the issue of death to their consciousness again and deal with it, experientially and philosophically, until they rid themselves of their irrational beliefs about it.

I would open up discussion of this problem by saying something like this to the group: "I find it very interesting that you are pretty much ignoring the problem of death that Jean has raised and that you are going back to discussing what would seem to be less important and less emotion-filled issues. I am wondering whether there is something you consider 'too uncomfortable' about this problem to deal with. Of course, some or all of you may really have faced it squarely in your own life and resolved it. But I wonder whether you, like Jean, have some real problems when one of your patients dies, and whether you are not avoiding dealing with these problems."

I would assume that, having directly raised this issue, some or all the members of the group would admit to having some problems dealing with issues of dying, and that some of them would recognize that they had deliberately avoided the topic that Jean raised, going back to discussing less important things. If so, I would then say: "Why do you think that you have so much trouble in dealing with the issue of death? What are you telling yourself when you think about it—as you momentarily did before when Jean raised the issue—and then sweep it under the rug?" By this kind of questioning, I would expect some of the group members to admit that they were horrified about death; that they did think it must not exist; and that they could not bear to discuss it openly. I would expect members to say it was very unfair that they and their loved ones had to die some day, and that the world was a pretty awful place for having this kind of unfairness in it.

As they brought out these ideas, I would actively dispute and challenge them; and I would try to get them to question each other's irrationalities in this respect. I would ask, "Where is the evidence that death *must* not exist?" and try to get them to see that it is really inevitable and *has to* exist, if it does. I would ask, "What makes it *awful* or *terrible* if you or one of your loved ones dies?" and try to show them that it is only highly inconvenient, only very sad—but not "awful," meaning *more than* inconvenient or sad and more unfortunate than it *should* be. I would ask them to prove that they *can't stand, can't bear* the thought of dying or having one of their loved ones die and attempt to demonstrate that no matter how much they dislike or feel greatly displeased about it, they definitely *can* stand it and can even experience a great deal of happiness while they still live on after their loved one has died. Finally, I would ask: "Why is the world a *terrible place* and life hardly *worth living at all* in view of the fact that we all die and cannot avoid this possibility?" And I would attempt to get them to see that this is not true: the world is a place where bad things exist—but is not itself, or in its entirety, *terrible;* and that as long as they live, they almost certainly *can* enjoy themselves to some considerable degree, even after suffering the loss of loved ones.

I would, in other words, actively try to get almost all the members of the group to see that they are not merely concerned or sad about death and dying but that they are distinctly *over*concerned and exceptionally anxious. I would show them exactly which irrational beliefs are giving them this overconcern, and show them how to learn the scientific method of logically and empirically disputing, questioning, challenging, and surrendering these beliefs. I would hope, in the process of my dialogue with the group members (and *I* would expect to be actively and directively engaging in a Socratic-type dialogue with the group as a whole, or at least with several of them), that I would jolt some of their current ideas about dying and death and help them get on the road of a more rational, self-helping philosophy of death. In the course of my talking with the group members, I would assume that many of their "hidden" or "unexpressed" concerns would surface (especially as they backed each other with *ir*rational ideas) and that some of these would begin, at least, to be worked through.

In order to get back to Jean's problem, and in order to show the members of the group that their fear of death was not the only issue involved, I would at some point take the conversation back to Jean by saying: "You seem very sad about the death of the 10-year-old boy who was your patient. I can well understand that since I am sure that you became rather attached to him during the past several weeks and that you also feel exceptionally sorry about the death of any 10-year-old boy, especially from a disease like leukemia. But I would like you to get in touch with your sadness for a short while and tell me what it really feels like, and particularly tell me if it is *only* sadness or sorrow about the boy."

Jean, in getting in touch with her actual feelings, would probably reveal other feelings, such as depression, guilt, and anger. If this were so, I would say something like: "Well, I can easily see how you would feel depressed. Most people, having gone through what you have just gone through, would feel about the same. But, perhaps very peculiarly, I would say that they were wrong and that you are wrong in feeling depressed. I would contend that you—and they—are very appropriately sad or sorrowful, but that you are inappropriately depressed. Do you know why I would say this?"

Since the group up to this point has apparently not been taught RET principles, Jean is not likely to know why I consider sorrow and sadness appropriate but depression inappropriate. If she acknowledged confusion, I would say: "Your sadness springs from your belief that it is more unfortunate, very bad that this 10-year-old boy has died of leukemia; that it is unfortunate for him, his parents, and you. And that is correct; we could rightly and empirically say that it *is* unfortunate. The boy wanted to live, his parents want him to live, and you certainly wanted him to live. And you are all not getting what you wanted—and are getting just about the opposite. It is, therefore, most unfortunate, sad, or regretful that this frustrating set of conditions exists; and you and his parents would definitely be foolish if you concluded that it was good or even unimportant. But depression—yours or theirs—comes from an extra, illegitimate idea that this unfortunate, sorry state of affairs *should not, must not* exist; that it is *awful* that it does exist; and that human life is pretty *horrible* and *useless* when such unfortunate events exist. Isn't that what you're really telling yourself—that the death of the boy *should not* have occurred and that it is *awful* that it did?"

Assuming that Jean admitted that she was telling herself something like this, I would show her that it is not the Activating Experience (A) of the boy's death that is creating her emotional Consequence(C) of depression; rather, it is her irrational Beliefs (B) *about* this experience that are making her depressed. And I would show her how she could change these Beliefs to rational or coping Beliefs, such as "I wish that boy had not died, but he inevitably did. Too bad!" "I can definitely *stand* his cruel death even though I'll never like it nor similar deaths of young children." "The world is a place in which bad things like this will always to some extent exist, but it is not *totally* bad; it still has a lot of good, enjoyable things in it. And as long as I still live, I can definitely lead a good, enjoyable existence."

I would try to get the other group members to join in with me, as we all tried to talk Jean out of, not her feelings of sorrow and sadness, but those of depression. Also, if she were guilty or angry, I would show her how she was needlessly creating these feelings—and how the happenings of her life, or what she had done or not done about them, were not the real issue. In getting the group members to help me show Jean that she was appropriately sad and inappropriately depressed, guilty, or angry about the boy's death, I would be helping them to face the problem that they have so far avoided—dealing with death. I would presumably also help some of them with their own expressed or unexpressed feelings of depression, guilt, and anger about death.

As this was going on, or after much of it had been completed, I would go back to the group's problem of ignoring the issue of death. I would try to show them that such defensive behavior covers up their underlying anxieties, and that if they faced these anxieties by finding their philosophic source and changing their philosophies so as not to make themselves anxious any longer, they could deal much better with their emotional and practical problems.

In several ways, then, I would take the current group situation, make a dramatic issue of it, and almost force the group members to expose, confront, and start to change their disturbed feelings. I would also give them some desensitizing homework assignments such as recording all their thoughts about death, visiting a morgue, or discussing death openly with a friend or with relatives of dying or dead patients. I might also give them the emotive exercise of Rational-Emotive imagery. I would ask them to think about a close friend or relative's death, letting themselves feel disturbed (depressed or anxious) about this intensely imagined fantasy; changing their feeling to one of keen disappointment, sorrow, or regret but *not* depression or anxiety; seeing what went on in their heads to effect this change in feeling; and then practicing doing this same exercise for, say, 30 consecutive days until they were automatically able to think about death and *only* or *mainly* feel sorry and regretful but not severely upset.

In various cognitive, emotive, and behavioral ways, therefore, I would work with this group on facing the problem of their own and others' death and of feeling appropriately about this. RET group therapy is one of the few forms of therapy that specifically tries to show group members the difference between appropriate negative emotions of sorrow, regret, frustration, and annoyance, and the inappropriate negative emotions of depression, anxiety, despair, hostility, and worthlessness. The group sessions and experiences would be employed largely as an educational device to dramatically help the members think about, feel about, and work on their disturbed reactions to death and dying.

# Reality Therapy

*Implemented by Thomas E. Bratter*

I would agree to provide a learning experience for the student nurses regarding their work with the terminally ill. Before accepting this challenging assignment, however, I found it most important to revisit my mother's death to discover if there were any unresolved issues and whether I had come to peace with the insensitive and at times unprofessional treatment of various hospital personnel.

This experience, though intensely painful to recall, is most important when considering running a group. Truthfully, the targets of my rage were the nurses who appeared so insensitive and incompetent. In addition, with the exception of a neurologist, all the physicians and medical consultants connected with the hospital remain objects of my contempt and hatred, not because my mother died, but rather because they did not render competent or caring treatment.

I would conduct the group, because at the appropriate time, I could provide a personal reaction of how a family member of the terminally ill viewed the medical profession. For reasons that will become apparent later for this specific group, I would apply a humanistic approach because the experience is more a learning one than a therapeutic one. But becoming vulnerable would in no way affect my credibility as the group leader while working with student nurses.

The group leader is more than just a member of the group. The leader retains the responsibility for determining the agenda so that both the individual who wants to work through a problem and the group can benefit. Generally, this can be achieved by restating the issue so that all either can relate to or identify with the person who is speaking. This, in brief, can be considered the art of being a group psychotherapist—that is, the ability to involve everyone while trying to achieve a solution. At times, a group leader may need to assume the role of catalyst when either the group becomes immobilized or begins to discuss topics other than therapeutic ones.

The student nurses who want to discuss "their personal difficulty with dealing with terminally ill patients and their families" present many interesting and somewhat unique challenges for the group therapist.

**First.**   The original contract which concerns the need to discuss difficulty with dealing with the terminally ill has been negotiated by someone other than the group with me. It is significant, indeed, that the head nurse contacted me rather than providing the group experience herself. My guess is that the student nurses would come to the initial group with varying expectations, with some confusion, with some resentment about being told by a person in authority that "each needed to attend a group." The leader cannot assume there is any consensus among the potential group members and any motivation to form a group.

**Second.**   It is important to recognize that the members already know each other and have many opportunities to interact both in competitive (academic) and cooperative (work) environments. Each person has an image and an identity which obviously impact upon the eventual cohesion and intimacy of the group. Each member already likes and dislikes, respects and disrespects, trusts and mistrusts someone in the group, which will complicate the formation of the group. The issue of confidentiality would become a crucial issue, since during inevitable daily interaction and power struggles, some of the data gained in the group can be used opportunistically and manipulatively.

**Third.**   A natural *we–you* dichotomy has been established prior to the formation of the group. While members have had some conflicts with each other, they do share a common experience of being student nurses. They will have some incentive to discuss occurrences which they have experienced during the day. The group leader will be identified as the "outsider," which means that there is more reason why I will need to prove myself as a credible and trustworthy resource person. Having been selected without any student nurse input by the head nurse also will need to be discussed prior to the group trusting me.

**Fourth.**   Before starting this group, I would know there would be some confusion and conflict regarding the format. One of the first demanding clarification would be the nature of the group—i.e., would it be therapeutic, didactic, sensitivity, problem-oriented, and so on.

I would be sensitive to permitting the student nurses to progress at their own pace. I would play a waiting game until one member would begin to relate to a relevant issue before attempting to focus attention. I would respect the members' right in this unique situation to determine when they felt sufficiently comfortable to disclose an intimate personal or professional concern regarding death. In an effort to stimulate this discussion, however, in all probability I would have suggested that the group read some of LeShan's works (1969, 1966, & 1959). If I knew of a television program about death, I would suggest the group watch it.

Jean showed both initiative and courage to confront her remorse about a 10-year-old boy's death. I would intervene on her behalf and attempt to redirect group attention and concern to help her with her grief. I would say: "I can appreciate your reluctance to want to focus on what Jean said because it is painful for us to accept the awesome realization that someday each of us will die and that sometimes we cannot help someone live longer. What I am wondering is what we can do to help Jean deal with her grief?"

Perhaps my most important contribution would be to serve as the architect or catalyst for the student nurses to form a supportive self-help group. Since the student nurses work daily with the terminally ill, they could rely on each other for consolation, guidance, and understanding. All personnel who are exposed to working with perpetual illness and dying should be provided with this kind of support system to help resolve the feelings of frustration and failure. If this model would be effective, I would think it could be implemented for all medical personnel and those who work with the aging and other subpopulations that tend to drain the psychotherapist. I believe, as does Glasser, that there clearly is a need for this type of self-help support system.

# Transactional Analysis

### Implemented by Herbert Hampshire

This situation points up the danger of the therapist colluding with patients in avoiding anxiety-laden issues. It would be unlikely that a first session would go by without my commenting on an automatic avoidance tendency, and I would early on provide a context in which the feelings involved in avoidance would be talked about and related to directly. Typically, I would, within the first 15 or 30 minutes of a group initiated for a specific purpose, comment that I understood the purpose of the group was to deal with the difficult issues of treating the terminally ill, that I appreciated that it was tempting to avoid them, and that the members might begin by talking about how they experienced being in a group set up for this purpose.

The same therapeutic dilemma created in the first session is again set up in the fourth session, with group members automatically responding to Jean's emotion by moving to "safer" topics. It is important, at the point that Jean moves the group to the difficult issues, for the therapist to side with that openness and not to side implicitly with the defense against it. Thus, Diane's comment must be responded to immediately. A simple statement, such as, "It is uncomfortable to respond directly to Jean's emotions," would be sufficient to direct Diane and the rest of the group back toward her feelings.

Since the series of avoidant comments have taken the focus away from Jean's reactions, the problem for the therapist is to bring the group back without being parental or critical, which would only serve to increase defensiveness and to produce a protective veneer of anger at the therapist. It is more effective to stroke what *is* wanted than to respond negatively to the avoidance. I would be likely in that context to ostensibly ignore other comments and address Jean directly. I might say something like, "Jean, I understand your anger and sadness. And you're right that it's natural for the group to want to avoid the difficult issues of death. But it's important to talk about it. Talk about your experience of talking to the boy's parents."

While Jean would start out talking directly to the therapist, and other members would avoid eye contact and direct involvement, it would very rapidly be possible to focus on the others' reactions and, by inviting them to verbalize them, to produce interaction among the group members themselves. Before long, it would be essential for other members to talk specifically about their experiences with death—either within nursing or in other situations. Part of the purpose would be to lead them to a realization that there are many personal connections, both through feelings and circumstances, that are automatically being suppressed. The additional aspect of purpose here is directed at dealing with not only the specific "forbidden" topic but also all the mechanisms of taboos in general.

Even groups that are not organized around a particular issue encounter this phenomenon at some point in their development. As one person attempts to deal with more intimate aspects of a sexual problem, or someone brings up sexual feelings toward the therapist, or a group member reveals a possible fatal illness such as cancer, all the prohibitions about openly discussing "taboo topics" become engaged.

In most instances, the primary task of therapy is merely to create an environment that supports open communication. It is not so much that there are conflicts in the area as the reactions to the issue are not verbalized within the context of the programming. Just to be able to "say it" is frequently sufficient to defuse it as a problem.

Another issue to be addressed in this group is how the members related to death as an aspect of nursing *before* they entered the profession. By dictating avoidance of areas, programming often keeps people relating to reality in a very ineffective and childlike manner. What is often revealed in situations like this is that people both know what problems are likely to occur and have the personal resources to cope with them. The problems lie in the sanctions against focusing on exactly what difficulties are likely to emerge. Unless the nurses accept this, they can unwittingly believe that they did not have the perceptiveness or sufficient grasp of reality to know that confronting death was likely to be an aspect of nursing.

# Theory Evaluation Form

1. Which theoretical practitioner did you most resemble?

2. Which theoretical practitioner did you least resemble? Why?

3. What does your response to *Question 1* tell you about yourself and your leadership style as a potential or present group therapist?

4. What does your response to *Question 2* tell you about yourself and your leadership style as a potential or present group therapist?

5. After rereading how the theoretical practitioner of your choice responded to the incident, how would you modify or change your response?

# *A Member Chooses to Leave*

How is a therapist affected when a member of a group suddenly discloses that this is the last session for him or her? Our theoretical practitioners are faced with this dilemma in Incident 4.

## *Incident #4*

This group is composed of four men and four women. Initially, each of the members of this group had come to you because they felt unhappy with their lot in life. They felt fate had dealt them a poor hand. Each of them presented themselves to you in ways that expressed a low sense of personal worth. Recognizing that they all seemed to have symptoms of low self-esteem, you invited them to join together in a group to deal with what appeared to be a common area of concern.

Briefly, the members are described as follows:

*Deborah* is 22 years old, single, and holds an Associate Degree from

133

the local community college. She is employed as a legal secretary.

*Peggy* is 23 years old, married for six years and has three children ranging is ages from 2 to 6 years old. She listed her occupation as housewife.

*Jean* is 34 years old, married, and had dropped out of school after 10th grade. She is short and heavy in stature. She drives a school bus.

*Andrea* is 28 years old and recently divorced. She had interrupted her college education eight years ago in order to help her then-husband pursue his Ph.D. She presently feels at a loss as to where to pick up her life.

*Jim* is 25 years old. He is single and was recently discharged from the Army. He is working as an automobile salesman until he can decide what he wants to do with his life.

*Bob* is 35 years old and married. He was referred to you by his family physician, who was concerned with the disclosures Bob had made about feeling "trapped and not going anywhere."

*Ron* is 32 years old. Recently divorced, he feels his marriage was a disaster and that he felt worthless because most everthing in his life seemed to go the same way as his marriage.

*John* is 30 years old. He is in his second marriage. He was unable to bring his wife with him when he first visited you. He explained that he felt lost in his marriage and was afraid it was going to end as the first onc had.

This is the fifth session. The first three meetings saw the group move through the initial stages of development, which included orientation, resistance, conflict (questions about trust), and a struggle for power and confrontation. Toward the end of the fourth session, there seemed to be signs of group cohesiveness and a readiness for self-disclosure. Peggy, for example, expressed her disillusionment with her present roles of mother and spouse. She said she was unhappy with herself and felt powerless to do anything about it. The group seemed ready to listen to her and willing to offer its thoughts on how she might be able to work out her problem. Andrea disclosed some deep-seated feelings of resentment toward her ex-husband, especially over the way he ignored the sacrifice she made on his behalf. In a similar way, the group appeared receptive to Andrea and demonstrated a willingness to offer assistance to work through her difficulty. This activity had the effect of encouraging other group members, including Bob and Ron, to risk disclosure as well.

Much of what had begun in the fourth session carried over into this session. Early in the meeting, Ron began by stating how much he valued the group's willingness to hear him out and that he had given much consideration to their suggestions. He no sooner completed his remarks, when John, taking advantage of the very brief silence, announced to the group that he was making this his last session. He said he planned not to return after tonight's meeting. You quickly noted the effect his words had upon the group members and that they appeared quite stunned.

# Client-Centered Therapy

*Implemented by William R. Coulson*

If anything could both stir my fears about being left alone and reinforce the suspicion that I am not a good therapist, this incident would be it. Why would John want to leave so soon? It is only the fifth session and he has hardly begun. If I were a better therapist, he would have been hooked before now.

Maybe I exhausted the need to be self-critical in responding to Incident 1, since my final notes for comments on this situation neglect such personal thoughts. I am prepared instead to write about the purpose of group therapy, about the importance of involving members of the group with John, and the key role of community in group work and life.

The bind I feel right now is similar to the one I sometimes feel in a group (and I suspect members often feel it about themselves, too): "Shall I be personal or not? It's embarrassing to be personal. I must sound like a baby." Yet, I want to be personal. I want you to know that I have my reasons for what I do, reasons having to do with my personality, my upbringing, and my likes and dislikes. I do not want to impart to group members all the reasons for my actions in leading the group.

With regard to John's announced departure, the therapist has to face the possibility that John is right; he should resign from the group. It is doubtful this is the proper moment since the group, including John, seems hardly to have gotten started. But *some* time will be a good time for him to go, and we shall have to anticipate that (a) because it is his life, John will know that time better than we and (b) even at the right moment for him to leave, we are likely to want to keep him. He will by that time have become a friend.

Even when there is a specified end to the group, some people will decide to leave before it is over. Sometimes they will come to you privately and announce their intention. This is a problem. If you support their departure, you deny what you may have been working for in the group: a community in which members care about what happens to one another. But John did not approach you in private. He brought it up in the group and, to his credit, did not wait until the last few minutes of the session. There is time to talk it over, time for the members to sort out how they feel about his announcement and discuss their feelings with him—which is precisely what I hope would now happen.

If people in John's group were not yet friends, they could use his announcement as the occasion to begin. I hope they would discuss with him his decision to leave, encouraging him to talk, give him understanding and respect. It would be hard for them not to mix up their wishes and his, but the therapist could help by remaining relatively objective. If the therapist could not be objective because of his or her own interest in John remaining in the group, the therapist should disclose this.

In any case, I would not want to rush in or deal with John's announcement as an expression of his psychological problems. I would hope for the members of the group to speak to him. Thus, I might remain silent at first.

John might yet leave the group. But in the end I cannot think of anything better than to trust his judgment.

# Gestalt Therapy

*Implemented by Mirriam F. Polster*

So far, John has been able to make it through the group sessions by listening and apparently not revealing much about himself. But the group appears to be moving into fuller levels of trust, responsiveness, and intimacy and his silence may become more and more noticeable. He wants out. Abruptly, and with no explanations given.

In the face of his terseness, we can only speculate about what lies behind his barebones statement. Of course he has every right to leave the group. Nevertheless, I want to know why. I also want to be sure that he is saying what he actually wants to say. Possibly John does not know how to express his despair without delivering an ultimatum, desperate as it may be, and then he has to stonewall it out and gets stuck with it. Perhaps he is discouraged and feels his problems are worse than anyone else's, and that even *if* he could talk about them, there are no solutions. His wife does not seem available to work with him on their troubles—why should strangers be any more sympathetic or helpful?

I might ask him to expand on his announcement by saying to the group, "Since I can't such-and-such in this group, I feel like leaving." Not only is this statement more *specific*, but it also brings him into relationship with the group. He is not alone and toughing it out all by himself, he is speaking *to them*. In a roundabout way, he may be telling them what hopes or expectations he had in joining the group in the first place and how he is not getting what he wanted. Maybe he feels that he has been wasting his time, sitting around with a bunch or losers and that they could not possibly help him. Maybe he feels that since he has not come up with any solutions or helpful suggestions for anyone else, he has no right to ask for their time and attention in his difficulties. The time has come to put up or shut up, and he does not feel up to it. He has one failure behind him, another in the making, and his experience in the group is going to be still another one. But if his announcement causes another member to ask him why he wants to leave, John could begin a different way of dealing with his despair instead of acting like a desperate animal, who, when caught in a trap, gnaws off his own leg to gain release.

John is only one of eight individuals who are affected by his announcement. The other seven, as we already know, have a "low sense of personal worth" and their reactions to his statement probably tap into some of their own fears and self-doubts. They may even suspect that their disclosures are partly responsible for John's decision to leave.

There is a remarkable element of omnipotence in the way their low opinion of themselves provides them with a perverse sense of power. They consider themselves to be poor souls of little value *but* here they are speculating that their words and their presence are so powerfully unattractive that they could drive John away. This is power, indeed, even if it is backwards. They are juggling a paradox between their grandiosity (I am so powerfully unattractive I can make John want to leave) and their sense of low worth (John doesn't want to be in a group with me). So they shuttle between feeling that they have no effect or that they have too much effect. John is surely not the only person in their lives with whom they oscillate between these two possibilites. Obviously, the need for a specific statement from John about why he chooses to leave the group is important to them, too.

If John responds to my request to explain his desire to leave the group by saying, "Since I can't talk about my trouble in this group, I feel like leaving,"I want to know why John feels he is unable to talk. Do other people begin quickly to talk about their own concerns, making it difficult for him to get a word in edgewise? Are his problems so much worse than theirs that they seem unapproachable? It is unacceptable for him to ask for and to accept advice; is he supposed to be able to handle his own difficulties by himself, "like a man?" Is it hard for him to talk about his fears in front of women?

Answers to these questions will provide links to parts of John that he has shoved in the background and kept unspoken. They are things he tells himself that keep him feeling inadequate and worthless and prevent him from talking about what troubles him. He does it here in the group; at home he may do much the same with his wife.

The act of regulating an individual's own experience with admonitions, slogans, rules (or any of the other forms that "shoulds" can take) is called introjection (Perls, Hefferline, & Goodman 1951; Polster & Polster 1973). By introjecting, John has given up the rights to the primacy of his own experience and tries instead to make a life out of secondhand, hand-me-down opinions, dictums, and beliefs. The energy that could go into using his personal perspective as a basis for interaction with other people is devoted to a silent struggle to keep down his protest against these alien standards. He has learned to swallow down the aggression he needs both to move out forcefully into the world and to restructure what is offered by the external authorities there. He has absorbed uncritically what others have told him he *should* think or feel or do.

In working with John's introjections, it is important to reawaken his criticism of and disagreement with these rules. He has suppressed his own bewilderment and confusion, and he has muted his ability to question to the point where he remains silent until he becomes scared or desperate and then feels compelled to bolt. These tactics may have served him well at some time when he was more dependent on remaining on peaceful terms with the important people in his life. Currently, they are not working well for him. This may also be true for others in the group.

I can bring John's internal struggle into the open by asking him to begin a dialogue between the part of him that habitually tells him what he "should" do and the part of him that wants to behave differently. Up until now, this has been a silent debate, debilitating and underground. Articulating it loosens the energy that John is presently using up in suppression.

If I choose to work with this as a group issue, instead of individually with John, I will ask if any of John's prohibitions sound familiar to others in the group. Is there a voice within them that scolds or dictates? The same kind of dialogue can be introduced between the warring factions within one of the people in the group, or one person could play the introjected dictator while someone else speaks for the rebellious underdog. This kind of dialogue can lead to a shared experience of members' feeling helplessness, sadness, rage, disgust, and, eventually, healthy protest. Their grandiose fear of the power of their unattractiveness can become apparent and we can begin to invent ways of feeling powerful without feeling worthless.

John may be in for some surprises when he hears the reaction to his announced departure. Depending on his response, he might want to reconsider his decision. It may have been his clumsy way of saying that he wanted to begin working in the group.

I would have responded in two other important, and different, ways to this group situation. First, I disagree with the basis on which this group was formed. All of these people have a low sense of self-worth. I look for more heterogeneity in forming a group. One of the most valuable elements in a group is diversity, the spread of opinion and reaction. Choosing a group because of commonality of self-opinion minimizes this. I know there are many ways to be depressed, but this is still an impoverished form of variety.

Secondly, I would have made a contract with the group when we began, agreeing that each individual may, of course, choose to leave the group, but that they must inform the group one week (if it is a weekly group) before they actually do leave. This allows time and opportunity for the group to respond more directly and fully to their reactions about the member's departure.

# Individual Psychology

### Implemented by Guy J. Manaster

Individual Psychology views each individual's development of personal and unique goal or goals as being within the individual's own framework of values of self and the world. Stress on the whole, indivisible, person does not prohibit Adlerians from seeing similarities between people's goals, styles, and values, but it does demand that the practitioner emphasize the unique perspectives of each individual. In this situation, where the similarities seem dominant, the non-Adlerian therapist may tend to proceed as if all members have the same problem and therefore a single answer or response would hold for all.

Each of the individuals in this group appears, in some way, to have come to the conclusion that life is too much to handle. Their views may be that they are not intellectually up to the challenge (Deborah, Peggy, or Jim may feel this way), or are physically deficient (possibly Jean), or generally of little worth (Andrea and Ron). They may feel that life and people "use" others (Andrea may see life this way), that life "controls" individuals (Bob seems to feel controlled), or that life is too confusing (Ron and John seem overwhelmed and confused). Through analysis of each group member's goal, views, and life styles, members would have some notion of their own views and goals. Moreover, all members, in the process of the group to date, would have explored, alone, with the group leader in private session, and in the group, their life styles as lived—the patterned pursuit of their unique goals in daily life with all its problems. In the group, we would have discussed the particulars for each person and the commonalities and similarities of perspectives and behaviors.

I would also have begun exploring and exposing members' expectations of life and of the group. During the initial three meetings, when questions about trust and conflict came up, I most probably would have begun this process. The question posed might have been, "How can we as a group trust anyone, especially a bunch of people as messed up as we are?"

The discussion that followed should have brought some affirmative statements about trusting: "I trust Ron" or "I sort of trust Jean pretty much." I would also be hoping for, and encourage, statements of worth from group members. So if, for instance, Peggy said, "We may be messed up but we're not all doing that badly, and we're here to work on our problems," I would respond with something like "You're the ones saying how messed up you are. I think you all have points of view that lead you to expect the worst and you often see to it that the worst happens. I think you are worthwhile and can make it. Peggy, it seems to me you're saying, 'We're not so bad, we're just not good enough.' I'd say, you're not so bad at all, you're just not perfect. No one is. What we need is what Adlerians call 'the courage to be imperfect,' the courage to take a risk and know that things don't always turn out right, but if we take a chance, participate by doing our best, things won't always turn wrong—but they will sometimes."

Again I am trying to show the group the Adlerian view of personality, social psychology, and mental health. If this view has begun to sink in when John makes his stunning announcement, then what will happen? The group will ask John why, and obviously his reason for leaving the group will determine to some extent the group's response to his leaving. The questions I would want answered are (1) how are John's reasons for leaving (or saying he is going to leave) the manifestations of his life style? and (2) how does the group react, analyze, and proceed with John's announcement?

From an Adlerian position, all behaviors illustrate life style—but this position, like any rule without exceptions, has its limits and pitfalls for its proponents in the extreme. If John says he cannot return to the group because he is being transferred to another city by his employer and both he and his wife are pleased with the move, it would seem to be a good break for him, encouraging, and we should wish him well. This reason for leaving would not illustrate his life style, although the manner of his announcement well might. If on the other hand, he says he cannot return for reasons such as his wife does not like him out at night or does not want him talking about their relationship to others, or, more likely from the brief description we have of John, he does not feel things will work out in the group and he does not know how to act in the group (which may take some probing to find out), we have a good example of a person living his life style in the group. The group, including me, must show John what he is doing and how this continues a behavior pattern rather than allowing the group experience to serve to break the pattern.

Within the give-and-take of the group's exchange, its interest in, affection for, and some dependence on John should emerge. Should this not occur early on, I would ask, "Does anyone here like John, want him in the group? How did you see him helping the group, helping you?" A general support for John will come, along with disappointment in and anger about his leaving. John can identify how he elicits negative as well as positive feelings. At the same time, the other group members can see how their reactions are, in essence, automatically programmed within their life styles by simultaneously responding to the intentions of John's behavior.

There is a good bit of time left in the session for the discussion needed to reach John and the other group members. For John, we need to end the session so that if he persists in his decision to leave, he knows his decision is reasonable (if it is), or knows why he is leaving, if it is part of his life style pattern. In either event, John will know that from the "group's mind" he has not been rejected and remains accepted and acceptable. If he decides to change his mind and stay, he should also know why, and we should help him discriminate between feeling coerced into staying and making his own decision.

Each group member should have the opportunity to state and investigate his or her own feelings and the reason for those feelings about John's leaving. My task for each person would be to make the reasons as clear as possible within their own life style framework.

However, the *overall* task for me is to convey a common sense lesson that, it appears, everyone in the group needs to learn: living in society, like being in a group, includes disappointments and failures that are to be met, learned from, and left behind. John's announcement and decision is not fate again striking us. His decision, whether we like it or not, is an individual decision that we ultimately must respect even if we quarrel with his rationale. Our responsibility is both to our self and to others. The joy is in the task, in the doing, for we cannot expect to perfectly answer, to perfectly struggle over the elements of the age old dilemma posed by Rabbi Hillel:

> If I am not for myself, who will be?
> If I am only for myself, what am I?
> And if not now, when?

## Rational-Emotive Therapy

*Implemented by Albert Ellis*
Because these group members are first of all humans, and because virtually all humans are exceptionally prone to feelings of inadequacy and self-downing; and because, secondly, these particular individuals have been placed in this group because they all seem to have "what was symptomatic of low self-esteem," I would assume that many or most of the members feel stunned by their sense of being rejected or deserted by John's withdrawal from the group.

They are probably putting themselves down for not having been more effective in the course of the group process, and thereby not helping John enough to keep him as a group member. They are perhaps angry at John for not giving them more of a chance, and perhaps also angry at the group leader for not getting things more organized sooner, so that John would not have seen fit to quit the group. Because John is also human, and perhaps a typical member of this self-flagellating group of individuals, I would assume that his quitting has something to do with his own feelings of inadequacy and hopelessness. Just as he has felt lost in his second marriage and concluded that it was going to end as the first one had, he also felt lost in this group process and has concluded that he is going nowhere in it and is wasting his time by staying.

I might first check out my assumptions by asking John his reasons for leaving the group. If he had "legitimate" reasons, I would mainly acknowledge these, and tell him that the group will probably continue without him, and invite him to rejoin if and when he feels inclined to do so. Even more important, however, because I know that the members of the group appear "stunned," I would probably work first with them and their emotional problems. I would assume, as noted above, that "stunned" mainly means panicked and self-flagellating; I would spend time checking to see if there is evidence behind this assumption.

If it proves that the members are indeed panicked and self-downing, I would take it that this is *not* directly caused by his proposed desertion of the group but by their overinvolved, personalized, and irrational reaction to that desertion. In accordance with RET theory, I would assume that the Activating Experience (A) of the group members, John's desertion, contributes to but by no means "causes" C, their emotional Consequences of shock, horror, and worthlessness. Rather B (their irrational Beliefs) about A are mainly "causative" of C.

I would more precisely tell myself: "The group members are probably assuming that they have done something wrong to merit John's desertion; that they *should* not, *must* not have done this wrong thing; that it is *awful* that they did; and that they are *pretty rotten* persons for having done it. These nutty *evaluations* or *conclusions* are driving them to a state of panic." I would find methods to get them to see this and to give up their absolutistic *musts* and consequent self-damnation in order for them to accept themselves with their wrong doings, assuming that these have actually occurred.

I would also assume that if the group members are indeed angry toward John or the group leader, they are foolishly *making themselves* irate about these people's "inequities," and that they can be taught, through the use of Rational-Emotive Therapy, not to anger themselves about this or about virtually anything else. I would be determined to show them what they are needlessly doing in this respect and how to make themselves unangry and only, instead, sorry and annoyed about John's or the leader's behavior.

I would ask myself where my interventions were likely to do the most good, and what specifically these interventions should be. I would probably choose the group itself, rather than John, as the focal point of these interventions. I would do this for several reasons: (1) The purpose of RET is to help as many people as possible in the most efficient manner, and helping seven group members seems more important to me than only or mainly helping John; (2) in focusing on the group members rather than on John, he might feel relatively unthreatened and therefore listen better to the RET problem-solving process, and be as much or even more helped than some of the other members; (3) John may well have made up his mind to quit already, and trying to help him at this stage might prove useless; and (4) if time permitted, the first focus on helping the other group members might be shifted back to John so that he might be focused upon too.

Although the group members might be both angry and self-downing about John's proposed desertion, I would probably choose to focus on the latter rather than the former emotional difficulty. For one thing, it seems more important, since it is related to the basic problems of virtually all the group members. For another, it is less dramatic (though perhaps deeper) and less likely to get the group members off on a melodramatic tangent, which would stir up their feelings, all right, but quite possibly sidetrack them from understanding what is going on in their heads and hearts and from doing anything definite about it.

Shuttling back between dealing with, first, the emotional disturbance of panic and, second, that of anger, is not considered de riguer in RET. Since we have a kind of quadratic equation with two unknowns, anger and panic, understanding and resolving either of these disturbances is likely to be impeded by dealing simlutaneously with both. I would therefore concentrate on only one of these emotions, and would probably choose self-downing behavior as a place to start.

Since this group has apparently been given no behavioral homework assignments as yet (because who knows what muddled theory of group therapy its present leader is following!), I would think in terms of *in vivo* desensitization assignments, both within the group itself and with outside assignments between sessions. On this particular occasion, I would begin this desensitization process by trying to incorporate some of it in this very session in which I am about to intervene.

I would start by addressing the group members along the following lines: "You seem positively stunned by John's announcement that he is about to leave the group. Am I right about this? How, exactly, do you feel about the fact that this is going to be his last session?"

I would then get more details of their feelings, including, probably, rage, depression, hopelessness, inadequacy, and panic. If so, I would first zero in on those involving self-recrimination and self-downing: "It looks like several of you are blaming yourselves for not having managed to build an effective group and therefore not helping John enough. Now, we could argue this point: no matter what kind of a group you build and how effective it generally is, John might not accept help or might not allow himself to benefit from it. But let's suppose the worst: that you really haven't worked hard enough to weld yourself into an efficient and helpful group and that John is rightfully quitting, because he has got little help from you. If so, why *must* you have been more efficient? Where is the evidence that it is *awful* that you haven't been? In what way can't you *stand* being so inept? How does your poor group behavior prove that you are basically *rotten people?*"

I would show these group members, in other words, that they were needlessly upsetting themselves about John's desertion of the group, and that the part they played in it, by irrationally—in point B (Belief System)—*muster*bating, awfulizing, whining, and putting themselves down as humans for their (assumedly) crummy and nontherapeutic behavior. I would try to convince them that, no matter how legitimately they were assessing their *deeds* and *performances*, they were very illegitimately rating *themselves* for these poor performances. And I would teach them, through individual and collective dialogue, to actively challenge and dispute each others' faulty thinking. I would attempt to get all of them—or at least as many as will dare to change their fundamental philosophies of life—to give up ego- and self-evaluation, and to keep their identity or the power to choose more of what they want and less of what they do not want. Otherwise stated, I would attempt to help them enjoy rather then "prove" themselves.

In attempting this (almost Herculean!) task, I would specify emotive and behavioral exercises for the group members. Emotively, for example, I might deliberately have John vent his spleen on them, and tell them how much he despised them for not being very helpful to him or to themselves. As the group members made themselves enraged or ashamed in the face of his tirade, I would try to help them change their feelings from anger to annoyance and from shame to disappointment, and make them see that they could probably only do this by radically changing their cognitions. Thus, if one of them first felt enraged at *John* and later only frustrated by John's *behavior,* he or she would probably be internally saying: "It really is too bad that John doesn't appreciate the help we've been trying to give him and that he is copping out by quitting the group before he gives us more of a chance to reach him. But that's his prerogative; and there is no reason why he *has* to give us a full hearing." And if another member first felt ashamed at John's tirade and then only disappointed by it, he or she might later think: "Maybe John is right, and I did not do everything I could to understand and help him. That's poor behavior on my part, and I'd better do something about it. But I am entitled to my errors, fallible human that I am; and there is no necessity for me being less fallible and having to help John." Seeing and practicing these new cognitions, after they had temporarily changed their inappropriate feelings (rage and shame) to appropriate ones (frustration and disappointment), makes these group members more likely to spontaneously feel less enraged and less shameful about the happenings in their lives when new difficulties arose.

In terms of behavioral assignments, if Andrea (let us say) was very angry at John for not speaking up sooner and letting the group know how he felt about its ineffectiveness, I (with the collaboration of the group) might give her the assignment of deliberately keeping in close touch with her ex-husband, at whom she might also be angry, and working on her feelings until she only disliked his behavior and refused to damn him totally for this behavior. And if Ron was notably self-damning because he felt that he and the group had not helped John sufficiently, I and the group might give him the homework assignment of disclosing to his friends some particularly foolish acts he had recently done, and working on not putting himself down in case they laughed at and denigrated him for these activities.

After dealing with the members of the group, individually and collectively, and after trying to see that they really understood that John was not upsetting them, and that they had the choice of reacting in appropriate or inappropriate ways to his leaving the group, I would try to spend some time helping John with his problem of wanting to quit the group. Assuming, again, that he did not have very good reasons for doing so, and that he was falsely concluding that he could not possibly be helped by the group, I would first try to show him that this was an antiempirical statement: he certainly might not be helped, because of his own and the group's inadequacies, but there was no evidence that getting help was impossible, and under no conditions would he ever be able to receive it or use it.

In the process of doing so, I would try to show him that—something akin to the reaction of the other members of the group—he was putting himself down and concluding that because he had failed in the past, he would *always* and *only* fail; that he was essentially a *rotten person;* and that, as such, he really deserved to keep failing and had no possibility of succeeding at therapy or almost anything else in the future. I would actively Dispute (point D) these irrational Beliefs (at point B), and would try to show him how to Dispute them himself, outside of the therapeutic milieu. As in the case of the other members of the group, I would try to devise (with John's help) some emotive and behavioral exercises that would also motivate and encourage him to make a basic philosophic change in his attitudes toward himself.

Thus, I might use rational-emotive imagery, in the course of which he would imagine himself seriously failing at some important task and being rejected by others for failing. After he imagined this, probably feeling severely depressed or even suicidal in the process, and after he was in solid touch with these feelings, I would get him to change them to feelings of keen sorrow and regret but not depression. When he had achieved this, he would practice, perhaps every day for 30 or more days, this process of rational-emotive imagery to reinforce these more appropriate feelings whenever he thought about failing or actually did fail at some project that he considered important.

If time permitted (or in subsequent group sessions), I would work with the members of the group (and with John, if he decided to stay in the group) on their feelings of anger at John, at the group leader, at the others. RET clearly distinguishes between people's legitimately feeling highly annoyed and irritated at the displeasing acts of others and their illegitimate total condemnation of these others as humans. This therapy attempts to get clients to make this kind of distinction and to feel and express intense displeasure or annoyance without being globally intolerant of the *people* who exhibit annoying *qualities*.

Would I, in the course of leading this session, neglect some important elements of the group process? Yes, I probably would. For I am not interested—except from a research or general psychological point of view—in group process half so much as I am interested in helping group members. Humans normally live in groups and are appropriately and inappropriately affected by group processes. My job, as a psychotherapist, is to help them live more happily; incidental to this goal is understanding what is going on in the group process. More important, I want to understand the group *members*, and how to intervene to aid these members overcome their emotional disturbances.

## Reality Therapy

*Implemented by Thomas E. Bratter*
The conglomeration of people and their presenting problems of being passive, feeling unfulfilled and worthless would constitute an ideal group for Reality Therapy. By virtue of their common problems, this group can offer participants an opportunity to identify with each other and form a support network to reinforce newly acquired behavior.

John is illustrating a central group concern. He is verbalizing a combination of resignation and impotence while feeling sorry for himself. Since no one apparently wants to respond to him, I would assume the initiative: "I feel sad to hear you are considering leaving the group because I both like you and think you can contribute something important. I do respect your right to choose whether or not you wish to continue. I believe you are confusing a crucial point. You may not be able to control the conditions which challenge you, but you certainly can control what you do. You mention you have been hurt in your first marriage and that your second one seems doomed. You may be right. Some relationships probably are best to end, though we do not know if this is the case with you. It is more than likely, although there are no guarantees, that we might be able to give you some suggestions which will help you revitalize your relationship with your wife. Since your announcement surprises me, I would appreciate it if you could give me the opportunity to think about your situation during the week and then we can discuss your decision next week. I am interested to learn some of the reasons for you wanting to leave us. Hopefully, then, other members will relate to what you have said."

In all probability, John would discuss how he feels. "I feel depressed, drained, discouraged, and defeated about everything. What is the use to continue?" While other schools of psychotherapy would consider these revelations to be significant examples of insight and "being in touch" with one's feelings, I would be unimpressed. I would prefer for John to describe what he does so that I could try to help him understand the correlation between action (behavior) and feelings. If, for example, John currently is not engaging in any responsible, productive, and gratifying behavior, there is no reason for him to feel particularly happy.

My guess is that John neither feels loved or loves, which probably is creating his unhappiness. John's decision to terminate creates a crisis that will jeopardize the continuation of the group. If John can be persuaded to remain and begin to work on his areas of concern, the group can coalesce and become a nurturing unit which will provide the incentive and support which John needs. While I would respond to John's comment seriously, I do not believe he really is committed to leaving. Instead he may be testing whether or not we sincerely care about him. He knows he has few options. I, nevertheless, would be prepared to verbalize my concern without feeling I have been manipulated.

## Transactional Analysis

*Implemented by Herbert Hampshire*

There are aspects of this situation that would not be likely to develop in a TA group. The most glaring one is the announcement that this is John's last session. Everyone, before joining one of my groups, is informed of the "operating procedures," which form the basis of the only "group contract" asked of members. One of its primary elements is the proviso that any member who terminates will discuss that intention early in one session and then in two subsequent meetings. One of the purposes of this procedure is to avoid exactly the situation presented in the incident. The agreement provides protection both for the individual who is terminating and for the other group members. Without it, it is likely that a rise in uncomfortable emotion or a confrontation that seriously undermines a member's defense structure will lead to impulsive "acting-out," which is destructive because of its relative nonreversibility. Patients frequently consider termination and see, through the process that ensues, how they are programmed to run away from intense feelings. The structure provides them an opportunity to look at their impulse and see what is behind it, and the "decision" to leave thus becomes an authentic and productive demonstration of their reaction. Without that structure, members are often out of the group before realizing they did not want to leave even though they were reluctant to express their hurt, anger, or fear.

The structure also protects the group from a form of emotional blackmail. Precipitously announcing one's termination from the group is tantamount within the group culture to threatening suicide. In this example, John has threatened the group with his disappearance, giving them one last opportunity to express any feelings they have toward him. No matter how pressing any other issue may personally be for another member, the situation creates a powerful pull toward dropping everything and relating to the imminent threat to the group.

The composition of this group provides an opportunity to note the value of individual contracts. Eric Berne advised against homogeneous groups, because he saw them as supportive of each other's game and racket patterns on the unconscious premise that "if you don't call me on mine, I won't call you on yours." Contracts provide a potential antidote since they highlight the individuality that exists beneath ostensible similarity.

The fact that the common element in the experiences of these patients is they are "unhappy with their lot in life" underscores shared resistance to assuming responsibility. From that statement alone, one would expect the individuals in the group to perceive the group, and to see things generally, as *happening* to them. Allowing them to begin without specific sets of purposes and goals supports the passivity of their patterns and enhances the probability of an outcome in which they are "unhappy with their lot in groups."

Since all group members share issues of responsibility, I would be cautious about doing something to "handle the situation." There is the danger in a "critical situation" that the therapist will implicitly agree with patients that they are powerless or incompetent and that intervention by the therapist is now needed. Highly charged encounters that have no simple or obvious resolution are, in fact, optimal both for members to discover how people actually function and to allow them to generate new response options. It is precisely these kinds of situations that cause problems in everyday living. A therapist who allows patients to sit around discussing problems in living in a relatively subdued fashion and then, when something upsetting happens within the group itself, rushes to the rescue, is doing what Berne called "making progress rather then producing cure."

In this instance, I notice immediately that two elements of the session have been group-directed. Ron has talked directly to the group members about perceptions of their responses and about reactions to their input. John's threat to leave is even more direct evidence that group members are beginning to connect emotionally to the group. This is a precondition to beginning to play out programmatic issues in observable form—rather than merely talking around them.

The first order of business for me when "something happens" is to notice quickly what each person's ego state is and what they reveal about their programming. Some will be afraid, some angry, some hurt, some aloof. Some may feel secretly pleased, relieved, or victorious. The intensity of each person's response reveals the degree to which the incident relates to their programming. A particularly strong response often provides evidence about large segments of the script mechanism. For example, I might in this instance notice that Andrea responds to John's announcement with the immediate fear response of a 4-year-old child, followed rapidly by a reaction of controlled grief and resignation. I might speculate that an important figure, such as her father, had died if not committed suicide when she was 4. That would relate directly to a script focused on Andrea working to please men only to have them desert her. When I see the response of this intensity, significance, and clarity, I frequently focus on it directly, ostensibly ignoring "the crisis at hand." This serves several purposes, one of which is to shift the context away from "crisis" to recognizing an event as simply an event. Also, it allows, by virtue of capturing the momentary re-experiencing of pivotal script situations, highly "efficient" therapy. In addition, this strategy consciously interrupts the flow of any game or script payoff that John is setting up. By the time we get back to John, his affect is likely to be more authentic and more genuinely related to the reaction he did or did not perceive himself getting.

Even when there is nothing as dramatic, there are always subtleties of reactions that reveal elements of programming. I particularly focus on identifying "intersections" and overlaps in individuals' patterns. Andrea is an obvious person to focus on, since she has experienced separation from a man before. Jean's reaction would be important since she has "dropped out" herself. Bob would "intersect" with John since his pattern is to remain "trapped and not go anywhere" rather than to take action such as John has. Ron's response is important to notice because he is the person who is being at least implicitly transacted with. At a Child-to-Child or Parent-to-Child level, John is communicating, "My problems are more important than what you are talking about now." Ron's work in the group has suddenly "turned into a disaster." I would want to know if he has a pattern of getting "overruled" by people whose feelings are more intense or whose problems are greater than his. Is the dissolution of his marriage related in any way to this? It is inevitable that he will have anger at having the rug pulled out from underneath him, and his response will clearly indicate the way he relates to competitiveness in relation to feelings. It is quite likely that Ron will reveal in this circumstance any problem he has derived from sibling rivalry.

It is significant that the pacing of sessions had moved toward self-disclosure and that women appeared to be "going first." Peggy and then Andrea had opened up, leading to Ron and Bob talking. Since there is a specific theme among the women of being victimized in relation to men, and among the men of not relating well to women, this pattern may be a powerful theme underlying the group process. Shared issues produce group process and must be individualized and related to directly to interrupt patterns. John may be feeling not only the increasing intimacy of the group but also some perceived pressure to "take his turn." His reaction may be related to coercion he feels from women as well as competitiveness he experiences with me. This area of speculation is rendered more viable by the recognition that John was "unable to bring his wife with him. . . ."

Since there is some element of transference in all responses in a group, I want particularly to focus on what reaction John is "pulling for" from me. I want to notice, for example, whether he makes his announcement directly to me or whether he pointedly did not look at me when he spoke. He may be inviting me to control him and "not let him go," or he may be challenging me to prove that I care about him. It is essential to know how John perceives me relating both to him and to other group members. It is likely that he is, after session number four, seeing that others in the group are beginning to "get to work," while he continues to feel "lost" and under pressure, as he has been in both of his marriages. If he had a pattern of parenting in which he concluded that he could never ask for assistance or rely on someone, I might ask John to focus on how isolated and unsupported he is feeling. If he had a parent who always rescued him, I might point out that it is all right for him to be in an uncomfortable struggle and to stay and work it out.

It is important to point out that most of the analysis in TA terms is going on in my head and not in the group. "Why" someone is behaving in a particular way is important for me to understand as a therapist but not for the individual to spend his or her time discussing. What is central for the patient is *how* their functioning blocks their satisfactions and *how* they can function beyond their programming and out of their script. I frequently share with new patients Eric Berne's dictum, "Change today; tomorrow we can figure out why it was so difficult to change the day before."

Concretely, in this instance, I would invite any group member to tell John how they were reacting, or I might ask John to tell group members how he wanted them to respond. Since the underlying issue of passivity and responsibility exists in the group, and since John has not opened up before, I would be more likely to go to John. I would do this, however, only if the "stunned" silence continued until it became unproductive, and it was clear that none were able to get themselves out of their paralysis.

John would proably require some encouragement to verbalize how he wanted people to react to him and how his perception of himself in the group led him to view leaving as his only option. As I moved him to a point of communicating clearly, I would invite him to speak directly to one or more group members. If the dynamics within the group were especially powerful, I would suggest John talk to a specific person whose programming would "automatically" interact with his, and therefore shift the context. Andrea would be a possibility, since she has demonstrated a capacity to verbalize her resentment, as distinct from John's wife, who simply pulls away. If John were more focused on his own dynamics at that point, I would simply allow him to select any person to talk to.

Whatever specific set of transactions were produced, the feelings related to and from John would be made apparent, and the group would individually and collectively move toward reacting to them in new ways.

Notice that it is not, in the final analysis, critical whether John actually leaves. What is important is that the issue be dealt with in a way that assures everyone of deriving value from its having come up, and that John is not left in a position of avoiding therapy, because of his programming. If his decision to leave is made from the Adult ego state, it ceases to be an appropriate focus for therapy.

## Theory Evaluation Form

1. Which theoretical practitioner did you most resemble? Why?

2. Which theoretical practitioner did you least resemble? Why?

3. What does your response to *Question 1* tell you about yourself and your leadership style as a potential or present group therapist?

4. What does your response to *Question 2* tell you about yourself and your leadership style as a potential or present group therapist?

5. After rereading how the theoretical practitioner of your choice responded to the incident, how would you modify or change your response?

# CHAPTER ELEVEN

# A Deep Disclosure Near Session Termination

In this incident, we find how our theoretical practitioners deal with the group when a relatively nonverbal group member suddenly discloses deep-seated emotional feelings near the end of the session.

## Incident #5

The group is heterogeneous in composition. During the preinterview sessions, the presenting areas of concern were somewhat similar. The group members appear to be having difficulty dealing with the significant others in their lives. Their relationships seem to be shallow and have very little meaning. The reason they sought you out was to find some way of bringing significance and value back into their personal lives. They all seem tired of bobbing like corks aimlessly on the sea of life.

The membership of the group is comprised of five females and three males, ranging in ages from 28 to 45 years old. Briefly, they are described as follows:

*Sally* is 28 years old, single, holds a B.S. in Biology. She is a laboratory technician and is engaged to be married.

*Francine* is 34 years old, divorced, and has custody of her two children. She is employed as a cocktail waitress.

*Janet* is 39, married and childless. She is employed as an elementary school teacher.

*Sarah* is 43 years old. Her husband is a pediatrician and they have three children; two of them are in college. Sarah has returned to college to get her M.A. in Psychology.

*Sandra* is 45 years old. Her four children have completed college and are on their own. She appears uncertain about the direction her life is going to take. Her husband has three more years before he retires at age 65 on a very substantial income.

*Samuel* is 29 years old. He is married, but is living separately from his wife. He is a successful sales representative for an international brokerage house.

*Jonathan* is 32 years old. He owns a very unsuccessful insurance agency in town. He has completed four years of college at the local university.

*Franklin* is 28 years old. He married his high school sweetheart 11 years ago. He has three profitable gas stations throughout the area and is president of the Chamber of Commerce.

During the first six sessions, which last for an hour each, much time was spent exploring each other's values, motives for joining the group, and the like. Of course, before any of the members joined the group, you had told them that there were five or six other persons who seemed to be expressing similar concerns and if they wished to, they could volunteer to join the group. The expressed goal, or purpose, was to share and perhaps work out what appeared to be barriers to enjoying more effective and meaningful personal lives. All of the members appeared quite agreeable to cooperate and join. Their general attitude was that they would like to do "anything" to get themselves out of the holes they felt they had dug for themselves and thus bring them closer to the people they felt they had a deep love for.

Through the first six sessions, the group had been relatively open. The members tended toward establishing acquaintanceships (orientation) during the first three meetings. Francine seemed ready and willing to move into personal disclosures. This proved threatening to the majority of the members. You observed their uneasiness in their rapid movement away from Francine to topics that seemed away from and outside of the group. Jonathan, for example, preferred to talk about the difficult time he has had building up his insurance business; the amount of hours spent on identifying new clients, advertising, and public relations. Franklin has discussed the difficulty he has contending with the major oil corporation (his supplier) in order to sustain his business. Samuel expressed more personal feelings early in the fourth session when he disclosed his discomfort and sense of personal failure for not making a "proper go" of his marriage. His confusion is further pronounced because none of the members have appeared to hear him.

Sarah seems to have demonstrated an ability to keep her involvement at an intellectual level and maintain her wits about her. Her disclosures have been very carefully articulated throughout the first six sessions. She has stated on numerous occasions that she believes she and her husband have an "understanding." She has her life to live and whatever she chooses to do is all right with him, so long as it does not interfere or disrupt the medical practice he has so diligently developed.

It is now the seventh session (week) and Sandra, who has remained rather silent over the past six weeks, has been fidgeting and looking extremely restless throughout the first 45 minutes. You are about to make movements to bring the group from an affectively oriented process to prepare them for the session's termination. Sandra has been a very quiet and inactive member of the group. You have attended to this form of nonverbal involvement on her part and felt it would be just a matter of time before she would choose the appropriate moment for herself to actively (vocally) participate. Of course, tonight's session was not very different from previous sessions in which the group had moved rapidly from socializing to confronting. They appeared to be establishing some overall cohesiveness when suddenly, without any warning, Sandra burst forth. Her exclamation was mixed with blame, bitterness, anger, and hostility for her lot in life. On the face of it, it appears she is directing all of her feelings toward the group. She claimed no one seemed to care about her anymore. They all just seemed to be "takers" who never give anything back. She was tired of giving herself for nothing and not being appreciated. After all, she had her own life to live too. She spoke directly to Jonathan when she said that all he seemed to care about was his business and it appeared that no one else in his life seemed to matter. As she continued to ventilate, her disclosure subsided into deep sobs, and tears rolled down her cheeks. She was visibly shaken by all that she had just experienced and said, and she was trembling. As your eyes scanned the members, you (the leader) recognized how immobilized the group had become. They had sunk into complete silence. All of them had turned their eyes from Sandra and were looking at the floor, fidgeting with their fingers, at a loss for what to do or say.

## *C*lient-Centered Therapy

*Implemented by William R. Coulson*
My first reaction upon reading this incident was to imagine, like the rest of the group, that I would be paralyzed by Sandra's outburst. I might

feel, "Good Lord, the group is falling apart." In other words, my first thought might be for myself.

I would not be proud of such a feeling. I doubt I would say it, at least at the time. (Later, when we were recapitulating the incident in the group, after the crisis had passed, and members might be reflecting on the moment of panic Sandra had given them, I might confess to my own.) It is possible that if I were really in the group, I would not have felt panic at that point. I might have had a more sophisticated or experienced reaction. But my first thought was that if Sandra scared other members of the group, she might have scared me, too.

I am often looking for a response in myself with which group members can identify. If I do this too often, it becomes a manipulation: I am drawing them out by guessing their feeling and claiming it for my own. I think when I have a reaction like "Good Lord, the group is falling apart," it is because (1) I really am not better than other people—if some group event is traumatic enough to scare them, it could well scare me, too; and (2) deep down, I am afraid that the group will fall apart—other people will have better groups than I, their groups will go on and on, and clients unfortunate enough to have secured me for a therapist will wish they had someone else.

I feel justified in letting you in on my thought processes, because it can illustrate the common fear that beginning group therapists have, that groups will run out of things to say. This fear is relatively unfounded. When I start thinking about what I feel, I find a bottomless well. If the immediate purpose of group therapy is for people to talk about themselves, and since I can assume they also have this bottomless well of reactions to group events, then I do not think we need worry about having enough to talk about.

Twenty years ago, Carl Rogers and his colleagues studied the effect of Client-Centered Therapy on a hospitalized schizophrenic population. There they made the discovery that when clients' reactions are not available (some of the research subjects in that study simply would not talk), the therapist can talk about his or her reactions. If feelings are the subject matter of psychotherapy, maybe the therapist's feelings are eligible for examination, too.

A basic learning of the "Schizophrenic Project" was that the therapist's internal reactions provide a wealth of data, which can potentially enrich the relationship with the client. Client-Centered therapists began to believe that it was as legitimate to listen to their feelings as to listen to the client's.

I think we overlearned the lesson. I know I did. When I read through the list of incidents in this book, my first thought was always for myself, such as, "That scares me" or "Now what do I do?" I can defend myself by saying the cues to which I would respond in actual practice would be far richer than I can see on paper. My behavior would probably be an integration of my present feelings, memories of group members disclosures in previous sessions, and learnings from my teachers regarding how clients look, carry themselves, sit, and so on.

There are technical reasons for listening and fostering the expression of feelings. Expressing feelings helps people become vulnerable to one another and ultimately helps the group cohere and removes barriers to growth in individuals. Sandra, in our situation, is in pain; if I am thinking of myself at such a moment or laying back and scanning the group for their reactions, then I might have become more selfish (or more the technician) than I want.

Feelings are the very stuff of therapy. When deep feeling is emerging, Client-Centered therapists will concentrate on facilitating the flow. If the group needs maintenance or if the therapists want to assess their own personal reaction, they can take care of those tasks later.

For me, group therapy at its best is a laboratory in which our common moral commitments are tested and strengthened. The power lies in stimulating the sense of community, in which there are multiple and crossing lines of influence, in which members share perspectives directly with one another, and in which leadership passes from member to member (even in crises), rather than resting always with the therapist. If I find myself using the group in order to do individual therapy, I hope somebody will inform me. In general, I do not think it is the best use of group time.

What consequence would I anticipate following my response? I hope my encouragement would move Sandra toward a deeper understanding of her feelings, eventually ridding her of those that present barriers to personal development and, perhaps more immediately, teaching how her own reactions to people in a group will illuminate her life situation. I would not point out such connections to her. I would assume that drawing connections would be more effective if she did it herself. However, I do believe that by listening closely and reflecting my understanding of her message, I would be able to help clear away the clutter of her feelings. For example, the evident confusion over Jonathan and her husband. Finally, I would be glad for her outburst. Had she kept her feelings to herself, it would have prolonged the confusion. I have found when feelings are openly expressed, they more nearly become self-correcting.

I would hope the other group members learned from the incident and in future sessions, when a group member is in trouble, they might respond rather than stare at the floor. If they can learn a bit of self-mastery and courage in the face of group trauma, they will respond similarly outside of group therapy.

I would want to be sensitive to not intervene too quickly. Though I turned toward Sandra this time (rather than joining the group in turning to the floor), I would hope the positive effect of this move would be taken to heart—and that the next time, I would find one of the other members attending to the distressed person before I did. (I don't mean pushing Kleenex at her, clucking over her and shutting down her feelings, but I mean *being with her* in her distress, being a companion as she moved through it. If I were in trouble myself, I believe I would appreciate such help. It could come from anywhere. It would not have to be a therapist who gave it.)

Now and then, I view all functions in group therapy as those of bridge building. In early sessions, I listen for connections between what individuals say now and what they said before and between what this one says and what that one said. I sometimes focus on and point to such connections: "That sounds a little like what Janet said earlier, too." I am hoping to build bridges between people.

Once these bridges become firm enough to walk on (I am not the only one building them, of course; the participants are doing it, too), I like to get out of the way. I do not want to be standing in the middle, at the highest point of the arch, blocking traffic while members are trying to get through to one another. I used to be so pleased when members made disclosures to the group, and particularly when I helped them get started, that I would "hog" the conversation. I would forget that my goal was to facilitate group development rather than focus on myself. So the second step in my bridge building program is to get out of the way—to participate, yes, but not to take over.

The third step comes when no more special leadership behavior is necessary, when members are crossing bridges to one another readily and when they are passing leadership. Then I might cross a bridge myself, for I believe it is a more adequate reflection of reality when everyone is interested in giving and receiving help rather than in isolating the therapist as a function of his or her training and title. I find what I share with group members—our common human inheritance—far more powerful in determining our happiness than my special training. Group therapy is a premiere opportunity for the tacit acknowledgement of that inheritance.

## Gestalt Therapy

*Implemented by Mirriam F. Polster*

Sandra's passionate denunciation of the group strikes me as welcome and not at all surprising. It is about time that someone called them on the tacit acceptance of non-listening and non-responsiveness that seems to have become a group norm. Since group interaction is a microcosm of how individual group members customarily act, the behavior here is not merely symptomatic, it is a fresh and present demonstration of how these people may act in the relationships that they have already described as troublesome and unsatisfying. They have stated that their outside relationships are shallow and meaningless. In this group interaction, we have all the elements that illustrate how they contribute to their unhappy situations. They do not listen, they look away, they make abstract or impersonal statements, and they become embarrassed when someone else refuses to play by the familiar but juiceless rules.

Contact is the relationship of an organism to its environment and is an essential principle in Gestalt Therapy. Laura Perls recently described contact as "the recognition of, and the coping with the *other*, the different. . . not a state. . . but an activity. . . ." (Perls 1978, 31–36). We are all open systems, depending upon our exchanges with our environment to nourish, interest, stimulate, and educate us—in other words, to keep us alive and humanly responsive. In order to make contact, we must have a sense of our own separateness, the individuality that is our contribution to making contact. Contact is a process that requires the ability, rooted in ourselves, to venture into unfamiliar territory and to risk a momentary loss of self because we are willing to engage richly with that which is not us.

Given a moderately benevolent environment, we grow up with increasing confidence in our ability to make contact with the world. We discard, bit by bit, some of our dependency on external support and learn to support ourselves in the risky but exciting game of meeting that which is outside ourselves. But the more we venture, the more likely it is that the world responds unpredictably. So we are sometimes rebuffed, hurt, or ignored. We begin to develop strategies for these responses. We try to support ourselves as best we can in the face of these disappointments. Often, we begin to distort or cripple the possibilities for contactful engagement. We draw in and constrict the excitement and arousal that might lead us to make overtures to that which is outside ourselves. It is this constricted excitement we experience as anxiety, which results in stilted and unsatisfying interaction with the world around us. This is the root of the difficulty the group was formed to address; their inadequacies in the specifics of contact, their inability to be with other people, to talk to them frankly without hiding, to listen to them without distortion, and to support the excitement and uncertainty of this human engagement.

Before looking at the role of each of the participants in the present interaction and my actions as group leader, I would like to note that one-hour sessions are too short for working with a group of eight people. There is simply not enough time for the taciturn or slow group members to jump in. Thus, the pace of the group is skewed in favor of the verbally agile or assertive members. The lively ones talk and the silent ones feel bullied, robbed, ignored, or out of it. Sandra's complaint, therefore, has some genesis in the shortage of time.

Even though it is affected by this scarcity of time, her complaint also has its own personal style and content. Some people have taken the time and she has *given* it. She has remained silent, her gift to the group, and others have taken up the time she might have used, they have filled it up with empty surface talk, ignored her, and not even felt grateful. So she bursts forth with an intensity that may be greater than the present situation calls for, but which is loaded with a charge of energy from six weeks of silence in the group and from her "lot in life" outside it. The way she enters is to accumulate a grievance and then come in with a sense of having been wronged, with accusations and complaints. Nobody seems to care about her.

This is not only a statement to the group, it is addressed to me as group leader. Her complaint has validity. How could I have sat here for six weeks without remarking or asking about her silence? How could I have sat for 45 minutes in the present session and be working toward termination of the session without noticing her restlessness? I have colluded in the noncontact atmosphere and, as leader, have contributed a lot towards setting up the apparent group expectation of "hands-off," which is a burlesque of the existential belief in self-determinism.

How have I done this? I have let Sandra stew in her own juice for six weeks and done nothing. I have let Sarah palm off sloganistic statements about the "understanding" between herself and her husband and done nothing. I have let Jonathan and Franklin talk about the energy they put into their business activities and not asked them to direct this energy to their interaction with the group. I have heard Francine and Samuel broach their personal concerns and I have seen the unease and avoidance with which these disclosures have been met and I have done nothing.

I do not believe that these people have come into group therapy knowing how to make contact. They are here to learn and one way they learn is from me as model. This is an undeniable aspect of group leadership. To ignore it is to ignore one of the most potent influences in any therapy. If I, as a gestaltist, value the ability to make contact, if I believe in awareness as a mobilizing and enriching attribute and if I see self-support as a central quality in these actions, then I respond from these beliefs. I cannot become less responsive as a group leader than I am as a human being.

The tricky issue here is how to use my awareness so that it becomes a resource in the group rather then a dictum of how people *should* behave or a judgment of their behavior. I am not in the group to dictate, but to explore alternatives, to remark on something that might otherwise go unremarked, to give a sense of the elasticity of our time together that allows for human contact, and to make it more likely that the group members will get better and better at doing this for themselves.

So, I offer two sets of responses to the situation presented in this example. First, what I might have done had I been there from the first session on, and second, what I might do if I just began work with this group in the seventh session.

In the first scenario, I would begin the group work with a short statement of my beliefs as a Gestalt therapist and what the people in the group might expect from me by way of observations or suggestions. I would also remind them that they can at any time either differ with me or say *no* to my suggestions. This suggests that reluctance to do something is to be respected and can be at least as informative as compliance.

After allowing some time, perhaps the first session and the beginning of the second, for group members to get the feel of each other, I would begin to attend publicly to the quality of their contact with each other. This might begin with what happens when Francine speaks about herself. I would observe who is listening, whether they are looking at her and she at them, whether they look interested or uncomfortable. When they tried to shift from her discussion to topics that seemed to be away and out of the group, I might ask her how she feels about the change of subject. I would be interested in how Francine has contributed to the lack of interest. Has she spoken lightly as if telling them not to take her seriously? Has her voice been inaudible or her language dull? Does she look down at the floor or a wall or the ceiling?

I can explore with the group the reciprocal nature of contact. The person who speaks to support him- or herself with energy, breath, and intention in order to make contact with those who listen. And the listeners, too, are not passive recipients. Their share in making contact is to listen actively, to see how Francine's manner corroborates or contradicts what she is saying, and to tune in to their self-awareness to detemine what her personal disclosures evoke in them. Samuel, too, has been confused by the apparent lack of response when he has talked about his sense of failure in his marriage. Again, it is important to assess how Samuel fails to arouse anyone's sympathy, anger, resentment, or identification. How can he continue to speak when nobody appears to hear or be moved?

Jonathan and Franklin do not seem to make the group uncomfortable. They talk about all the energy it takes to make a go of their business. But where does all that energy go when they are in the group? I want to discover ways in which that good energy could go into lively interactions here in the group. When they talk to one of the people in the group, do they talk with the same liveliness and concentration? Do they leave space for responses or an interested question, or do they just continue with the recital of their problems as they might to a Chamber of Commerce meeting or to a group of business associates? Can they shift gears? Or are they so rigidly locked into a businesslike form of contact that personal feelings leave them not knowing how to respond?

What do they feel, for example, in direct response to Samuel's discomfort?

And what is Sarah's reaction to Samuel? She, who has such a good working "understanding" with her husband. And how does Francine, who might be closest to responding feelingly to Samuel, remain silent and apparently unhearing? There is much interplay here that could lead to contact among the group members if the ground work for expecting to be heard can be made clear. By this, I mean the shared responsibility in any communication; the person who is speaking intends to be heard and supports this intention with voice, language, breathing, body movements, in short everything he or she has in order to make contact. And those listening are active participants in the two-way process of contact, too. This means they do not change the subject and pretend the uncomfortable word was not spoken. They look, and are willing to see and hear clearly what is before them, even if it makes them uncomfortable. They support their own discomfort and can move from that into contact even with unwelcome news.

But here we are in the seventh session, and Sandra has burst out in a way that is hard for them to ignore. They become immobilized; they are stunned. Her grievance, as I said, has built up in the time she has spent silent in the group, but it also is loaded with what she feels is her lot in life. She is addressing Jonathan, so we need to sort out specifically what emotion she directs at him and what may be leftover or excess baggage from someone else. She can make specific statements to Jonathan about her complaints. I might also ask if there is anyone else in the group she would like to say something to. Her initial move was spawned by her own distress and desperation. But to make it into a contactful interaction, she needs to say what she has to say to the very people she would like to confront, instead of remaining silent and waiting, like Sleeping Beauty, for someone to discover her, and resenting them when they do not.

Clearly, this kind of confrontation is hard for Sandra. She is unaccustomed to it, her habitual mode is silent resentment, and she needs experience in supporting her drastic emergence. There are three sources of support that are hers to muster. First, she can call on the support that her body can provide. Is she supporting herself physically? How could her gestures and posture corroborate what she is saying rather than deserting her and leaving her trembling and shaken? Second, how does her breath support her emotion? Does she take in air adequate to meet her needs for speaking and crying, or is she trying to make do with only a scant supply? And third, she can support herself by what she knows. What is there in particular, about Jonathan that has triggered this in her? What does she want that she is not getting? How does she collude in this? What does her silence do for her that allows this to happen and enables her to build up the grudge that she needs to get into the action? Is this the only way she might choose to become more active in the group?

After focusing on Sandra's experience, I would move on to Jonathan and his reaction to her outburst, and to the feelings of the other group members as they witnessed it. This is an opportunity to break into a newer and deeper level of feeling than had previously emerged and to look at the fears and doubts of the others. Sandra's expression of emotion is an opening to be explored, not an aberration to look away from and pretend did not happen. The other members do not know how to deal with intensity. They need practice in knowing their response and in being able to articulate it to others. The leader can serve here as a temporary support also, something like a scaffold that allows the work to go on, but which will be removed as soon as the structure can support itself.

## Individual Psychology

### Implemented by Guy J. Manaster

At the critical moment in this situation, with all eyes to the floor and all ears to Sandra's sobs, I would do nothing. I would wait until one of the following events occurred: (1) one of the group members came to Sandra's rescue, in whatever manner; (2) Jonathan, or whoever else felt implicated by Sandra's accusations, spoke up in defense of themselves, the group, the process to date; or (3) time ran out, the hour was up. These three options seem most likely although other things could happen, such as a member beginning a new discussion without regard for the incident.

My hope would be at this point, after more than six sessions, our combined efforts under the umbrella of Adlerian theory, would have resulted in a group feeling, a feeling of and for us as a group, a community, not as an assemblage. I would hope to have conveyed, directly in an educative manner and indirectly by my example of attention to individual group members and their behaviors, that in our group, as in everyday life, we have a responsibility to ourselves *and* to others. This moment in the group is a time for our responsibility for, our feelings for, *an-other* to take precedence. This is a moment when social interest, social-community feelings, is called for and would, I hope, emerge.

Moreover, Individual Psychology's purposeful, functional view of behavior and emotions should also have been transmitted during the previous sessions. The group members should have developed some inkling of the purpose of Sandra's behavior. They should be able intellectually to discriminate at some beginning level the two messages in her outburst: "I am different, not like, not a part of you, individually, or you the group," and "I feel sad—look how bad I feel, I am crying."

Sandra is asking for a response to her verbal and behavioral messages. The question is what response does she get from the group—not from me, if at all possible, but from the group.

If these most basic, and crucial, Adlerian concepts have become part of the group mentality, the first possible event will occur: someone in the group—I expect Francine—will respond to Sandra's call. Inferring more than I should on the limited information I have, I expect Francine to say something like, "Come on, honey, everyone here likes you. We've just been waiting for you to join in. We all feel crummy about the same things, so come on and feel crummy with us. When we're together it doesn't feel so bad and we can get better. It's when you feel you're by yourself that you feel worse. At least that's the way it is for me."

This would probably be greeted by a chorus, not unanimous, of agreement. The discussion would then move, possibly with me posing it, to the questions, "How did we come to this juncture, Sandra's part, the group's part?" and "Where do we go from here?"

But what about Jonathan? He might have followed up a positive response, such as Francine's above, with his defense, or he might have preceded anyone else's reaction with his defense.

In the context of the group as described, that is, not as an Adlerian group to this moment, Jonathan might well say, "I haven't been doing anything wrong, or against you, Sandra. I've been doing what I thought you were supposed to do in this group." From the description of the first six sessions, I think he might well have presumed that.

But if some of the notions and *values* of Individual Psychology have been instilled and Jonathan interrupted the silence with "Don't holler at me—I'm telling about my reasons for being here—you tell yours," or something like that, we have the grounds for exploring two people's reasons for behaving as they have, possibly with sides taken.

But what if Samuel, who apparently has not been heard in the past, starts things up again by going back to his own story. If no one else jumps in to keep us involved with the current important issue, to help and understand Sandra and what is going on, I would. I might say, "Samuel, it seemed that no one has heard you, and now it seems you aren't listening. What just happened? What about Sandra?" If he cannot answer, which seems probable, I would ask the same questions of the group, maybe adding "and what about Samuel?"

If Samuel had taken another tack, or no one had spoken, and it was almost time to break, I would have continued:

"We don't know what to do about, to, or for others! We are all here because we want to find some way of bringing significance and value back into our lives, or into our lives for the first time. I am not sure 'back' is appropriate for all of us—I think, probably, values and significance, at least in interpersonal relations, have never been very much part of our lives.

"We have, as a group, characterized ourselves as all being 'tired of bobbing like a cork aimlessly on the sea of life.' It looks to me as if we have been doing the same in here, occasionally 'bobbing' or 'bumping' into one another. But it looks to me as if each of us had been primarily fighting to keep afloat. And we each have our own ways of keeping our heads above water. It is usual for people to try to keep themselves above water, above others, in some way because they think if they are not better than others, above others, they will be below them, they will sink. We have been almost pretending to be a group, and not even pretending to be a group of equals. We've been perfecting our own ways of being superior—like Francine has by showing she's the most open, or like Jonathan has by showing how good and hard working he is, or like Samuel by showing his good intentions in spite of his confusion, or like Sarah by controlling, or trying to control, herself and all around her.

"And now what have we come to? Finally Sandra has added up the time we've been in group, the slights she sees from everyone and concluded, and now affirmed, her place—her usual place and her place again here—she's been 'took,' she's been 'had.' Is this true, Sandra? I know you feel very bad right now, but is it the same bad way you have felt often for a long time when you've been taken by your kids who used you and went on to their own lives, by your husband who has had a good career and used your quiet help in the background?"

This abbreviated summary should, as I have said, been a part of the group process from its inception, and the specifications of life style goals for each individual inferred in the group and discussed individually and privately with each group member prior to the beginning of the group, as well as in infrequent, but regular, one-to-one sessions concurrent with the group.

What if I had summarized in this fashion at the end of the session? There are two thrusts to it. The first is generalized to the group, providing framework for each member to understand his or her own reasons and goals for not assuming some portion of the group responsibility, and taking responsibility for another person. The second thrust is directed to Sandra with the same message as that directed to the group. The purposes of this summary are to illustrate (1) how each person is attempting to elevate him- or herself in their own special way from their own unique perspective; (2) how this strategy does not serve the articulated purposes of the group, but does serve their lifelong life style goals and perpetuates their nonbelonging; (3) how responsibility for and interest in others is essential for group living and individual growth as part of a therapy group; and (4) how this holds true also for being part of the human group. I probably did not, nor could not, convey all of that in the summary, but it is the essence of what I would want to impart. And the question remains as to what effect would accentuate and applaud the commonality of the problem and the attempts by all who attempted to modify their self-glorification for the common good and for Sandra's good.

At the same time, I would have to be watchful of Sandra being too effective and gaining the unreserved sympathy and apology of the group. If she did, and everyone responded with something to the effect of "I'm sorry we have overlooked you, we've only talked about us," I think I would break in with real applause. I might clap my hands and congratulate Sandra as one of the all-time great guilt purveyors, turning the incident into a lesson in purposeful behavior, in people getting what it is they want.

## Rational-Emotive Therapy

### Implemented by Albert Ellis

This critical incident is quite predictable in groups that are nondirectively misled in the manner that this one has been up to now. The therapist, who has not only been trained in typical psychoanalytic and client-centered nonsense but has also unfortunately gone along with this pap, does not seem to have the foggiest idea about how people generally block themselves from enjoying a more effective and meaningful personal life. The therapist also does not appear to have any notion of what an effective group leader can do to help the members unblock themselves in this respect. Consequently, he or she is too scared to really take charge and try to be (and risk failing at being) truly *helpful*, and so is desperately hoping against hope that the group members will somehow muddle through and magically help themselves. As normally happens under these dismal conditions, these members have nicely wasted virtually all their time in the group, and have been beautifully diverted from helping themselves in almost any way. Almost all of them are probably now the worse for needless wear and tear, and more confused about their goals in life and how to achieve them than they were when they began this form of "therapy."

Sandra, being older than the rest, and perhaps recognizing that her precious time is being wasted away in this kind of group process, complains bitterly, in her own natural ineffectual way, about what has been going on in the group. Rather than blame the group leader (who she thinks might possibly attack her back), she blames the group in general. This may well represent her usual tendency to blame external people and events instead of squarely shouldering the responsibility for her own thoughts, emotions, and actions; or it may represent the fact that she accurately sees that she has been done in to some extent by this inefficient group process. Of course, Sandra has stupidly and silently consented to this situation for the last several sessions and now she knows no better way to vent her feelings about this perfidy than to whine and scream. Usually, she does this internally; but in this case, she feels that enough is enough, and she atypically lets her inward anger out.

Sandra, moreover, seems to be even more self-hating than hostile to others, and she foolishly believes that she *has to be* approved, loved, and helped by others—particularly by those for whom she has some feelings and whom she may have herself succored. She (like most "adults") has always been a baby and is determined to be one for the rest of her life—if she can possibly get away with it. She rather envies the "takers"—such as Jonathan—who at least seem to care for themselves and go after (or at least worry about) what *they* want; but she also at times hates them for not recognizing *her* weaknesses and for not making sure that *she* gets taken care of.

As Sandra lets herself go—with feelings of anger, self-loathing, and abysmal self-pity—she recognizes that she is doing the "wrong" thing, since no other group member has "broken down" like this. So she does what most people do at this turn of affairs: takes her primary symptoms (anger and self-pity) and creates a set of severe secondary symptoms about them. Her fundamental irrational beliefs are: (1) "I *must* do well and be approved by others! And isn't it *awful* if I am not!" (2) "You *must* treat me considerately and fairly! And isn't it *terrible* if you do not!" and (3) "Conditions *must* be easy and give me exactly what I want quickly, without any hassles! And isn't it *horrible* when they are not!" After creating her primary emotional symptoms of self-downing, anger, and self-pity with these foolish absolutistic ideas, she then uses the same basic irrationalities to create her secondary symptoms.

Thus, when she sees that she has an angry outburst, instead of rationally telling herself, "I wish I wouldn't be so angry and break down in this uncalled for manner; how unfortunate!" she irrationally tells herself, "I *must* not break down in this uncalled for manner; how awful! What a perfect idiot I am!" She then feels depressed and self-downing about her anger (rather than accepting *herself* with *it*), and she exacerbates her state of emotional dysfunctioning.

If the group leader had any sense of competence, he or she would not have permitted this kind of situation to go this far in the first place. Once it occurred, however, the therapist should recognize that this kind of "therapy" will usually lead to outbursts of this sort and help exacerbate people's problems. The therapist would then, at least, *do* something about showing Sandra, and the group as a whole, what her real problems are, how she (and not the group process itself) is creating them, and what she can do about overcoming them.

Taking over the leadership of this group, I would immediately say to myself, "Shit! What a therapist-caused mess! However, it does have some good points about it because at least I can use this situation to show Sandra and the other group members what they are doing to upset themselves, and how they can more assertively, in the future, refuse to go this far with an incompetent leader and try to get themselves some real help. Too bad that I am, as it were, given an already half-drowned person to try to resuscitate. But it is quite a challenge for me to use this near-disaster to illustrate some of the main points of human disturbance, and perhaps to dramatize them to Sandra and the other group members."

In other words, in consulting in a bad situation like this one, I would first use Rational-Emotive Therapy principles on myself, to make sure that I did not anger or otherwise unnecessarily upset myself about this needless disaster. If I did feel angry at the incompetence of the group leader, I would quickly do the A-B-Cs of RET on myself: "At point A," I would say to myself, "let us assume that this leader has behaved incompetently. At point C (emotional and behavioral Consequence), I feel angry. What am I telling myself, at B (my Belief system) to make myself angry? Obviously: 'This therapist should not have acted so incompetently! Any leader like that deserves to be drawn and quartered!' But on to D (Disputing of irrational Beliefs): 'Why *should* not, *must* not he or she behave so incompetently—then that's the way they are! Tough!' And why does he or she deserve to be drawn and quartered for incompetence?' Answer: 'They don't—he or she is only a confused, fallible human who acted incompetently in this situation, not a totally bad human who deserves to suffer for incompetence. Too bad—but not awful!' "

I would show myself that Sandra's problems come from her own A-B-Cs, and not from A, the Activating Experiences, in the group, that happened to her. I would recognize that she has one or more profound, absolutistic *shoulds, oughts,* or *musts* by which she creates her problems—that she (like most humans) is a strong *mus*turbator. And I would guess from her highly disturbed emotional reactions, what her *musts* were. I would also look for her awfulizing, her I-can't-stand-it-itis, and her global labeling of herself and others as rotten people (instead of as people who behave rottenly in this instance). I would ask myself whether she had both primary symptoms (anger and self-downing) and secondary symptoms (self-downing about her own anger) and would quickly conclude that she definitely seemed to have both.

I would then start determining what emotive and behavioral interventions and homework assignments I would use to help Sandra and the group see how they were disturbing themselves and how they could stubbornly refuse to do so in the future.

I would recognize the group elements in this situation—but mainly see them as being at point A (Activating Experiences) in the A-B-Cs of RET. Sandra, even on her own, has a basic philosophy of perfectionism and intolerance of others' imperfections that would normally get her into emotional difficulties. But when she is in any kind of a group— even a supposed "therapy" group—she tends to use this philosophy about how she behaves in the group and how the group members behave toward her. Thus, she tends to think that *especially* when she is in front of other people she *must* act as well as they do and impress them with her goodness or competence; and she tends to think that they (especially the group leader) *must* come to her help and rescue, seeing what a weak ninny she is! So the irrational Beliefs and the dysfunctional emotions and behaviors that I would work on in Sandra's case would be even more prevalent and would tend to be shown more intensely in the group situation. But, following RET Theory, I would not delude myself that the group *makes* Sandra disturbed or *causes* her outbursts. The group and the group situation *contributes* significantly to her emotional problems, but they really do not "cause" them.

As a group consultant or therapist, I would keep in mind that I am primarily an educator—since, whatever I do with one member, such as Sandra, will be seen and heard by the other members. As a group educational setting, then, perhaps I can help several or most of the members by talking directly and incisively to one or a few of them. I also keep in mind that I want Sandra not only to understand herself and her own emotional problems, and how to cope with them, but also to understand how other people continually disturb themselves, and how she can accept them with their disturbances and perhaps help them overcome their malfunctioning. I would ideally like all the group members to talk each other out of their irrational beliefs—and thereby automatically and "unconsciously" talk themselves out of their own. So if time permits, I shall try to get Sandra to work with the other group members in a rational-emotive manner, along similar lines to those I use in working with her.

I would first say to Sandra: "I'm glad you spoke up like that! I think that this group has been run quite abominably and antitherapeutically so far. I think that your outburst shows that you tend to recognize this, too. You are showing your hostility to the group members, and especially to Jonathan. But I wonder if you are really quite angry against the group leader for allowing the group to wallow around like this, in a muddled and virtually unled fashion, for so many sessions? Do you think that you are angry about that?"

Assuming that Sandra replied that, yes, she was angry about the group process and the ineptness of the group leader, I would then continue: "Well, let's assume that you and I are right about this: that the group leader has been sadly remiss and has helped screw up things and waste your and the group's time. Now, you and I may be wrong about this, because maybe the leader really acted well, and your very outburst and what it may lead to therapeutically may prove this. But let's assume that the leader has been quite wrong—stupid, incompetent, unhelpful. In RET, we call that A—your Activating Experience. And at point C, the Consequence you feel in your gut, you experience extreme anger. Now you may think that the leader of the group makes you angry by his or her incompetence. But this is quite false! Actually, you *choose* to anger yourself about this; and you do so at B—your Belief System *about* the leader's incompetence. Now what are you telling yourself, at B, about what has been happening to you, at A, that makes you feel so angry at C?"

For the next few minutes, I would continue this dialogue with Sandra, trying to convince her (and the other members of the group who are presumably listening to the two of us) that no one has ever upset or angered her in all her life—but that she, instead, angers herself about things like people's incompetence. And, as briefly as possible, I would also try to get her to Dispute (at point D) her irrational Beliefs that create her anger, and thereby to surrender these beliefs. If she did not understand what she was telling herself to anger herself, and what she could do to make herself unangry, I would also try to get other group members to supply these answers, rather than supplying them myself, so that they, too, would see how to Dispute, at point D, their own irrational Beliefs, and to give them up.

After speaking with Sandra, I would ask Jonathan, "How do you feel about Sandra's attacking you?" Assuming that he said that he felt hurt, depressed, angry, or otherwise upset, I would try to show him that he created these feelings, and that Sandra, no matter how badly she might attack him verbally, could not make him feel disturbed. I would say to him, "Let's assume that Sandra is wrong about your caring only about your insurance business, and that no one else in your life seems to matter. Let's assume that she has accused you unfairly and unjustly. Her accusation merely constitutes an Activating Experience—point A—and cannot, in itself, upset you unless you tell yourself something irrational, something foolish about it. Now, what did you tell yourself, at B, your Beliefs about what Sandra did at A, to make yourself angry or hurt at C, your emotional Consequence?"

Again, I would get Jonathan, as well as the rest of the members of the group, to see that he upset himself about Sandra's accusation, and that she could not possibly make him feel anything (except physically, of course, in case she actually assaulted him) unless he told himself some strong evaluative sentence *about* what she did.

I would then ask all the members of the group, "Why did you all let this wasteful group process proceed as it did? Why did you not speak up earlier and try to help the group proceed in a manner that would have been more useful to you? What were you telling yourself about the way things were occurring?" I would get them to see that they were probably afraid to interrupt the ineffectual group process and risk confrontation with the leader, and that they were telling themselves that they could not stand his or her criticism or disapproval if they did so. I would get all or some of them to challenge this irrational belief. I would also show them that some or all of them had abysmally low frustration tolerance to allow things to go on this way, and to take the easy way out, because they had irrational ideas, such as, "If I speak up about what really bothers me, that will be very hard. In fact, it will be *too* hard! I *can't stand* facing hard things like this! I *must* have immediate comfort and ease and must avoid all real unpleasantness, even though it would help me in the long run."

I would show the group, in other words, that many or most of the members went along for the leader's foolish ride because their own irrational fears of disapproval and their natural tendencies to take the easy, and less effectual, way out of their difficulties. I would get them to see, and to help each other see, the precise self-defeating beliefs they told themselves to create their evasive and heads-in-the-sand feelings and behaviors; and indicate how they could question, challenge, and dispute these beliefs, and finally surrender them. I would give them emotive and behavioral homework assignments to help them rip up and keep annihilating their basic irrational philosophies.

Thus, I might give Sandra the homework assignment of asserting herself promptly and directly in any group situation she happened to be in during the next week or two, no matter how uncomfortable she felt in the process. If she carried out this assignment, she could reinforce herself with something she found rewarding; and if she failed to carry it out, she could penalize herself by engaging in some distasteful activity (such as cleaning her house or burning a 20-dollar bill). Similarly, depending on how the other group members reacted and disturbed themselves, each of them would preferably be given a homework assignment that would help them act and work against their self-defeating ideas and feelings.

Rational-emotive group therapy includes a good many emotive-evocative exercises, which may be given during the group sessions or as outside homework assignments. Since Sandra and most of the other members of this particular group seem to feel ashamed of expressing themselves and acting in a "foolish" or "humiliating" manner, I might give the group one of the RET shame-attacking or risk-taking exercises. In the group itself, they might all be asked to do something that they consider risky, such as saying something negative to another group member, confronting the group leader, or acting in some "ridiculous" manner. As outside homework, they might all be asked to do something "shameful" during the week, such as telling a stranger that they just got out of the mental hospital, walking a banana on the street, or yelling out the time in a department store. They would then be asked why they considered this task risky or shameful, how they felt about doing it, and how they could get themselves to do it without feeling ashamed, embarrassed, or humiliated.

The above interventions are suggestive of those that I would make in this group or in one of my own regular RET groups. The main goal is to show all the group members that they do not *get* upset but instead *upset themselves.* They do so by devoutly believing in absolutistic and unrealistic shoulds, oughts, and musts. To change their irrational beliefs and the dysfunctional emotions and behaviors that derive from them, they had better persistently and actively (not to mention vigorously!) force themselves to think, feel, and behave quite differently. As a RET group leader, I vigilantly question, challenge, teach, direct, assign, intervene, and—in a very real sense of this term—*lead.*

# Reality Therapy

*Implemented by Thomas E. Bratter*

The first task which confronts any Reality Therapist would be to establish a meaningful working relationship among group therapy members and the group leader. After achieving this task, which can take a few sessions, I would help and encourage each group member to evaluate their behavior, and in so doing, define their presenting area of concern. If possible and appropriate, I would attempt to reformulate these individual concerns into a few commonly shared group goals for purposes of attaining some kind of consensus as to which issues would be discussed. The group participants would have an explicit understanding as to what to expect from their shared experience. I would attempt to determine an agreement regarding individual and group priorities. Once this task is negotiated, the Reality Therapy group leader functions more as a catalyst-resource person who can facilitate group process so these issues and concerns are addressed and resolved.

I would attempt to establish an agenda with the understanding that members would confine their attention and comments to the "here and now." Discussion about persons outside the group, the past, or events not related to the group, would be discouraged unless a relationship existed to current group behavior. Generally, a gentle reminder from the group therapist can suffice to redirect the focus to a situation which has dual relevance for the individual and the group. While defining group goals is a shared concern, the group leader retains the prerogative to confront individuals when the group is not working effectively. It is unlikely that seven sessions would elapse before any member would verbalize a concern, because any skilled Reality Therapist would help the group relate. More specifically, during the first sessions, the group leader apparently decided to remain relatively passive and uninvolved. Since the group had determined "that they would like to do 'anything' to get them closer to people they felt a deep love for," I would, in all probability, have pursued Francine's personal disclosure before the seventh session. If the group responded as they did in the critical incident—i.e., "their uneasiness in their rapid movement away from Francine, to topics that seemed to be away and outside the group"—I would recognize the reluctance of the group to relate to Francine and remind them of their commitment to help each other become closer to people as well as to keep the discussion focused on relevant concerns.

Let us assume that no group leader is infallible and for some inexplicable reason, I missed Francine's earlier disclosure. During the seventh session, Sandra has provided the group and me another opportunity to discuss the central theme. I would pursue the issue by saying: "I sense, Sandra, that you have felt unappreciated for some time. I had hoped that you would begin to confront those painful feelings. I'm glad that you trust us to share your hurt. I think if the group so chooses, we can proceed at least two ways with what you have said. *First,* I think we can help you examine your behavior so that people will appreciate you more. *Second,* I think if both you and Jonathan consent, we can try to help you understand your reaction to him. I think both points are directly related to your sense of being unappreciated. Well, what do you think, Sandra?"

Sandra: "Well...okay...yes, it is all right with me. I think I would like to."

I would further comment, "I am wondering if there is anyone who would like to tell Sandra how they have experienced her so far in our group." Sarah might comment at this point by saying, "Sandra, you really surprise me. You have not participated as much as some of us. In fact, you could almost be considered a silent member. I really had no idea you wanted our approval, our acceptance, our appreciation, our respect. I have experienced you as being aloof. But I know what you are feeling because, like you, my family now is self-sufficient and independent. They no longer need me the way they did several years ago. Truthfully, this is what motivated me to get my Master's degree so that I can do something useful and worthwhile. What I have learned is that I needed to change or else I would have become as obsolete as the dinosaur. The truth of the matter is that your family has grown up and no longer needs you to do things for them. I guess you have a choice: to stay as you are and feel sorry for yourself, or to change and find some activities which will give your life meaning." In turn, Francine might say, "Hey, I appreciate you. I really do. You risked a whole lot by being honest. Maybe now we can begin to discuss some important and intimate issues. I think what you did took a lot of guts."

I would then summarize these comments by stating, "Sandra, maybe we can combine both Francine and Sarah's comments. Sarah, I think, is suggesting that you try to change some of your behavior so people will begin to need and appreciate you. Francine is suggesting that you risk becoming involved with people."

Sandra needs to renegotiate her relationships with her family and friends, and may need to establish new acquaintances. Unwittingly, Sandra may be relating to her four grown "children" as if they are juniors in high school rather than to their current status as college graduates. Perhaps, Sandra now is demanding that her family "repay" her for all the personal sacrifices she made on their behalf.

It is important for the group leader to recognize the tremendous age differential (28 to 45) in the group, which could be counter-therapeutic since each age group has different developmental needs and concerns. If the group is approached correctly, however, there are many creative opportunities for interaction which can benefit everyone. The group can be utilized as a therapeutic tool to help Sandra not only understand her situation but also to devise a constructive plan. Both Franklin and Jonathan, for example, have verbalized concerns, which, in all probability, parallel those of Sandra's college graduated young adults—i.e., adjusting to their chosen occupation or profession. Significantly, Sandra spoke directly to Jonathan in a criticizing and condemning manner. If the leader and the group could help Sandra "appreciate" Jonathan's realistic concerns, Sandra could be viewed as a resource-advocate by her family. The group leader could attempt to place Sandra in a position to offer some pragmatic advice about improving his business, which simultaneously could teach her a more relevant, humanistic way to relate and help her to be seen as an asset by her family. The group could assume a consultative role to both Sandra and Jonathan, which the young man would appreciate and which would help the wife-mother be more appreciated by her family.

While the exchange for both Sandra and the group has been an emotional one, an implicit responsibility of the group leader is to provide some kind of closure. The areas of concern for both Sandra and Jonathan will require more than the allocated time; the Reality Therapist needs to terminate the group, and, perhaps, set the agenda for the next. Rather than provide the solution, I would prefer to end the group by saying the following: "We will need to end in a few minutes because all of us have other commitments. Sandra, I think it would be important for you to consider ways you can suggest for Jonathan to expand his business. My guess is that Jonathan's concerns probably are similar to your family's. I would hope that you (the group) also will think about Jonathan and Sandra during the week. In addition (said with some humor and casualness), we can help Sally to help her fiance, and, of course, Samuel and Franklin. Perhaps, we can let Sarah assume responsibility for the next session so she will gain some counseling experience. We finally have discovered a common group concern. I am not sure how Sandy and Janet fit into the picture, but by next time, I assure you, I will know. I think it has been a productive, if painful, session. Perhaps it marks the first time we functioned as a group. Does anyone have anything they wish to add? (Long pause.) Have a good week, and I am looking forward to seeing you next Wednesday at 4:30."

My intention is to help the group coordinate its resources and function as a cohesive problem-solving unit. The collective wisdom of the group always exceeds that of the individual Reality Therapist. In a Reality Therapy group, members remain people from the beginning to the conclusion. The passive role of patient is totally rejected. It is assumed, therefore, that individuals have the capacity to discover for themselves creative and constructive solutions for their concerns. The themes mentioned in Situation One certainly lend themselves to the concrete problem-solving action approach to Reality Therapy.

## Transactional Analysis

*Implemented by Herbert Hampshire*

There are some elements of the situation that are unrepresentative of a TA group and the way it would be set up. Since TA is a contractual form of therapy, each person in the group defines a specific problem and related outcome that they and I agree to work toward. Thus, the purpose of the group would never be construed as "to share and perhaps work out...barriers." The TA emphasis on the personal agenda of each member is important in undercutting the normal tendency at the outset to move toward cohesiveness through the identification of more or less superficial similarities. Therapeutic movement is impeded to the degree to which a group member is blocked in experiencing his or her individuality. If individuality is given priority, then the natural similarities of shared emotions and experiences becomes supportive. Where the order is reversed, the similarities work to block individuation and depth.

Another basis for focusing on individual and specific contracts is the emphasis on personal responsibility. Each person is led to a recognition that he or she is in a group for his or her own *purpose* and is responsible, with the therapist, for achieving that *purpose*. The only responsibility each has to other group members is to recognize that any interpersonal situation involves some resources (such as time) that are finite and others (such as support, assistance, and love) that *appear* limited. It is essential to structure the group situation to allow each person to recognize and move beyond his or her programming, which impels them to "be nice," "take turns," or "let others talk when they are dealing with problems that are important or more upsetting." All of these programmatic constraints result in people living in unfulfilled ways, experiencing deprivation and building up feelings of futility and resentment toward an ungiving world. Allowing each person to be responsible for him or herself enables the development of an orientation toward others that comes out of a mature, autonomous recognition of "the way the world works" (for example, the realization that not everyone can get assistance simultaneously).

One of the outcomes of this difference in "set" created by TA is that the first three sessions of this group would not have been spent "establishing acquaintanceships." My most frequent opening for a group session is, "Who has something they want to work on?" Someone begins to deal with an issue of personal significance, and any attempt to move into idle conversation is identifiable as defensively motivated pastiming and begins to reveal how people relate to important issues in their lives. The group process is thus used rather than fostered.

A difference that is more structural is the use of one hour for a group of eight. Eric Berne's rule-of-thumb was to allow time equivalents(s) of 15 minutes multiplied by the number of members. A group of six would meet for an hour and a half and a group of eight for two hours. This ostensibly minor point has broad significance, in the sense that the therapist is literally responsible for the "reality" existing for the group. If structural properties of the therapy situation are, in fact, productive of negative emotional outcomes, such as deprivation or frustration, it is difficult for an individual to discover, and move beyond, how they unwittingly set up situations in ways that deprive or frustrate them. A situation that does not work, actually reinforces a life script that is based on the conclusion that life and relationships do not work.

By the seventh session, I would have made a number of interventions to alter the interpersonal gestalt of the seventh session. I would have commented on Francine's pattern of early self-disclosure and on the various patterns of moving away. If I had the sense that Francine was actually "coming on too strong" as an unwitting way of driving people away, I might have explored the possibility that she was revealing her script mechanism and replaying an early childhood circumstance. I would explore, for example, whether she had a remote father, who, like Jonathan, escaped emotion by tending to business, and whether her mother dealt with personal frustration by pushing Francine toward her father. Mother's behavior would effectively pressure father into distancing behavior, thus reinforcing mother's unconscious decision that getting anything from men is hopeless. It would also, implicitly, "instruct" Francine in the futility of relating to others, especially men. In addition, it would demonstrate how to keep that kind of decision looking like a "truth" about the world. We would have shifted away from Francine's "content" about herself to a focus on her feelings about the responses she was getting in the here-and-now from individuals in the group.

It would have been possible to use Francine's revelations or other members' contributions to focus on the ways in which the interpersonal situation of the group recreates the family dynamics in which their programming was formed and script decisions were made. Sarah might have been led to see how she has always "had" to keep things on an even keel and how intellectualizing and "being reasonable" blocks her from any deep, meaningful contact with others, including her husband. Samuel might have been encouraged to see how he empathizes with Francine when she seems to be working toward opening up and relating, yet with little success. He could use her behavior to see how he also does "what he's supposed to" and ends up feeling victimized by others' lack of responsiveness. Since he is so removed from his own anger at others, he might be able to see its existence by focusing on how Francine must feel.

There is a sense of choreography in group transactions in which the therapist is able to focus people on what they see and react to in others. Through this, they are led to relate to each other and the therapist in ways that are inconsistent with their own programming and script. Constantly being sought is a way to shift the context of transacting so that the affective experience underlying relating no longer reinforces the script but rather produces more authentic and autonomous functioning. Cathecting a different ego state, identifying an unconscious game setup, or producing an encounter that is contradictory to a script decision is always in the service of effecting this "contextual shift," the mechanism of therapeutic change.

One of the main differences that would occur in the group if conducted as a TA group, relates to Sandra, who would not have been supported in remaining inactive for so long. I might, as a matter of fact, have encouraged Francine to speak directly to Sandra. My purpose would have been to draw Sandra out, to increase the probability of Francine being responded to directly, and to allow Sandra to discover how she feels about people who, unlike her, are able to speak up for themselves and go after responses from others more directly. I might also have simply noted that she seems to be having difficulty getting what she came in for.

Given a different time frame, the circumstance described might occur. Sandra might manage, particularly if there were enough happening of therapeutic value, to play out her passivity and to remain silent for the better part of one or two sessions. That would occur, most likely, if these were her initial sessions in an open-ended, ongoing group and she were being given a chance to "ease herself" into working.

One of the first things I am aware of is the time, noting that only 15 minutes remain. Within the therapy situation, time is the equivalent of reality, and my purpose is to make sure that optimal functioning occurs *within* reality and is not blocked by reality. It is not therapeutic, for example, to end the group with Sandra so upset that, functionally, she does not have an available Adult ego state. That would be the equivalent of allowing the group members to "discover" that letting yourself feel things deeply ends with negative if not destructive consequences.

I would be noticing that Sandra's nonverbal behavior had been indicating her emotional responsiveness to the group. This suggests that her feelings and reactions are likely to be related directly to script issues. The group situation always replicates at an emotional level the conflicts that a person experiences "on the outside." When someone resists getting affectively involved and talks about things outside the immediate situation, the way Jonathan and Franklin do, we know they are resisting the involvement that would trigger the experience of the underlying conflict.

Most important, I would be diagnosing Sandra's ego state. If she is in a Critical Parent ego state, I would know I am seeing a picture of a parental influence that she dealt with as a child, probably her mother. I would then look for the child feeling that was too frightening to experience directly and which led her, internally, to "run to her Parent" for protection and for a solution. If she is in an Adapted Child ego state, then I would know that she is manifesting game behavior that reveals the nature of the underlying script. My hypothesis would be that she is in a racket since an emotional racket is by nature exploitative and the group members provide ample evidence that they have been effectively thrown into a guilty silence, feeling accused for not having given Sandra something that she had not been asking for. My guess would be that Sandra is programmed to do things for others and ends up depriving herself and then falling into an angry, resentful, accusatory racket, which results in giving herself sympathy and the implicit demand that others express sorrow over the deprivation and guilt over their insensitivity.

I would be diagnosing the others' ego states, particularly Jonathan's since he has been specifically invited by Sandra both to feel guilty and to become more directly related. Therapy always occurs in relation to the Child, shifting the executive function from Adapted Child and Parent to Natural Child and Adult. If I see someone in a Parent ego state, I want either to get at the underlying Child feeling or to wait until their ego state has shifted. To invite someone in group to transact from a Parent ego state is to pull for conflict or adaptation. If Jonathan is in his Parent state, he may accuse Sandra in retaliation and criticize her behavior. If he is in his Child state, it may be very therapeutic to get him to express his hurt feelings when Sandra accuses him of being insensitive to her.

I am also aware that if I do something that "takes care of" Sandra's upset and defuses her effect, I will run the danger of communicating to the members that intense feelings are not okay and should be suppressed, and also that when things seem to get out of hand, I will rescue the group and handle the situation.

Thus, I would be likely to say something to Sandra, such as, "I'm glad you're letting people know that you are wanting to be related to. How about letting someone know directly how you want them to respond to your feelings right now." This intervention would stroke Sandra for participating, and would also let others in the group know they are not to blame for Sandra's plight and that they need not become immobilized by guilt.

In all likelihood, Sandra's response would be to respond directly to me, saying something like, "I just want them to understand that I have feelings, too," at which point I would suggest that she speak directly to Jonathan. Jonathan, as well as the other group members, would thus be released from paralysis and could begin the process of relating to Sandra's feelings and to the feelings generated by Sandra's blaming and challenging the members. I would be likely to end the session by encouraging Sandra to take the initiative in the next meeting and to talk about her feelings. I would also acknowledge that the other members had important feelings to explore in future sessions.

By demonstrating Sandra's characteristic patterns of relating and emotional responding in the here-and-now, this incident allows for the beginning of therapeutic analysis. Through identifying the sources of patterns in her past and seeing how she unwittingly participates in setting up situations that keep them intact, she can begin to experience options that avoid them. As other people transact with her, more of their patterns will emerge and be identified, analyzed, and altered.

# *Theory Evaluation Form*

1. Which theoretical practitioner did you most resemble? Why?

2. Which theoretical practitioner did you least resemble? Why?

3. What does your response to *Question 1* tell you about yourself and your leadership style as a potential or present group therapist?

4. What does your response to *Question 2* tell you about yourself and your leadership style as a potential or present group therapist?

5. After rereading how the theoretical practitioner of your choice responded to the incident, how would you modify or change your response?

# CHAPTER TWELVE

# *A Member Maintains Distance*

In this situation, the theoretical practitioners examine the ways of dealing with a group in which one of the members sets himself apart from the rest of the group. There are a number of ways to interpret the individual's behavior. Similarly, there are numerous ways to interpret the behavior of the other group members.

## *Incident #6*

This is a group of four women and three men. During your pregroup interview sessions, you discovered that each of the members had expressed a personal concern over their inability to be assertive. This is what prompted you to offer them an opportunity to deal with the issue in a group setting.

The members are briefly described as follows:

*Francie* is 35 and married. Her husband drives trailer trucks for long-distance hauling. She has two teenage daughters. When she first met with you, she explained that she had the primary responsibility of raising her children. She is having difficulty dealing with her parenting role and wants more active support from her husband.

*Kathy* is 28 and employed as a librarian. She lives at home with her parents, both of whom are in their 70s. She is the youngest of five siblings. Her concern is that she feels she would like to live a life of her own, but feels obligated to take care of her parents. This situation has also caused her much consternation in other areas of her personal and professional life.

*Michele* is 42 and has been married for 22 years. She has disclosed her dissatisfaction with spending the rest of her life at home as a homemaker, but she has been under considerable pressure from her husband and children to remain at home.

*Jaqueline* is 30 and lives apart from her husband. She has custody of their 6-year-old son. Jackie is employed as an executive secretary for a large corporation. The job demands that she be decisive and work independently. She is experiencing a great deal of anxiety since her new boss has not acknowledged her abilities or defined her responsibilities, yet she fears confronting him. It seems this symptom is also appearing in other phases of her life, particularly with her husband.

*Troy* is 36 years old, single, and presently employed as a senior high-school science teacher. He has tried, on a number of occasions, to obtain an administrative position and not succeeded. He says he seems and feels very inept at expressing himself, especially in areas where he must compete or take a stand on what he believes.

*James* is 28, and has recently married. He sought you out because he feels he has always been taken advantage of. This is especially true with significant others in his life. He is very upset with himself for not being able to say *No* when others ask him to do things for them.

*Joe* is 33 and has been married for six years. He is a foreman at a local brewery. He has expressed discontent with himself and his job. He says he does not know whether he is "fish or fowl." His subordinates demand one thing of him, and his superordinates another. He feels as though he must serve two masters.

This is the seventh session. There has been a great deal of disclosure on the part of all members except Joe. In previous sessions, whenever the others would share their concern about not being able to speak out on their rights or their own mind, Joseph would insist that he had no such problems. Now, it is the middle of the session and the group has been grappling with the difficulty of holding different opinions and taking a personal stand on important issues. Joe again states that this is not the case for him. He no sooner completes his statement when the entire group attacks him and accuses him of not being honest. Jackie leads the attack by stating that people such as him scare her and that if she could, she would not have anything to do with that kind of person. Jim followed by offering that he had taken some big risks in saying some of the things he had about himself. It was people like Joe whom he thought took advantage of such information and made it hard for Jim to be his own person. The interaction gained intensity, and the more the others accuse Joe, the more he states that he has no problems. This in turn only serves to increase their attack. Throughout this exchange, Joe has given no clues as to how this whole series of events has affected him.

## Client-Centered Therapy

### Implemented by William R. Coulson

The group is working on Joe and I am tempted to join in. I think I see an opening. He is saying he has none of the problems of the others—yet he wanted to join an assertiveness group. "Okay, Joe, why did you join the group if you don't have these problems?"

I don't say it.

I think of other ways to make Joe humble ("I think Joe wants our attention"), but again resist.

I never like it when I am argumentative, and I never like it when the group is working on somebody and I join in. It is tempting, to be sure. There is something Joe cannot see, but that everybody else, apparently, can. Each, in turn, wants a crack at straightening him out. We are having a contest to see who can make Joe confess.

Working on somebody like that wastes group time. In that sense, Joe disrupts the group. My tendency when such things happen is to wait them out. I have said before that the leaders have a good deal of initial authority because of their title. If they do not play games, such as "Let's fix Joe," such activities tend to run out of gas on their own.

If group members persist in going after Joe, I might ask one of them about it: "It sounds like you want to get Joe to confess." And if the member agreed with me, I might say something like, "I thought so. I felt that way myself, until I realized we could have a group without having to make Joe the same as us." Maybe if Joe sees what a group is, he will want to join in. Maybe it just takes him longer than seven weeks to feel safe.

By and large, I like to go around disruption. Dealing with it directly can add to the disruption: we are fighting over fighting. I have seen groups that were very slow to develop because they spent so much time arguing about how to be a good group. I would rather see if we can come to it without talking about it. I would trust it more if we discovered it rather than ordered it.

If we went on with the group without requiring Joe to confess, I think we just might find him joining in later. Generally, people do not change because of attack. They dig in and defend themselves.

"If sharing problems is a good thing to do, Joe will come around to it." That would be my attitude. I would also have considerable curiosity about Joe. I would assume he had joined the group for a good, even pressing reason, and I would find it interesting that he did not seem to want to reveal it. I might make a date with him (maybe just inside my own mind) to discuss this in the future, when the pressure is off. But I would not push it, even then. As far as I am concerned, he never has to tell. Sometimes people who participate very little say later that they got a lot out of the group. I believe them.

When I give in and push people, it is sometimes for my own sake. I want them to know I do good work. I make them cooperate so I can help them. I would want to try to avoid doing this with Joe, or with anybody. I have made more mistakes in the name of "helping" people than in the name of being patient.

I can reach some people in therapy groups and not others. Some I cannot reach because I do not like them. I think I would like Joe, however. I would like his orneriness. In fact, I might say, "I kind of like your stubbornness, Joe. You seem like you're not going to let anybody make you say you're different than you want to be." That I cannot reach everybody in my groups does not matter at all if other members can reach them. Usually someone in the group will be able to get through.

# Gestalt Therapy

*Implemented by Mirriam F. Polster*
Joe appears to be doing pretty well what the rest of the group have said they would like to do, namely hold different opinions and take a personal stand on important issues. Here he is, holding all of them off and insisting that he has no problems in the face of a direct confrontation by two members of the group.

The possibilities for contact between the three main actors, Joe, Jim, and Jackie, are clear and arousing. The rest of the group, too, has some investment in what is going on here.

First, and most obvious, there is Joe's insistence that he has no problems. Now, in the pregroup interview, he did express some discontent with his life and his middle-management position at work. His present system of self-support requires that he deny and cover up what problems he may have, clearly deflecting contact with others who have been admitting their difficulties. There are several options open to the group leader. I could point out that while they may disagree with him, Joe is being assertive and standing up for himself. In confronting him they, too, are being assertive. How do they feel to be doing this? Do they speak crisply and are they stating their opinions clearly? What do they want from Joe?

I might ask Joe that if his presence in the group signifies that he had identified some personal problems that he wanted to work on, has anything anyone else has said meant anything to him personally? He is dealing right now in the group with some of the same pressures he may experience on his job, where people are demanding something from him that he may either be unready or unwilling to give. This might provide a chance for him to express some of the frustration he experiences when he tries to reconcile demands of others with his own needs. Previously, I speculate, he has handled such situations by clamming up and by not knowing whether he is "fish or fowl." Not supporting himself adequately, and getting no support from his marginal position as foreman, he turns silent and puts up a good front. But now, I can ask, does he feel he is being attacked by the group? Does he feel he is being pushed prematurely into taking action?

Taking time for himself is a luxury which he presently does not claim for himself, which illustrates an important point about assertiveness. One of the most basic needs in assertiveness is to establish one's own pace and move when one chooses to move and not merely at the prodding of others. It is important to me that Joe not be made a scapegoat, and that the members see his actions as an act of self-regulation and not capricious stubbornness. He has come to his predicament through a long and painful history of trying to do the best he could in the circumstances he was in.

The rest of the group members have much to learn in directly moving from their customary roles as victims to the unfamiliar opposite roles as bullies. How might they explore this?

Jim is telling Joe that Joe makes it difficult for him to be his own person, whatever that may mean. The underlying message is unclear and unspecified. He tells Joe that he believes he took great risks in saying some of the things about himself that he had just said. But is that not what being his own person means? Joe has given no indication that he is going to go around blabbing about what people have been saying. There is no indication that he disrespects the privacy of the group's communications with each other.

It seems likely to me that when I ask Jim to be more specific in his requirements from Joe, it would become more apparent that what he is seeking from Joe is easy agreement and confluence (Polster & Polster 1973). For Jim to be his "own person," he may be saying that Joe has to be just like him! Joe has to "own up" to his problems at the same time that Jim does and to take risks in revealing himself, otherwise Jim feels taken advantage of. Jim is scared that differing with others indicates that something is wrong with him. So, from his fright, he insists on similarity as the only way to reassure himself. This is both dangerous (because this kind of confluence is illusory and temporary) and presumptuous (because it compels another person to overlook some very real differences and bow to Jim's need for similarity).

I might ask Jim to expound on his wish from Joe by telling Joe how this silence hampers him in his search for assertiveness. If I wanted to heighten the drama of this interaction, I might ask Jim to deliver a lecture or sermon or a pep talk urging Joe to shape up. Perhaps when Jim starts to listen to himself telling Joe how important it is to him that Joe agree with him or be like him, he may also begin to recognize the absurdity, tyranny, and dependence of his own position. Jim can, after all, do what he needs to do in the group regardless of whether Joe conforms to his wishes. If this means revealing something about himself, so be it, without Joe's doing the same thing. It is quite possible that Jim's need to have the support of others, before he can stand up for himself, impedes him from doing it because it sets up an impossible situation. Here, in the group, he has the opportunity to begin to function independently, to go about the business of saying what he is moved to say and getting what he needs or wants, irrespective of whether the rest of the group supports and endorses him.

Jackie's spunky confrontation of Joe is somewhat different. I suspect that what she wants and finds supportive is Joe's approval. She doesn't know how to get it for herself and ends up scared, silent, and intimidated. She hears Joe's repeated insistence that he does not have any problems as an implicit statement about her own inferiority because she does have problems. She projects onto Joe her own doubts and disapproval of herself and then says that she is scared of him. She has given up ownership of her own low opinion of herself, and of her discontent with the way she acts, and inserts it into Joe's denial of his problems and, possibly, her boss's lack of acknowledgement of her job performance. This situation can be the cornerstone of movement out of her stuck position. I might direct Jackie to go over and stand behind Joe's chair and to speak for him and tell Jackie what (she imagines) he thinks of her. She may come up with harsher statements than Joe himself might make. She can check this out with Joe right there and determine if he is actually looking down on her as she fears. Or, instead of checking with Joe, Jackie could return to her chair and reply to the words she has put into Joe's mouth. When she does this, we have the beginning of a dialogue that is long overdue. Jackie may have been seeing her own self-disapproval in other people, such as her husband and her boss, for a long time. By having nothing to do with them, by remaining silent, she has refused to engage in dialogue with them and

confront her fears. It is time for her to speak aloud in her own self-dis-
paraging voice and to mobilize her response to this retroflected criticism (Perls, Hefferline, & Goodman 1951; Polster & Polster 1973). She
has taken over the criticism that she dreads getting from someone
else and redirected it toward herself. She does this selectively. After all,
if she is projecting in the face of someone else's silence, she could
conceivably imagine that they were approving of her. But this she does
not do. In the dialogue, we can begin to trace the one-sided nature of
her self-doubt.

The reactions of the other group members is not made clear, and so I
can only propose what I might do in principle, rather than a specific
reaction about each of them. I would ask the rest of the group what
they are feeling about the interactions among Joe, Jim, and Jackie. I
would hope that there would be some support among them for Joe. He
is accustomed to standing on his own, feeling isolated, and it could be a
very warming experience to have an ally when he is feeling attacked. It
may be that he needs this before he can admit to having difficulties.

James, for example, might feel pleased that Joe is able to say *no*. He
might express a wish that he could do likewise. Troy might identify with
Joe's inability to express trouble and might recognize and identify with
Joe's denial as an easy way out of trying to say something that is just too
complicated for him to express. Francie may have something to say
about the importance of getting support from someone when dealing
with personal decisions.

## *Individual Psychology*

*Implemented by Guy J. Manaster*
I have no more information about Joe than the brief description given,
and know no more about him than do the other group members. The
group assumption, predicated on the reasons given for organizing the
group, is that all members have "a personal concern over their inability
to be assertive." The group's consternation at this point is over Joe not
"fessing up," not acknowledging that he has this concern.

In my opinion, it is fallacious to asume homogeneity in a group
designed to be "homogeneous," that is, a single-problem group. As
stated earlier, from an Adlerian position, people may appear similar
and be categorized, labeled, and grouped together, but they are not the
same—each person, personality, and life style is unique.

At this point in the group, we know very little about Joe, but we do
know something about the group process, and, in my opinion, both our
knowledge and lack of knowledge lead to the same response—the
leader had better step in and find out what is going on with Joe.

"Joe, can I ask something? It looks now, to me, as if everyone in the group feels like they have some things in common, some positive and some negative, and they are working together on the negatives. You have not been participating. Everyone wants you to. I guess I wonder how you feel about what's going on right now? And I also wonder what you want from the group—is there an issue or concern you have?"

Joe may be so entrenched in his "no problems" position that he cannot graciously express any concerns. So he may say, "This is all right. I'm all right," and nothing more.

If, in fact, I had more information from the pregroup interview with Joe, I might not draw on it. Nonetheless, I would press on, trying to read the goal of his behavior from the way he spoke and sat, trying to assess the reaction he wanted, not consciously, from his behavior.

"Joe, do you want to know what I think?"

I expect an affirmative grunt.

"I think your problems are not the same as everyone else's. Is that right?"

(From this point on, I will go on as if Joe agrees. If and when he does not, I would try other tactics until I was correct, until he joined me in the effort, or until I would not figure out what he was after, in which case I would probably say, "Joe, I don't think you want anyone to know what you are about," and then I would expect a smile of recognition.)

"Everyone in the group is unsure of what to do, but you know, don't you?"

"But you don't do what you know to do. Is that right, Joe?"

"What would happen if you did?"

If Joe agreed to this point, I would wait for his response, which would, grudgingly, reveal the essence of his fear, and his reason for his "he-man" coverup.

This might look like a short one-to-one therapy interchange in the midst of a group therapy session. That is what it is. I think this is perfectly permissible and in this situation demanded. If we do not get to Joe so that he can begin to benefit from the group, we may lose him. Moreover, his obstinacy to the point of this incident shows great distancing, denial, and defense. Joe is not only not a part of this group, neither "fish nor fowl" at work, but also, I suspect, not a part of any group. His behavior and the attitude it reflects is quite worrisome. My immediate concern would be to give Joe a handle on his goals and an inkling of the warmth and joy of having others interested in you, and you interested in them. Without a dynamic and dramatic intervention, the prognosis for Joe could be quite negative.

This instant in the group is critical for the group *and* for Joe. The rest of the group has each other and, for the moment, their common anger at Joe. My regard for Joe, his feelings, the compassion I show, will be considered by the group and be part of the discussion, which I hope includes Joe, at the end of our one-to-one interlude.

The worst outcome of the exchange with Joe would be his agreement that he does not want anyone to know what he is about, followed by stony silence. I would try to get him to agree to a private session with me to see what he wants to do from here on.

A less drastic outcome would reveal some understanding of Joe, but it certainly might not include Joe's wholehearted support for the group's goals and further participation in the group. However, the group will also have learned something about Joe and in the process, learn about themselves. I would ask: "How do you feel about Joe now? How do you feel about what has happened?"

I expect that someone, possibly Kathy whose life seems devoted to taking care of others, will say that she, or he, did not understand Joe and is now sorry for attacking him. Others will probably agree, but someone will still say, and I will if no one else does, that with the information we had, the way Joe was behaving, they had no choice, he was asking for it. "How?" The discussion might lead to the conclusion that seems warranted—he wasn't behaving according to the group norms that had developed—he wasn't behaving as he "should."

A number of "lessons" for the group should be clarified in a summary at the end of the session. Among these "lessons" are: (1) People usually get what they want, and what their life style, goals, and behaviors bring, from situations—Joe got what he wanted; (2) people often, maybe usually, do not consciously understand what they want, do not understand their goals—again, Joe did not; (3) but this understanding, although not conscious, is readily accessible, what Adler termed "dimly envisaged"—note Joe's recognition (which I must admit I confidently included); (4) other people react to you as you want, and react in a group as the group wants, to the degree that it also suits their purpose; (5) the way one feels (emotions) depends on one's perspective on, and understanding of, a situation or another person—as when everyone was angry at Joe when they thought he obstinately would not behave as he "should," but felt differently, not angry, when they better understood his behavior and plight; and (6) sometimes people will go beyond their personal limits in emotional vehemence when they are part of a group (but that is probably for next session).

# Rational-Emotive Therapy

### Implemented by Albert Ellis

I would assume, as usual in situations of this sort, that the group members are not merely healthfully confronting Joe (and trying to see that he admits to some of his major problems and tries to do something about them), but that they are also angry at him, and that they feel that he *has to* disclose himself to them and admit that he is holding back displaying his feelings, and that he should do his best to change his ways. I would tell myself that they are quite probably correct about Joe's holding back and about his sabotaging himself in the process of doing so, but that they are wrong about making themselves seriously upset about what he is doing or not doing.

I would also tell myself that, in accordance with the theory of Rational-Emotive Therapy (RET) their hostile and confrontative manner toward Joe will in all probability encourage him to be angry at them, to become more defensive, and to avoid, rather than to seek, looking more intently at his own problems. I would therefore first choose to talk with the group members about their anger, and would try to get them to surrender it. I would keep in mind that using their disturbances in this manner might help Joe see more clearly some of his own problems in them, since one of the advantages of group therapy is that people can often understand others' problems more clearly than their own; and in getting them to do so and to work to help these others, they can frequently be persuaded to work, consciously or unconsciously, on their own emotional difficulties.

I would therefore first say to the group, or to one or two of the more hostile members of the group: "I can see that you are quite upset about what you consider to be Joe's holding back, and his refusal to acknowledge some of his deep-seated problems. And let's assume, for the moment, that you are right about him. Jackie, let's assume that Joe acts in a 'scary' manner and that people like him scare you and put you off, so that you want nothing to do with them. Even if this is so, you are still condemning Joe for his holding back and for his so-called scariness. Now, why *must* he not hold back and be unscary? And in what way does he become a louse or a rotten person if he continues to be the way that he is?"

I would try to show Jackie that whatever Joe's deficiencies may be, she is commanding and demanding that he not have them; and by her unrealistic and irrational demands, she is foolishly upsetting herself, making herself exceptionally irate at him. I would first try to get her to give up her demands, while keeping her strong desire that Joe not act the way he is acting, and then try to help her work with Joe to get him to change some of his ways.

I would also try to show her that Joe's behavior may be bad or self-defeating, and that it may be against the group's best interests, but that it is not really "scary." She *makes it* scary by needlessly frightening herself about it—by contending, in her own head, that she cannot stand his acting that way, and that she cannot allow herself to be comfortable and unscared (though still distinctly displeased) if he continues to act that way.

I would work with Jackie, with the help of the other members of the group—whom I would induce to join in and to question and dispute

Jackie's irrational beliefs about Joe's being "scary"—to give up frightening herself about his behavior and of having to give up her own openness and honesty just because he chose to be closed. At the same time, I would get Jim into the center of the stage, and show him that he, too, was taking Joe too seriously, and was *making it harder for himself* to be his own person, and then assuming that Joe was making it hard for him to act openly. I would particularly try to get Jackie to see that Jim was upsetting himself needlessly about Joe, and get Jim to see that Jackie was gratuitously upsetting herself about Joe. I would assume, while talking with both of them (and the other members of the group), that Joe really had a serious problem of defensively keeping himself closed; and I would show Jackie, Joe, and the other group members that they *still* viewed this problem in an overdramatic light and still *made themselves* upset about it.

I would also try to show them that if they really *wanted* (and not *needed*) Joe to be more open, they would hardly persuade him to act in this new manner by beating him over the head, complaining viciously about the way he was acting—and thereby encouraging him to be even more defensive. If they were more open themselves, in spite of Joe remaining closed, and if they mainly ignored his shut-off qualities for the moment, he might well take after their good modeling and make himself more open and honest.

I would, in other words, show Jackie, Jim, and the other group members that although their goals and desires (to have Joe be more open and to feel safe in opening up themselves) were highly desirable, their method of achieving these goals was not very efficient or productive. They were really asking Joe to be open *first*, and then they would begin to be so themselves. But they could make themselves open—as they actually had been doing up to now—whether or not Joe was acting in the same manner.

I would show the group members who complained about Joe that in some ways they are probably right, that he may well be defensive and may be doing himself little good by holding back, and that he may also be harming the group process. But I would also show them that he has a right to be wrong—as have all humans, and that although his behavior may be "bad" or "harmful," *he* is not a *bad person*. I would try to show them that unless they accept this kind of philosophy about Joe and his errors, they are unlikely to accept themselves when they do badly. I would try to get them, as well as Joe, to see that all humans are fallible. Most of them have a very difficult time opening themselves to others and admitting that they have serious problems, but if they stop putting themselves down for *having* such problems (and stop denigrating others for having similar problems or for denying such problems), they will be able to face themselves much more openly and clearly.

In the process of talking with members of the group, I might tell them something of myself and some of the difficulties I have had, to show them that, I too, am fallible and have screwed up during my lifetime. I would probably give them a specific self-disclosure exercise, such as, thinking of something secret they have not revealed to anyone in their entire lives, and revealing this secret to the group right now. I would show them that, whatever they revealed, there is nothing to feel ashamed of or to put themselves down for, even though their act may well have been immoral or reprehensible. And I would show them how not to feel ashamed or embarrassed, now that they have revealed this secret to the group. In the course of this exercise, I would especially try to induce Joe to reveal something "shameful" or "humiliating," and try to show him that he could do so without damning himself for having done it or for revealing it.

I might also give all the members of the group some kind of shame-attacking or self-disclosing homework exercise, such as revealing some "shameful" act (including ones they have already revealed in the group) to an important person outside the group who might condemn them for this disclosure. If Joe, in particular, was not able to do this kind of thing, I would try to induce him to think, during the week, about something that he has not yet revealed to the group about himself that he would hesitate to reveal, and to do so next week.

In various cognitive, emotive, and behavioral ways, such as those just listed, I would try to keep the group centered for awhile on this problem of disclosing oneself to others. I might even spend several sessions trying to get the members to see what they tell themselves to keep themselves closed up, how they could dispute these irrational ideas that make them secretive and defensive, and how they could actively push themselves to become more open with members of the group and with significant people outside the group.

## Reality Therapy

### Implemented by Thomas E. Bratter

I believe the group experience can provide optimal conditions for individuals to experiment with new roles and concurrently become more self-confident and assertive. Since the group is a homogeneous group, whose members have similar presenting problems characteristic of their inability to be assertive, I would be prepared to use some newer and more innovative techniques to help the group. I certainly would incorporate, at appropriate times, some behavior therapy and psychodrama techniques, such as: modeling, which has been described by Bandura (1971 and 1969) and Rachman (1972); behavioral rehearsal, which has been described by Wagner (1968 a&b); and role playing, which has been described by Greenberg (1968). These are responsible and effective therapeutic adjuncts which can serve as catalysts to help people become more assertive. In addition to the more traditional discussion and didactic group session format, for this specialized group I would adapt the four-phase process for problem solving developed by Siegel and Spivack (1976), which incorporates the major components of Reality Therapy:

1. The ability to recognize problems.
2. The ability to define problems.
3. The ability to think of alternative solutions.
4. The ability to decide which of the alternative solutions is the best way to solve the problem.

The objective of this approach is to help individuals solve problems by providing practice and reinforcement. This approach assumes that the desired behavior change can be achieved more effectively through planned therapeutic action rather than by the acquisition of insight.

The group leader in Situation Six, however, appears to be unaware and may be unwilling to modify his or her approach to accommodate the group which individually has verbalized a desire to become more self-assertive. Unfortunately, the group leader apparently did not orient members before forming the group. Wolpe and Lazarus (1966) explore whether a person would be a good candidate for assertiveness training by asking the following questions:

Are you inclined to be overapologetic?
Are you able to contradict a domineering person?
Are you able to openly express love and affection?
If a friend makes what you consider to be an unreasonable request, are you able to refuse?
Is it difficult for you to compliment and praise others?

Had these questions been specifically addressed to Joe, it is doubtful whether he would have refused to acknowledge a problem. Joe, in fact, has the insight to recognize his "problem"—i.e., "he feels he must serve two masters"—but, while he may wish implicitly to change, the group leader never requests he make any commitment to change by becoming more assertive. Joe does not know whom to please. Rather than risking alienating either, he decides to do nothing. He, thus, becomes trapped in his own game and remains reluctant to change. Bugenthal (1965) would view Joe as saying, "Since I can't control everything that will determine what happens to me, I have no control at all." Experiencing the unpredictability of his life, the patient gives up and enacts this feeling of having no possibility of affecting what happens to him. He makes himself totally an object. Olden (1943), who writes from a psychoanalytic reference, has conceptualized a person who refuses to change as being obstinant, one whose efforts are to maintain feelings of supremacy even though such feelings may have no bases in reality.

The group leader in this situation may have inadvertently placed everyone in a "no win" situation. Jackie and Jim have begun to assert themselves by confronting Joe about his denial of his problems. This confrontative behavior needs to be reinforced since it represents a significant and positive achievement. In contrast, Joe's refusal to be manipulated also is being assertive. Obviously, the group is correct by assessing that no one is problem-free. Yet the existence of the group is threatened by a power play. Apparently, the group leader has failed to create a climate where people can honestly relate to their vulnerability and contemplate adopting more self-fulfilling behavior.

In all probability, most Reality Therapists who work with unassertive individuals would avoid the potential dilemma of having one person adamantly deny having any problems while the group insists he does. The group would become frustrated with Joe's denial and condemn him for refusing to change. Even though Joe's assertion is less than positive for him, most mental health workers would agree the individual retains the right to select any life style as long as it does not interfere with anyone else's attempts to be responsible and productive. Joe's decision, while annoying to the group, certainly harms no one but himself. As the leader, I would defend Joe's right not to change, which, of course, could provoke other members. I would try to maintain an atmosphere conducive to candid examination and creative change. I would take the opportunity to make the following points:

"Joe, I respect your right to make a decision regarding which issues you wish to discuss and then determine whether or not you choose to change. Every person basically is accountable only to himself. You do not owe us any explanations. Some members obviously are less than happy with your assertion that you do not feel as if you have any problems, which is their right. There is no reason why we need to achieve consensus. I would be interested to learn what caused you to join this group and also what your goals are."

If Joe continued to deny he has any problems, I would suggest that he spend the next week evaluating whether he could justify the expenditure of his time and money to continue with the group. I would hope to deescalate the malignant and counter-therapeutic *ad hominem* attacks by other members and give Joe some time without feeling pressured to make a decision. The only commitment I would attempt to get from Joe would be for him to return next week and share his thoughts with us. At this juncture, depending how much time remained, I would switch the focus to another member. I would try to reinforce the most rational and reasonable member who disagreed with Joe. I might say:

"Gee, Jim, you shared with Joe some candid feelings. Maybe you can tell us your reaction to your comments. Do you think it will be easier for you to do this in the future and in different settings?"

In an effort to diffuse the tension, I would suggest that the members might wish to consider sharing with someone whom they trust and respect a not so pleasant opinion. They could report back to the group at the next meeting.

Before concluding the group, I would volunteer either to see or to speak with Joe, individually if he wanted. I would also point out, though I may disagree, that in his own way Joe was being assertive.

If Joe did not attend the next group, which might be likely, I would set aside 15 minutes of discussion time. I then would ask if anyone would volunteer to call Joe to invite him to return. I would do this in such a way that someone would become assertive in a protective way because it would help both the volunteer and Joe.

Assertiveness training and Reality Therapy are closely aligned.

# Transactional Analysis

*Implemented by Herbert Hampshire*

Working with problems of assertiveness can be particularly tricky, if not treacherous. A lack of assertiveness functions as a racket, which with great effectiveness, justifies a life of "unwanted" outcomes and avoids the direct experience of uncomfortable effects. The lack of assertiveness constellation is difficult to deal with because it has the illusion of being the problem when, in fact, it is not. When someone comes in for treatment saying they want to be assertive, I always ask if they will be satisfied if that is all that happens. If they become assertive and nothing else changes, will they consider their goal accomplished? Would Francie be happy if she became assertive *and* her husband still supported her no more than he does now? Would Troy consider therapy successful if he became assertive and *still* did not get an adminstrative position?

Underneath the identification of the problem as one of assertiveness, is the implicit assumption that the "real" problem (for example, the lack of support from Francie's husband) will be cleared up simply by the acquisition of assertive behavior. If not very careful, the therapist will give tacit agreement to this assumption, often without being conscious of doing so. At the outset, it is critical to determine if the patient's analysis is correct. Does it appear the problems being encountered in the patient's life would be resolved if a more assertive life style were available? In my experience, this conclusion is unjustified and comes from a contamination of the Adult. While there are definite advantages that accrue from developing a more assertive style of relating, it seldom includes obtaining immediately what the patient claims to want.

In arriving at a clear understanding of the underlying dynamics that hold the life pattern in place, one often sees the potential "costs" involved in cure. There are philosophical and ethical problems involved in proceeding with treatment when the patient is unaware of these dynamics. There is a very real necessity for obtaining "informed consent" on the part of the patient. It is important, for example, that Francie's development of assertiveness in relation to her husband may undermine the stability of the marriage. The same holds true for Michele. When major changes in life circumstances of a patient are possible, concomitants of a cure of the presenting problem, both therapist and patient are well-advised to enter the process with awareness and a specific contract around the issue.

These considerations arise particularly when problems presented initially by the patient are obvious results of the patient's behavior. Francie marries a man with a job that is likely to keep him away and relatively uninvolved in the family and ends up unhappy that he is not more actively supportive. Kathy stays at home with her parents and ends up feeling that she would like "a life of her own." Michele embeds herself in a stereotypically sexist marriage and, after 22 years, is unhappy at getting opposition to going out on her own. All of these are examples of problems resulting from operating within a self-defeating script. The rule-of-thumb for identifying script-driven behavior is that a problem is set up by someone who, if they were observing another person, would clearly be able to identify the inevitability of the undesirable outcome. Thus, to deal with the overt problems is to confront the script; therefore, it is essential to know all the elements of the matrix, including what the patient is likely to do to themselves if they defy the injunctions of the script.

Joe is the patient in this group who evidences the greatest degree of connectedness to the underlying anxiety associated with breaking out of the scripted patterns. His resistance to even acknowledging the existence of the conditions bringing him to treatment is indicative of a great deal of fear. At the outset, I want to be sensitively aware of his level of affect. This concern is augmented by his denial of the effect that group members' attacks are having on him.

When a group member is being attacked and does not have the available resources to effectively handle either the attack or the feelings generated, my priority becomes that of defusing or deescalating the situation before significant damage is done to the individual, the relationships, or the context of therapy. This can often be done by recontextualizing the interactions.

One possiblity is to stroke Joe for not submitting to the group pressure—evidencing the kind of power that he does not experience at his job. It is also possible to focus on Jackie or Jim, who are responding with great force and assertiveness (if not aggressiveness). It is often useful to point out to patients that they are manifesting the very behavior they consider themselves incapable of. They are so accustomed to thinking about themselves in a particular way that they tend to ignore inconsistent observations. Jim is doing a good job of relating directly to "being taken advantage of," one of his presenting complaints. I might ask if he was aware that he was dealing with Joe more directly than he typically dealt with people who "took advantage of him." He might also be focused on his feelings in the process of confrontation to get him to shift toward acknowledging his own experience rather than continuing to relate to Joe as his persecutor, thereby maintaining his own position as victim. Were it not for the importance of keeping the attention of the group on the volatile situation within the session, it would be possible to ask Jim if he ever talked to others—his boss or his wife, for example, the way he was talking to Joe.

As usual, my underlying motive would be to foster interaction that produces contextual shifts through the meshing of issues and programming. Since Michele is likely to be a caretaker for her family, as well as for others, I would be watching her for signs of discomfort at open conflict; the same would be true for Kathy. It is also an opportunity to work with Troy on his ability to express himself in the midst of an affect-laden circumstance.

In the final analysis, my response would be determined in this circumstance by my awareness that the situation had developed to this point out of my at least passive collusion. Optimistically, Joe would have been invited much earlier than the seventh session to relate to his resistance to becoming involved with the group and to deal more openly with his anxieties about sharing his problems. Thus, I would be likely to say something to him, such as, "You're under a lot of pressure now. Is this the way it feels for you at work?"

This intervention would, first, acknowledge the reality of what was going on, and second, create a context in which Joe could begin to verbalize his feelings and be involved, admitting to the problem he was having right then, without either submitting to or rebelling against Jackie or Jim. My intention would be to get him to relate directly to the "problem" and to his feelings, and then move him toward transacting directly with the group members. At that point, it would become possible to begin to relate the experience to the programing and issues of the others in the group.

## Theory Evaluation Form

1. Which theoretical practitioner did you most resemble? Why?

2. Which theoretical practitioner did you least resemble? Why?

3. What does your response to *Question 1* tell you about yourself and your leadership style as a potential or present group therapist?

4. What does your response to *Question 2* tell you about yourself and your leadership style as a potential or present group therapist?

5. After rereading how the theoretical practitioner of your choice responded to the incident, how would you modify or change your response?

# PART THREE

# *Where Have We Come?*

# CHAPTER THIRTEEN

# Congruence of Theory with Practice

In the preceding chapters, we have observed how theoretical practitioners (TPs) with differing theoretical orientations have responded to six critical incidents that may occur during the life of a therapy group. Central to our mission has been the desire to underscore the important role that theory plays in guiding group therapists as they lead their groups. The purpose of this chapter is to provide an analysis of the degree of congruence between theory and practice. We will do this by interpreting the responses our TPs have made to the critical incidents, in light of their adherence to the various constructs that comprise their respective theories.

Our approach will be to understand how the TPs determined the action they chose and to see if they anticipated the consequences of their intervention. Above all, we shall try to observe how the TPs' actions and thoughts relate to the primary principles undergirding the theories they espouse. We shall also try to see the amount of variability or license the TPs have taken in interpreting the theoretical principles as they encounter the critical incidents.

# Client-Centered Therapy

If there was one approach to group therapy in which the therapist had the broadest interpretive range in applying theory to practice, it is Client-Centered Therapy. Remember that Rogers himself said that he did not want to develop a theory of group therapy. He also told us that he makes no effort to differentiate his approach to group therapy from that of individual therapy. With these criteria in mind, we approached the observation of our Client-Centered TP. We looked to see the extent to which the three key variables—external, group member, and group therapist—were considered, and the degree to which our Client-Centered TP employed any or all of the 15 techniques (stages) identified by Rogers.

It becomes immediately evident that our TP's approach to each of the six incidents graphically illustrates the Client-Centered approach to group therapy. He adheres vigorously to the basic tenets of the key concepts related to group member variables and group therapist variables. For example, there is strong evidence in virtually every critical incident that he trusts the group to develop its own potential and to set its own directions. As the therapist, he does not hesitate to employ empathic listening, disclose his feelings, share personal issues, and maintain a very low profile by trying to join the group as a participant.

We also see how our TP in Incident 5 moves to set the climate by trying to be empathic and by joining the group through identifying with and accepting Sandra. We also learn how strongly he opposes making process observations, as in Incidents 1 and 2. Similarly, we see that he expects the group to mill around and avoids preplanning or exercises (Incident 1). This is in keeping with trusting the process and relying upon the members to provide the group's motivation and direction.

Throughout each situation, we see our TP attending very carefully to members' expression of feelings. It is perhaps among the most pronounced differences we have witnessed between each of the therapeutic approaches. Since he considers himself a member, it is like him to present himself as vulnerable and subject to experiencing feelings of discomfort. During the moment of group attack (Incident 2), he permits us to understand the tendency to want to become "psychological" and his resistance to this by directing his focus to what the group members are trying to say about him and perhaps themselves as well.

Another characteristic of Client-Centered group therapy that our TP demonstrates regularly is the attention the *individual* gets, as opposed to the group. It is through modeling behavior during these one-to-one encounters that the TP transmits the basic tenets of the theory (such as, unconditional positive regard) to the rest of the group. He does not hesitate to admit that he does not expect to reach everyone in the group. Yet, this admission serves only to further underscore his belief that the healing potential of the group rests with the group itself.

Our TP's approach to responding to each of the incidents is characteristic and reflective of the theory he espouses. He has chosen to be unique by not following any preset rules. In this way, he stamps his own peculiar brand of therapy to the task at hand. Our Client-Centered TP's very way of responding to each situation is a model of his theoretical orientation.

## Gestalt Therapy

A crucial variable in Gestalt Therapy is for the therapist to be a model of that which the theory espouses. In this case, we need to ask ourselves, for example, "Was our TP demonstrating such things as spontaneity, emotional responsiveness, sensory awareness, and self-support, and was she expressing a 'juiciness' and freedom from barriers to effective living ("Was she integrated?")?" It seems that indeed, in her responses to each of the critical incidents, she reflected her own aliveness; including ownership of times when she had not been helpful (for example, Incident 5, "I colluded in the noncontract atmosphere. ..." and Incident 3, when she disclosed the effect Jean had had on her). On the other hand, she was quick to say when a situation (2) was one she would not have gotten herself into, thereby implying that her own awareness would not have permitted the group to have reached such a point. It appears that our Gestalt TP's approach to each of the six situations graphically illustrated the intuitive, creative, and imaginative way in which she used her abilities. There is clear evidence that she adhered, for the most part, to the rules of Gestalt Therapy. However, there were some subtle interactions that suggested she also took the liberty (license) to interpret the rules in order to fit the role and function of the therapist as she viewed them. For instance, in her approach to Incident 6, she encouraged the group to engage in an interactive experience through dialogue with each other. If you recall, this is not usually seen as the norm in Gestalt Therapy, but is one which she developed (Polster & Polster 1973, 287).

In every response to the incidents, then, it can be observed that our Gestalt TP was not so concerned with techniques as she was with experiencing each moment of the group, and that from such experience, the technique(s) that she employed evolved. Note that while we were exposed to what appeared to be an "intuitive" feeling regarding what technique (or game) she was to employ, we were able to know the kind of interpretive thoughts she was making almost at the very moment of the interaction. Such activity (rationalization), while occurring at a subvocal level, leads to interventions that are far from what may appear as "flying by the seat of one's pants." Clearly, there was an effort to blend experience with reason in order to select the "game" that she felt would most help the members face themselves.

# $\mathcal{I}$ndividual Psychology

Perhaps in none of the six theoretical models of group therapy presented, are the parameters for the therapist's role and function, as well as group member interaction, so flexible as in Individual Psychology. This TP exposed us to the way in which little or no focus is given to members' emotions; while simultaneously showing how a therapist acknowledges reasoning and cognitive power over affective and emotional power.

In considering the behavior of our Adlerian TP, we should keep in mind how *purposeful* each of his behaviors were in helping group members achieve the primary concepts of Individual Psychology. We can also examine the extent to which he has exemplified being both a model of effective living and a creative and imaginative strategist and technician.

In Incident 5, our TP has opted not to acknowledge the affect tone of the group; instead we learn that he has hoped to appeal to group members' intellect through his model or direct instruction. This appears to be most pronouced in the way our TP draws our attention to the fact that he is less interested in terminating on an emotionally positive note, but is more concerned with teaching group members the ways they engage in purposeful behavior. Furthermore, it apparently is like our Adlerian TP to "up the ante," so to speak, by purposefully engaging in a behavior that "teaches" the intended lesson. If it appears paradoxical, it should, for Adlerian therapists are the masters of paradoxical intervention.

In Incidents 1 and 4, we see a consistency in our TP's behaviors. He continues adhering to Adlerian principles. But what seems to receive subtly different emphasis is the amplification of the concept of life style. He instructs members on the risk of being imperfect as human beings, on basic life tasks, and he makes an effort to create a feeling of community among group members through the sharing of reasons for their feelings. By instructing them through their differences, they can find a commonality that will lead to group cohesion. Achieving this cohesion prepares the environment for facilitating group work.

In Incidents 2 and 6, our Adlerian TP underscores his adherence to the theoretical principles that emphasize the development of group members' self-esteem and equality. For instance, in Incident 2, he attempts to accomplish this by reducing his status as a leader and demonstrating his respect for the group. Then again later, he follows in Incident 6 by helping an individual member establish the goal of his behaviors. Of particular significance is the way our TP has demonstrated his own spontaneity and creativity by freely engaging in individual therapy in his analysis of the situation. By so doing (for example, giving Joe individual attention), he hopes to establish the member's sense of dignity, self-worth, and belongingness to the group.

In Incident 3, more so perhaps than in any other situation, we see a deliberate and obvious use of the *paradox* in group therapy. We also witness how leader-centered the group can become, and our TP even tells us how directive he, as an Adlerian therapist, can be. Instruction takes a very didactic form and increases the pressure for individual action and decision making. We can conclude from this action how Adlerian therapy came to be known as Individual Psychology.

## Rational-Emotive Therapy

The critical incident responses of this section are unique in that our TP is the founder of the theory he espouses. It was interesting to see how congruent he was with his theory. We looked to see how our TP was a model of his theoretical orientation and also tried to observe how the techniques he employed determined the degree of success he had in getting group members to challenge their irrational assumptions and beliefs. It is important for us to remember that *the technique* (cognitive, emotive, and behavioral) was named central to the RET TP's functioning as a group therapist, and that less emphasis was placed upon attending to group process.

We were immediately faced with our leader modeling the principles of RET. In fact, in Incident 5 he actually employed them on himself. He also moved very quickly in establishing a rapport with his members that would sustain the eventual confrontation they would have to face. This was done through instruction of basic RET principles. In some respects, we became his group members. He attacked our own irrationality by allowing us to be privy to his innermost thoughts as they related to his interpretation of each situation. We were challenged as to how we might employ ourselves as group therapist. For example, how many of us would orally state to our group members that our predecessor (previous therapist) was ineffective and that the preceding sessions had been wasteful? Perhaps we might have thought it but not have considered stating it out loud. As we continued, we found our TP made efforts to help members see how they were responsible for behaviors that evolve from unrealistic (irrational) directives, which ultimately lead to dysfunction. Our TP did not hesitate to be a living example, in every way, of the person who follows the precepts of RET.

Again, throughout these sections, we were privy to our TP's inner thought processes. He explained, in RET terms, how he viewed and assessed the incidents and, within the context of RET principles, how he then chose to intervene. In each situation, our TP was seen employing instruction, offering directives, and proposing homework assignments. All of these were contextually developed, not predetermined. They were the consequence of his assessment and experience of the incident in regard to each member's response to it. It is significant to note that he did not hesitate to engage members in individual dialogue and then to move to group work. In every instance, we found that the means were justified by the desired ends. This fact is underscored by the statement our TP made at the conclusion of his response to Incident 4. He informed us that group process did not receive his focus of attention, rather his concern was more to help group members to live happier lives. Earlier in Incident 1, we learned that our TP had disdain for attending to group process. Instead, he hastened to share his delight with being able to structure the initial group session by engaging the members in didactic instruction. He also moved the group members (individually and as a group) to employ RET principles in the very first session. He assigned homework and used bibliotherapy, which he felt would appeal to and reinforce the rational side of group members.

In Incident 2, we found a subtle difference from the way in which our TP had previously behaved. He confronted and became quite transparent with one of the members. This particular action typified how our therapist had employed himself within the context of the situation. We got to see *him*. It was hard to disassociate technique from the person and person from the technique. The whole process dealt with the immediacy of the incident. Instruction was evident and the lesson to be learned was framed within the context of the incident.

We can conclude that our RET TP indeed maintained a high degree of congruency between the stated principles of his theory and his behaviors as a group therapist. In fact, we are more apt to add that in this instance, more than in any other, the theory personified the therapist and vice versa.

## Reality Therapy

As we learned in the chapter on Reality Therapy, the group therapist role and technique are synonymous with group process, which in turn is identified by the seven stages a group must pass through. As we observed our Reality Therapy TP work, we tried to see how extensively he adhered to acknowledging these seven stages. In addition, we examined how he integrated the key concepts that support Reality Therapy into his work. Finally, we looked at the extent to which our TP appealed to our rationality, and if indeed he chose to do this by engaging the group in some pedagogical dialogue.

In terms of his style, our TP did not disappoint us. Throughout each incident, we found him attempting to engage each group or group member in some dialogue. He appealed to their sense of reason and avoided becoming enmeshed in their strong feeling states by not acknowledging them. However, this did not come at the expense of not becoming *involved* with the group. In fact, in nearly each situation, there was strong evidence that our TP made an effort to become *involved*. Throughout each incident, we also found that our TP modeled the basic tenets of Reality Therapy. He was not reluctant to reach out and make contact. He used self-disclosure to establish a degree of intimacy within the group. In a number of incidents, he did not hesitate to take the initiative and assume responsible behavior (as in Incident 1); he arrived early to meet, greet, and introduce members to each other, while communicating the significance of starting on time.

We also saw that our TP is not reluctant to be himself, that is, he used his way of interpreting how Reality Therapy might be applied to a given incident. As he did in Incident 2, he permitted us to see his directness, while also allowing us to see an alternative way that not only demonstrated responsibility-taking, but how to confront subtly, but again directly, group members to take on more responsibility for themselves.

We were able to see how our TP applied the use of dialoguing. He did so with us, as though we were in his group. He continually made us aware of the rationale that supported his every move and drew support from various sources. This gave us some insight into our TP. He appeared to strongly value the pedagogical position of the therapist. We also learned that there was an eclectic orientation in his approach. This may be viewed as separating himself from the purists. For example, we did not see him acknowledge any of the seven stages of Reality Therapy that the group must have been through, which in turn might have affected his style or the intervention he employed. But perhaps it can be argued equally as strongly that this is precisely what Reality Therapy is about. If it works, and it does not violate the basic tenet for responsible living, then use it.

## *Transactional Analysis*

Throughout the TA responses, we saw the significance of the therapist's personhood within the therapeutic relationship. As we considered our TP, we were conscious of a number of factors. He should model humility, equality, and openness. Furthermore, his behavior should demonstrate a strong commitment and responsibility to the group as well as to any contracts that had been agreed upon. Being creative and imaginative is another very strong orientation for TA leaders. He must demonstrate an ability to collect and quickly evaluate data. He then has to analyze ego states, transactions, games, and scripts and transmit those skills to group members, while simultaneously determining which standard or creative TA techniques will be appropriate to apply.

In Incidents 3, 4, and 5, we find our TA leader at work restructuring his groups according to TA precepts (by stating that none of these incidents would have developed). He was quick to teach us how and why he, as a leader, would have employed a variety of standard TA techniques as he tried to instruct group members. We were also shown his diagnostic thinking processes and how they lead to the type of interventions he used. Our TP used his personhood (in Incident 4), when he referred to the "element of transference" that a member held for him. How our leader chose to respond to the member in this instance was reflective of his disallowance of getting trapped in the member's game, while also modeling healthy functioning behavior.

As we advance through each of the situations, we learn that our TA leader was not reluctant to move quickly to work. We also see that he was not afraid to be himself and interpret how he chose to behave as a TA leader. In Incident 1, for example, it was typical for him to stop a group member's work, in order to provide some instruction in TA, while also taking care to avoid moving into a cerebral, TA concept-oriented relationship with his members. Our TA leader has successfully communicated his analysis of ego states, transaction patterns, games, and scripts of each member. He then translated his interpretations into interventions, which would help his group members to move to a healthy ego state.

## Conclusion

At this juncture, we can conclude that each of our TPs adhered to their respective theories. More important, however, we need to note how much significance can be placed upon not only what Yalom (1985) had referred to as the *core* of group therapy but also the *front.* In our efforts to determine the degree of congruence therapists had with their theories, the personhood of each of our TPs seemed to emerge with a degree of frequency. In virtually every instance, the way each theory was applied was determined as a matter of how each TP chose to make it "fit" their personal style, thereby giving us subtle yet significant variations between theory and practice. This suggests that therapists' rigid adherence to theoretical principles not only may be unrealistic to expect, but also would be restrictive to the development and implementation of interventions needed to deal with the moment-to-moment interactions in a group.

# CHAPTER FOURTEEN

# Comparison of Theoretical Practitioners' Interventions

Historically, practitioners have been faced with the question of whether one theoretical approach is better than another. In the previous chapter, we concluded that there was a degree of variability between theory and practice, which in large measure was attributable to the characteristics of the therapist. We had an opportunity to explore this issue within the context of how our TPs have presented themselves. What we set out to emphasize in this chapter is that effective leadership is more a matter of choice and blend, rather than determining which theoretical intervention is the best. The manner in which we will address this task is to introduce briefly the central issues elicited by each critical incident, comparing similarities and differences among TP interventions by identifying specific group therapy concepts or procedures and concluding with an assessment of the primary intervention emphasis of our six TPs and a brief synthesis of what we have learned about effective leadership as suggested by our TPs' interventions.

# Critical Incident #1

Critical Incident 1 addressed the issue of beginning a therapy group with brief introductions, which was then followed by an initial silence.

With the exception of the Client-Centered and TA approaches, all TPs initially addressed the group silence with varying amounts of structuring comments aimed at "getting started," or "ground rules" directed to the group. Our RET TP was the most explicit in outlining his goals, motives, RET theory, and determining if members could commit themselves to his therapy group. In a similar but briefer fashion, the Adlerian TP informed members "why" they were there, particularly the need to belong. The Gestalt TP, like the Adlerian, believed members were reluctant to talk because they felt their concerns were different or unique, but she did not verbalize them as did the Adlerian. She asked the group "What pleases them?", "Who do they miss?", and the like, while the Adlerian asked them to specify their concerns. Both our Adlerian and Gestalt TPs focused on the "universality" of concerns of group members, the importance of group cohesion (comradery for the Adlerian or environmental support for the Gestalt therapist). Our Gestalt TP, however, emphasized the importance of balancing "individual differences" with environmental support. The Reality TP *self-disclosed* his experiences and feelings as a beginning college freshman as a means of facilitating member disclosures regarding their concerns as freshmen.

The Client-Centered TP treated silence with silence, which, in effect, is a *group as a whole* intervention, eliciting ambiguity and individual member's tolerance for ambiguity. He believes "not talking will give us something to talk about later." Assumption of responsibility for involvement was, therefore, left to group members. In contrast, the TA TP began by giving his name and, sequentially, noted members' discomfort (body language) in response to the silence and invited them to verbalize their feelings. *Contracting* with *individual* members was begun immediately to define *what* aspect of behavior they wanted to change. He required clarity and specificity of concerns in these individual transactions and, consequently, "contract negotiations" could take up most of the beginning session since members' concerns are often unclear. The Gestalt TP, like our TA TP, stressed clarity of communication ("sharpening their language"), *how* members listen and express themselves (body language), and "saying clearly what they want."

Both Gestalt and RET TPs utilized *role playing* as an intervention during the latter portion of their sessions, although the methods and purposes differed. The Gestalt TP employed role playing as "experiments" in interpersonal transactions with others to make individuals more aware of their behaviors. In contrast, the RET TP selected a member who presented a concern and, in a fashion similar to our TA

TP, conducted an individual transaction with the member. However, he demonstrated the process of RET problem-solving with this member to the group (imitative learning) as opposed to the TA TP's contracting process. Our RET TP *involved* other members to challenge and question the problem-solving member and involve themselves in RET problem-solving. Therefore, our RET TP employed the *universality* of experience around the process of problem-solving, and, further, he was the only TP who required *homework* assignments for his group members for purposes of practicing new behaviors.

### Summary of Critical Incident #1

Clearly, all our TPs were interested in having members talk or participate in the beginning group session. With the exception of the Client-Centered TP, all the others were active in providing varying amounts of *structure* or *direction* to get group members talking. The crucial difference among TPs was *how* and *when* they decided to involve group members. For instance, the RET TP demonstrated the most explicit form of structuring, while the Client-Centered TP demonstrated the least amount of structuring. It might be inferred that these two interventions reflected the extremes of *therapist-centered* (RET) and *group-centered* intervention styles (Client-Centered).

Specific TP similarities were the Gestalt and TA TPs' emphasis on specifying members' concerns and members expressing strong feeling, RET and Gestalt TP uses of role playing, and the Adlerian, Gestalt, and RET TPs' emphases on cohesion and universality (group processes). Specific differences among TPs were the introduction of *contracting* (TA), homework (RET), and "group as a whole" intervention (Client-Centered).

## *C*ritical Incident #2

Critical Incident #2 addressed the issues of group members' views and complaints regarding the therapist's competency to conduct the therapy group.

To varying degrees, the Client-Centered, Reality, Adlerian, and RET TPs openly acknowledged some responsibility for having been uncaring, cold, and distant toward the group, while the TA and Gestalt TPs initiated interventions at slightly different rates and styles toward members expressing the most *intense affect.*

The Client-Centered TP clearly assumed the most responsibility by disclosing ineptness in previous sessions and contributing to the current state of affairs (self-disclosure). He invited criticism from the group and viewed it as an opportunity for learning about his errors. Implicit in the invitation, he used himself as a *model* so that "criticism eventually shifts to group members as we move to higher forms of individuality." He implied by his statement his *collusion* (group process) with the group in avoiding more important interactions. Apart from disclosing substantially less responsibility for the "group's floundering," the Adlerian TP, like the Client-Centered TP, invited group criticism to "learn about myself and how I come across as a leader," and viewed the incident as an opportunity for group development. He differed from the Client-Centered TP by *structuring* group feedback, asking what he should be doing and what would a real therapist be doing. Clearly, his structuring comments served to dilute the *affective* components of members' complaints, while the Client-Centered TP's "open invitation" allowed for affective components to be expressed.

Our RET and Reality TPs used self-disclosures that assumed "half of the responsibility for the group's floundering." The Reality TP validated, "in part," the group's reaction and recommitted himself to contribute more, but was curious as to *why* the group "wants me to run the show." The RET TP viewed the group as "copping out," admitting he "didn't structure the process well enough," and going on to reeducate the group on the purposes of RET; unlike the Reality TP, however, he explained the *why* of their avoidance.

Unlike the other TPs, our Gestalt and TA TPs did not disclose responsibility and discounted the group's attack. The Gestalt TP viewed the group's waiting for a member to present a therapeutic "opening" in the present session; she invited responses to "unfinished business," or addressed a member with "spoken vehemence" from the previous session. Similar to the Client-Centered, Adlerian, and Reality TPs, the Gestalt TP viewed the incident as an opportunity for group movement or "new emotional territory" (norm development).

The TA TP, like the Gestalt TP, viewed the group's "small talk" as a continuation of "revealing patient's programming," and either attended to those members displaying the most intense affect in the current or previous session. Both TA and Gestalt TPs, in terms of shaping and initiating their interventions, acknowledged the importance of the *group's history* (previous sessions) and members who displayed the most intense affect. In addition, the Gestalt, TA, and RET TPs focused on individual transactions between leader and member to demonstrate their therapeutic expertise and discounted attending to *group processes,* which were more characteristic of the Client-Centered, Adlerian, and Reality TPs.

Our TA TP was the only one who addressed the issue of *extra-group socializing* (between husband and wife) and how the interaction *outside* the group influenced subsequent group behavior in the form of a *subgroup.* He also noted the importance of "endprogramming" this subgroup with the group.

## Summary of Critical Incident #2

Four of our TPs (Client-Centered, Adlerian, Reality, and RET) utilized varying amounts of therapist self-disclosure to account for ineptness in conducting prior group sessions in order to dilute the growing attack (emotional contagion) in the current group session. In contrast, the Gestalt and TA TPs *covertly* acknowledged the influence of group history (group processes) on the current session, but chose to attend to those members displaying the most intense affect.

A critical but subtle difference among the six TPs was the extent to which each allowed a specific member or the group as a whole to express affect. Clearly, the Client-Centered TP permitted the most expression of affect, while the Adlerian and RET TPs exhibited control over the amount of affect expressed.

Most of our TPs viewed the incident as an opportunity to shape new *norms* and enhance group movement. Interestingly, our TA TP introduced the possible existence and influence of two group processes—extra-group socializing and subgrouping—evolving in the current incident.

## $\mathcal{C}$ritical Incident #3

Critical Incident #3 addressed the issue of group denial in response to a member's discussion about death.

All TPs agreed that the issue of death, as verbalized by Jean, must not be avoided (denied) by the group, and all viewed Jean as needing support. In dealing with the group's denial, the Gestalt and Client-Centered TPs focused primarily on Jean. The Adlerian and Reality TPs focused largely on the group, while RET and TA TPs attended both to the group and Jean.

Although both the Gestalt and Client-Centered TPs attended primarily to Jean's distress and had similar outcomes for the session, the manner in which they intervened varied significantly. Both were intent on serving as *the* providers of support for Jean, since the group appeared immobilized or traumatized at the time, and both were concerned with creating group support and reducing fear in members by means of their individual interactions with Jean (imitative learning).

Our Gestalt TP went through a series of confronting interventions with Jean, which attended to Jean's *feelings* about the group's response to her sadness. Her interventions required Jean to disclose her feelings, by having her *fantasize* and *dialogue* with the dead boy while the therapist simultaneously observed her body movements. She viewed this intense encounter (emotional stimulation) as "support generation momentum" (instillation of hope) in having provided other group members with the ability to face the issue of death.

Our Client-Centered TP saw Jean as a "human in pain" and became "absorbed" in her pain by means of empathic interventions and *modeled* to the group (imitative learning) appropriate responses to help members overcome their fears (instillation of hope). Unlike the Gestalt TP, he did not attend to Jean's body movements, but, similar to the Gestalt TP, he offered no guidance other than modeling for the group members. The Client-Centered TP, in contrast to the other TPs, talked about his desire to cry and "why" he decided to avoid it.

Although the Reality and Adlerian TPs directed their interventions primarily toward the group, the way they viewed and treated the group was quite different. The Reality TP, in conceptualizing his interventions, considered the "formation history" of the group in that nurses were "told" to attend and, consequently, *individual* differences existed among nurses regarding their expectations of group. He emphasized the therapist's ability to recall personal history (recall of pain) in dealing with issues of death. In sum, the therapist must respect individual differences among members.

In contrast, the Adlerian TP confronted the denying group by the use of *paradox*, with little concern for group history or individual differences among the nurses. He confronted the group as a whole by describing their avoidance and stated the paradox "Why not work at figuring out how we can be nurses who only work with well people?" (emotional stimulation). He continued the paradoxical intervention using *provocative* statements until, hopefully, a member recognized the paradox and the denial subsided. If, even after repeated interventions, the group still did not recognize the paradox, he would dismiss the group, leaving them with a final paradox to discuss the next session, but would invite Jean to meet with him *privately*. The Reality TP, in contrast, invited the group as a whole to focus on what Jean said, acknowledged their pain, and asked members what "we can do to help Jean deal with her grief." Clearly, his intent was similar to the Gestalt and Client-Centered TPs. The RET and TA TPs also elicited support for Jean *by means* of generating immediate *group* support, as opposed to therapist support. The Adlerian TP, in contrast, tried to evoke (provoke) group support for Jean.

Both the RET and TA TPs initially addressed the group as a whole, as did the Reality and Adlerian TPs. However, the TA TP quickly refocused the group from safer responses to joining Jean's feelings, ignored any group comments, and began working with Jean. The RET TP, in contrast to the TA TP, first spent time *interpreting* the group's resistance ("unconscious cop out") and subsequently attempted to *link* members with Jean (universality). "I wonder if you, like Jean, have some real problems, when one of your patients dies like hers did." He continued to prod members to question the *whys* of their fears and "overconcern with death" at the expense of more personal issues. Thus, he created a form of "environmental support" similar to Gestalt, TA,

Reality, and Client-Centered TPs but by addressing the group. Once support was mobilized, he directed his attention to Jean.

Interestingly, our RET TP was the first of the TPs to acknowledge the role of the *unconscious* and *subconscious* in influencing group behavior.

### Summary of Critical Incident #3

All TPs believed the issue of death, as expressed by Jean, should not be avoided (denied) and that she required *support.* The critical difference among TP interventions was *how* they chose to provide support for Jean. Specifically, support for Jean was provided by the therapists (Client-Centered, Gestalt, Reality), by the group (Adlerian), and by both the therapist and the group (RET and TA). Interestingly, all of our TPs believed their respective interventions would simlutaneously *reduce* group members' fears of talking about death while providing support for Jean.

Unique procedures suggested by our TPs in this incident were fantasy and dialogue (Gestalt), group interpretation of unconscious behavior (RET), and a private therapy session with Jean (Adlerian).

## *Critical Incident #4*

Critical Incident #4 addressed the following issues. First, we have a member announcing departure from the group in the beginning moments of the fifth session. Second, there is the resulting group silence. Finally, we are faced with the decision-making process regarding termination or continuation in the group.

The Client-Centered and TA TPs' initial response to John's announced departure and consequent group silence was his own silence. Our Client-Centered TP used the silence to *internally diagnose* his feelings regarding the announcement, assumed a group response would eventually occur, but was unclear what he would do if the group remained silent. Our TA TP used the silence to conduct an internal diagnosis of those members exhibiting "intense ego states" in response to John and what they meant theoretically. In sum, for the TA TP, the *why* of member behavior was important to the group therapist, while the *how* was important for the members. The TA TP's subsequent strategies, unlike those of the Client-Centered TP, called for inviting John to tell members "how he wants them to respond" and for members to respond to John (feedback).

Our Gestalt and Reality TPs bypassed the silence and initiated action with John. The Gestalt TP, unlike the TA TP, wanted to know specifically *why* John was leaving, for his benefit as well as the group's and wondered whether "Since I cannot such and such in this group, I feel like leaving." Similar to the TA TP, our Gestalt TP was concerned with the intense member reactions to John's announcement, but more in terms of their *identifying* those feelings (helplessness, sadness) that were similar to John's (universality).

The Reality TP initiated action with John by self-disclosure "I feel sad to hear you're leaving" and showing caring "because I like you and think you can contribute something important." He continued working with John by stressing the crucialness of the decision to leave the group, and how it related to doubts regarding his second marriage (insight). Our Reality TP, unlike other TPs, viewed it as imperative that John express his feelings and see the correlation between action and feelings with the group "waiting in the wings" until John saw the *why* of his behavior.

Both the RET and Adlerian TPs directed their interventions to the group. Our RET TP wanted details regarding members' feelings about John's departure for purposes of identifying their self-blaming, hopeless feelings and *teaching* them not to "illegitimately rate themselves." Unwittingly, later in the session, when our RET TP focused on John's "self-blaming" behaviors, he also initiated the process of universality, as did the Gestalt TP. The RET TP was similar to our Gestalt TP in attempting to elicit the *why* of members' behavior, but different from the Gestalt TP in that he *explained* the why (imparting information) by means of RET Theory. Our Gestalt TP generates the *why* from John. Both the RET and Gestalt TPs also relied on the use of specific exercises (imagery and dialoguing) for members to dispute faulty thinking as well as a means of clarifying John's faulty thinking.

Our Adlerian TP asked the group, "Does anyone here like John, want him in the group? How would you see him helping the group, helping you?" His group intervention paralleled the RET TP by having members present *feedback* to John regarding his behavior and simultaneously relieving members from being responsible or blaming themselves for John's departure. This intervention also gave John the opportunity of *seeing* what was and was not likeable about him, so that he could make a responsible decision regarding termination. Being placed in the position of being responsible appeared to correlate with the TA TP's notion of John being in an Adult state when making his decision to leave group.

## Issue of Dealing with Member Termination

The Reality TP stands alone in having asked John to *think* about his decision to leave group for one week and return the following session before making his final decision. In contrast, our Client-Centered TP appeared to leave or "trust" the decision to John. The remaining TPs seemed to take a "middle of the road" position by initiating process either towards John (Gestalt and Reality) or towards the group (RET, TA, and Adlerian) for purposes of helping him make a responsbile decision in the current session. It is also important to note that at varying degrees, these five TPs were concerned that the remaining group members *not* feel a sense of being *responsible* if John chose to leave.

### Summary of Critical Incident #4

The outstanding similarity among five of the TPs in Critical Incident 4, with the exception of the Client-Centered TP, was their concern with the *why* of John's behavior or the group's behavior (silence) and *how* they employed or discounted the group silence in making their interventions.

The Gestalt, Reality, and Adlerian TPs were concerned that John *discover* the why of his behavior, although their strategies differed. In contrast, the RET TP *explained* the why to John, while the TA TP *internally diagnosed* the why and was more interested in John knowing the *how* of his behavior. Interestingly, the Client-Centered TP internally diagnosed the why of his *personal reactions* to John.

Both the TA and Client-Centered TPs used the silence to complete their internal diagnosis, while the remaining TPs bypassed the silence to work on the why of John's announced departure by attending to the group or John.

Unlike the other TPs, the TA and Gestalt TPs confronted these members who showed the greatest discomfort with John's behavior, even though the TPs' view of *why* was *different.* Both RET and Gestalt TPs employed specific exercises to clarify John's faulty thinking.

With regard to John's termination, most TPs left the decision to him. The Reality TP differed by asking John to attend one more session before making a final decision to leave the group.

## $\mathcal{C}$*ritical Incident #5*

Critical Incident #5 dealt with issues concerning an emotional outburst with 15 minutes remaining in the seventh session of a therapy group, as well as group closure within the prescribed time limits of the group.

With regard to the emotional outburst, *all* TPs acknowledged the importance of Sandra's outburst by attending to her directly. Four of the TPs (Gestalt, RET, TA, and Reality) specifically chose to *reward* Sandra for her expression of feeling.

Our Adlerian and Client-Centered TPs chose not to reward Sandra's behavior. However, all TPs seemed to encourage Sandra to continue verbalizing and exploring her thoughts and feelings to the group, to specific members, or to the therapist. The Client-Centered TP encouraged Sandra to continue exploring her thoughts and feelings *(self-exploration)* and *rewarded* continual exploration. He appeared content to allow members to respond "at will," without direction, *hoping* that some "bridge-building" (linking/identification) would occur naturally among members. The Adlerian TP assumed a similar approach to focusing on Sandra's outburst, but differed from the Client-Centered TP by summarizing her behavior and providing a framework (framing) for purposes of having Sandra compare her current group behavior with similar behavior with her husband outside of the therapy group (insight). Our RET TP assumed a similar posture to the Adlerian TP in that he provided a framework for *explaining* and *educating* Sandra about the "why" of her behavior according to the A-B-C theory of personality. However, he chose to *involve* group members in helping Sandra by answering some questions he posed to her or Jonathan. Therefore, he elicited *group involvement* at a cognitive level, unlike the Client-Centered and Adlerian TPs, and also indoctrinated or taught members to understand and apply principles of RET theory. The TA TP, like the Adlerian and RET TPs, had an *internal framework* for understanding Sandra's and members' behavior (ego states), but did *not* employ his internal framework to explain member behavior, as did the RET TP. Rather, he had Sandra *act* on the framework by suggesting she let Jonathan and other members know specifically "how you want them to respond to your feelings right now." Our TA TP, like the Client-Centered TP, assumed member involvement might occur without direction, but unlike the Client-Centered TP, he acknowledged that "members had important feelings to explore in future sessions."

The Gestalt TP, like the TA TP, encouraged Sandra to make *specific* statements to Jonathan (feedback) and other members of the group by *confronting* them directly with her complaints as opposed to *asking them* to respond to what she wanted them to respond to. The Gestalt TP, unlike the Client-Centered, TA, and Adlerian TPs, facilitated member involvement *after* dealing with Sandra by asking John and other members to verbalize their feelings regarding Sandra's outburst.

In contrast to other TPs, the Reality TP acknowledged Sandra's pain (empathy) and , subsequently utilized *self-disclosure* about himself and his family as a means of providing a *framework* for Sandra to understand her current behavior. Unlike other TPs, our Reality TP posed two alternatives for Sandra and the group to choose from to pursue examination of her behavior. In addition, he first solicited Sandra and Jonathan's *permission* (consent) and, subsequently, other group members', regarding their desire to participate in examining Sandra's behavior. In making the statement "If the *group* wishes...," the Reality TP employed a *group as a whole* intervention as opposed to the primary emphasis on *intrapsychic* interventions and to a very lesser degree *interpersonal* interventions by other TPs. Our Reality TP clearly tended to emphasize the importance of group involvement by actively soliciting members' input.

## Session Closure and Preparation for Subsequent Session

Closing a session within a short period of time following an emotional outburst by a group member was dealt with in several ways by our TPs.

Clearly, the RET, Reality, TA, and Gestalt TPs explicitly noted the need to give closure to the group and some direction (structuring for the subsequent session).

Both the TA and Gestalt TPs encouraged Sandra to initiate the next session by addressing her feelings, while our TA TP emphasized the importance of ending the current group by having an available "Adult ego state" or some control over her behavior instead of her present "Child state." The Reality TP and, particularly, the RET TP were more explicit with regard to preparing *all* group members for the subsequent session by giving them homework assignments. Inherent in these four TPs' approaches was a concern with *ambiguity reduction* for Sandra during the closing 15 minutes and varying amounts of direction for members during and following this session. In contrast, the Adlerian TP viewed the closing 15 minutes as a "beginning" for this group and that "important and personal work" had only begun. Therefore, closure was not necessary at this time and a state among members was a prerequisite for "some hard self-analysis" between sessions. The Client-Centered TP, like the Adlerian TP, did not provide direction for the subsequent session, but assumed members would learn to respond to each other as a function of witnessing his interaction with Sandra (modeling).

## Summary of Critical Incident #5

Clearly, all TPs agreed that Sandra's emotional outbursts with 15 minutes remaining in group must be attended to. *How* they chose to *involve* her participation in exploring her thoughts and feelings demonstrated both *intervention* similarities and differences. More specifically, our TPs interventions were directed either to the group (RET, Reality), to specific members (TA, Gestalt), or to the therapist (Client-Centered, Reality). Our TP strategies for involving Sandra's participation included self-exploration and reward (Client-Centered), behavior summarization and framing (Adlerian), questioning and educating (RET), group as a whole intervention and leader self-disclosure (Reality), and confrontation (Gestalt and TA).

With regard to closure of the group session, the RET, Reality, TA, and

Gestalt TPs agreed that some closure or preparation for the subsequent session was necessary, while the Adlerian and Client-Centered TPs viewed closure and preparation for the subsequent session as unnecessary.

## *C*ritical Incident #6

Critical Incident #6 addressed the issue of a group attack on a denying member during the middle of the group session.

All of our TPs seemed to agree that Joe (denying member) was being scapegoated and needed support and protection. Further, they thought the group attack on his behavior should be diluted or deescalated since the attack would only increase his denying behavior.

To dilute or deescalate the group attack, our TA, Gestalt, Adlerian, and Reality TPs focused initially on Joe, for varying periods of time, before attending to group members, while our Client-Centered and RET TPs directed their early interventions toward the group.

Both the TA and Gestalt TPs viewed Joe's behavior as assertive (more so than the group members) and attempted to *define reality* or provide a *framework* for Joe by means of comparing the group's demands with demands he experienced in his work setting (insight). The TA TP, moreover, assumed a more protective role for Joe than did the Gestalt TP since he believed he had colluded with the group (group history) by not inviting Joe to work on resistances in previous sessions. While the TA TP focused on defining reality, helping Joe express himself more openly and subsequently interacting with other members, the Gestalt TP assumed that Jim and Linda (two intense reactors) *were not* as open as Joe and confronted them to be specific about *what* Joe did that frightened them (feedback).

Our Adlerian and Reality TPs conducted "individual therapy" with Joe apparently seeking causes (why) for his behavior in group. The Adlerian TP spent time *explaining* and *interpreting* the goals of Jim's behavior, until Jim "agrees," which, in turn, would elicit *different* responses than anger from group members. The Reality TP, in contrast, asked Joe *why* he joined the group and *what* his goals were. Continual denial would have led the TP to ask Joe to evaluate his decision to stay in the group, but also to commit himself to returning the following week.

Our Adlerian, Reality, and Client-Centered TPs advocated an individual or private session outside of group to assess Joe's current group behavior, while our Gestalt, TA, and RET TPs did not view an outside session as necessary or his behavior as requiring special attention.

Both Client-Centered and RET TPs directed their primary attention to the group, but their strategies differed. The Client-Centered TP initially conducted an internal dialogue to avoid colluding with the group attack on Jim. His strategy was to wait, believing that "disruptions are a waste of time"; and he did not want to "fix Joe." However, if the attack increased (emotional contagion) he would *interpret the group's behavior* by saying, "It sounds as if you want Joe to confess!" Later, he acknowledged Jim's right to his behavior, "Maybe it takes him longer than seven weeks to feel safe." In contrast, the RET TP viewed the group as "Not healthfully confronting Joseph!" and asked them to "surrender their anger." He, like the Gestalt TP, focused on those two members (Linda and Jim) who displayed their disturbance although he worked with Linda first. However, the RET TP, like the Adlerian TP, explained the "why" of Linda's behavior as self-defeating, and then described Joe's behavior as self-defeating, thus attempting to link the two together in a cooperative working relationship. The RET TP, like the Gestalt TP, attempted to address Linda and Jim's fears and simultaneously attempted to reduce Joe's fears, although their leadership behaviors differed. Unlike the other TPs, the RET TP invited group members to challenge and question Linda and Jim.

Our RET and Reality TPs assigned *homework* to group members related to their current group behavior. The Gestalt TP, in contrast, had group members do homework *in the group* by means of various verbal and nonverbal techniques.

### Summary of Critical Incident #6

Our TPs agreed that Joe was being scapegoated and needed both support and protection. The critical issue was *how* the TPs chose to deescalate the attack on Joe and move the group in a more productive direction.

To deescalate the group attack, two TPs (Adlerian and Reality) intervened by conducting individual therapy with Joe, while the Gestalt TP asked the two members showing the greatest discomfort to provide feedback to Joe. The Client-Centered and RET TPs directed their interventions to the group, but differed in terms of the degree of structure they provided for the group. Our TA TP intervened by helping Joe express himself more openly.

Interestingly, our TA and Gestalt TPs viewed Joe's behavior as assertive, while the remaining TPs viewed his behavior, in general, as *defensive.*

## $\mathcal{P}$*rimary Intervention Assessment*

The primary intervening emphasis by our six TPs to the six critical incidents elicited interactions between the therapist and a specific member(s) or the therapist and the group. In some instances, therapist-centered interventions (self-disclosure) were utilized as primary interventions. Secondary or sequential interventions varied in terms of emphasis on a specific member, the group, or the therapist.

It is also clear that the six TPs' primary interventions paid the *least* amount of attention to group processes (group dynamics) and, consequently, negated their influence on leader, member, or group behavior. On a few occasions, some of our TPs did attend to group processes, but largely in terms of conceptualizing the critical incident and not in terms of their stated intervention. Instances of *actual group process* interventions were the TA TP's emphasis on extra-group socializing and subgrouping; the Client-Centered, Adlerian, Reality, and RET TPs' emphases on group history; and the Gestalt and RET TPs' emphases on unconscious or subconscious group behavior.

Of equal and related importance is the fact that very few of the TPs' primary *or* secondary interventions required members to *interact* with or give *feedback* to each other. The Gestalt and TA TPs pursued member discomfort and encouraged feedback on several occasions, as did the RET and Reality TPs, but more in terms of cognitive feedback rather than affective feedback. The Reality and Client-Centered TPs utilized therapist self-disclosure and introspection, respectively, as intervening styles to general interaction among members. The Reality TP was *overt* with his disclosures, while the Client-Centered TP's introspections were *covert*, leaving the group to deal alone without direction in several incidents. The Adlerian TP generated some member-to-member interaction, but largely by helping them discover the goals of a member's behavior.

It is our contention that group processes such as interpersonal learning, consensual validation, cohesion, subgrouping, family reenactment, emotional contagion, and the like, contribute to and affect the development of a therapy group and influence member and leader behavior. Further, to elicit and deal with these group processes *requires* interventions that have members interact with and give feedback to each other, while some group processes require interventions that acknowledge their presence and influence. Therefore, a limitation of the primary intervening emphasis of our six TPs was the deemphasis on group processes.

Our current TPs have provided us with a variety of strategies and procedures reflecting therapist-member(s), therapist-group, and therapist-centered interventions when encountering critical incidents in group therapy. We encourage the student of group therapy to give equal credence to the existence and influence of group processes when developing their theory of group therapy and, subsequently, formulating their primary intervening emphasis.

# Conclusion

The central task of this chapter was to emphasize that effective leadership is more of a choice and blend rather than a determination of which theoretical intervention is best. In comparing and contrasting the 36 TP responses to the six critical incidents, it is clear that our TPs have provided us with some important *learnings* regarding effective leadership and demonstrated that effective leadership *is* more of a choice and blend. The following *learnings* from all of the responses are:

1. TPs of differing orientations do intervene in a similar fashion.
2. TPs of differing orientations focus their interventions on one of the following: the leader, the member(s), the group, or the group processes.
3. TPs of differing orientations *vary* their interventions on the leader, member, group, or group processes during a specific critical incident.
4. TPs of differing orientations employ a *series* or *sequence* of interventions during a specific critical incident.
5. TPs of differing orientations may base their current interventions on the basis of *previous group sessions* (group history).
6. TPs of differing orientations may intervene to generate affect (emotional contagion) or dilute affect in a therapy group.
7. TPs of differing orientations conduct individual therapy with group members during or between group sessions.
8. TPs of differing orientations *educate* members regarding the "why" of their behavior through a variety of strategies.
9. TPs of differing orientations differ more in terms of *how* and *when* they intervene than *why* they intervene.
10. TPs of differing orientations may conceptualize the existence and influence of a group process but may or may not acknowledge its existence in their intervention to the group.
11. TPs of differing orientations employ individual therapy interventions in therapy groups.
12. TPs of differing orientations may employ interventions based on members' physical responses (body language).

# CHAPTER FIFTEEN

# Considerations in Developing Your Theory of Group Therapy

Just as we began this text by explaining the reasons we believed a theory of group therapy was important, we can now address how a beginning group therapist might undertake the development of his or her own theory and rationale of group therapy. In this final chapter, we have provided you with some of the primary elements that you should consider fundamental to an evolving theory of group therapy.

## Steps to Developing a Theory

In developing a theory of group therapy, the first step is to define what group therapy is and how it differs from other systems of therapy, such as individual or family therapy. In other words, it is necessary to determine what is unique about group therapy as a therapeutic system that sets it apart from other therapeutic models, and to ask "What characteristics or properties of a therapy group do not exist in other therapeutic modalities that contribute to therapeutic change?" More simply stated, we need to understand why it may be more beneficial to place clients in a therapy group instead of individual or family therapy.

In defining group therapy, the fact that five to ten people are meeting with a therapist suggests an inherently different system for conducting therapy, understanding client behavior, and generating therapeutic change than does a system that employs a two-person interaction.

Second, a group provides the therapist an opportunity to *see* how group members interact with each other, as opposed to just interacting with the therapist in individual counseling. More specifically, the group therapist is able to see what clients do and how they behave in their relationships with others. In other words, the process of group therapy provides the group therapist with behavioral data on member interactions that are unavailable in individual therapy. This behavioral laboratory provides data on verbal and nonverbal behaviors emitted by members in response to each other, the therapist, and the group. An adequate definition of group therapy must take into account the unique contributions of group dynamics, the therapist and group members and the way each affects the therapeutic process.

Properties unique to groups—such as cohesiveness, "group generated affect" (emotional contagion), power distribution and influence, proxemics, subgroups, group development, and norms and standards—have been identified as evolving or existing processes within the group system. The question arises as to how these processes interfere with, or contribute to, changes in a therapy group, group development, the learning of new behaviors, and to the success or failure of the therapist's interventions. The group therapist's theory of group therapy must account for these unique processes in order to understand, control, and predict group movement and member behavior.

In addition to defining what group therapy is and what those properties are that make group therapy a unique system of change, a theory of group therapy must address three elements: the therapist, the member, and the group. To ignore one or more of these elements is to neglect a potential explanation for unexplained occurrences or events during the course of group therapy.

Among the group therapists presented in this text, clearly none address explicitly the contribution of the *group dynamics* to therapeutic change. Our TPs primarily focused on the theoretical characteristics of the leader or the member. It is our position that *all* three elements must be given *equal* attention when formulating a theory of group therapy. We have, therefore, developed a series of questions that should help you identify features of the three elements that will help you establish your theoretical "map" of group therapy.

## Elements of Group Behavior

1. How does group therapy differ from individual therapy?
2. How do nontherapeutic groups (support groups) differ from therapeutic groups?
3. How do groups go through specific stages and how do the stages (phases) of groups reoccur?
4. In what ways does the history of the group affect its current operation and future development?
5. How do norms and standards influence *what* is talked about (content) and how it is talked about (process)?
6. Explain how emotional issues exist in groups and how they are manifested by the group process.
7. In what ways do group processes interfere with or contribute to therapeutic change in a group?
8. How do group processes contribute to helping determine a member's readiness to leave group therapy?

## Elements of Member Behavior

1. How does group member behavior differ in group therapy from individual therapy?
2. How does group member behavior differ in nontherapeutic groups (support groups) from therapeutic groups?
3. In what ways do the group members' pregroup histories influence how they experience the group process?
4. How do the members' historical behaviors in groups affect their current behavior in the therapy group?
5. In what ways do the group members' behaviors influence what is talked about (content) and how it is talked about (process)?
6. How do group members' behaviors elicit emotional issues in the group, and how are they manifested by the group process?
7. How do group members' behaviors contribute to therapeutic change, and how do group members' behaviors interfere with therapeutic change?
8. How do group members' behaviors determine their readiness to leave group therapy?

## Elements of Therapist Behavior

1. In what ways does the therapist's behavior differ in group therapy from individual therapy?
2. In what ways does the therapist's behavior differ in nontherapeutic groups (support groups) from therapeutic groups?

3. How do the group therapists' pregroup histories influence the way they experience the group process?
4. How does the therapist's historical behavior influence the group's current operation and future development?
5. In what ways does the therapist's behavior influence what is talked about (content) and how it is talked about (process)?
6. How does the therapist's behavior elicit emotional issues in a group, and how are they manifested by the group process?
7. Explain how the group therapist contributes to therapeutic change and how the group therapist interferes with therapeutic change.
8. In what ways does the group therapist determine a member's readiness to leave group therapy?

# Conclusion

From the beginning, we have emphasized the need to observe the value of the *core* of the therapist. That is, we have argued for the value of each individual developing his or her own theory. Our primary mission, of course, was to urge you to demystify this phenomenon called *group process* by placing it in your terms. Our intention has been to underscore the fact that there are reasons for all events that occur in groups, and the way you choose to experience and interpret them will be determined by the theoretical reference point upon which you rely. Furthermore, your choice of leader response (intervention) will also be dependent upon this theoretical frame of reference.

As a result of witnessing our TPs' approaches to each of the critical incidents, we hope you have come to realize that effectiveness may well be a matter of choice and blend of concepts as opposed to trying to find which theory is better. We also hope that you have come to recognize the flexibility and imaginative fluidity in each of our TPs' particular approach. We hope that you have observed how their particular interventions of choice evolved from their *core*. In other words, that there was a theoretical framework that guided their perception of a given event, which subsequently determined the technique they employed to deal with it.

We see the development of your personal conceptual framework of group dynamics as analagous to Yalom's *core* concept. Taking it a step further, we contend that techniques evolving from one's *core* will tend to be more effective than those applied in a serendipitous fashion. It follows therefore, that it will be to your *disadvantage* to enter group therapy with simply a kit bag of procedures and techniques as opposed to a formulized theoretical perspective.

# REFERENCES

Adler, A. (1956). *The individual psychology of Alfred Adler*. New York: Basic Books.

Allen, T. (1971). "The individual psychology of Alfred Adler: An item of history and a promise of a revolution." *The Counseling Psychologist, 3(1)*, 3–24.

Allen, T. (1971). "Adlerian interview strategies for behavior change." *The Counseling Psychologist, 3(1)*, 40–48.

Bandura, A. (1969). *Principles of behavior modification*. New York: Holt and Company.

———. (1971). "Psychotherapy based on modeling principles." In Bergin, A.E., and Garfield, S.L. (Eds.), *Handbook of psychotherapy and behavior change*. New York: Wiley.

Barnes, G. (Ed.) (1977). *Transactional analysis after Eric Berne*. New York: Harper's College Press.

Becker, B.J. (1972). "The psychology names of analytic group psychotherapy." *The American Journal of Psychoanalysis, 32(2)*, 181.

Berne, E. (1964). *Games people play*. New York: Grove Press.

———. (1966). Principles of group treatment. New York: Oxford University Press.

————. (1976). *Beyond games and scripts.* New York: Grove Press.

Bickhard, M., and Ford, B. (1976). "Adler's concept of social interest: A critical explication." *Journal of Individual Psychology,* May: 27–49.

Blakeney, R. (1977). *Current issues in transactional analysis.* New York: Brunner/Mazel.

Bowen, M. "Family systems theory and society." In Lorio, J. B., and McClenathan, L. (Eds.). *Georgetown family symposium: Volume II (1973–1974).* Washington, D.C.: Georgetown Family Center, 1977.

Bratter, T.E. (1975a). "Group psychotherapy: A restructuring of the probation process." *Corrective and Social Psychology, 22(1),* 1–5.

————. (1975b). "Responsible therapeutic eros: The psychotherapist who cares enough to define and enforce behavior limits with potentially suicidal adolescents." *The Counseling Psychologist, 5(4),* 97–104.

Buber, M. (1967). *A believing humanism.* New York: Simon and Schuster.

Bugenthal, J.F.T. (1965). *The search for authenticity.* New York: Holt, Rinehart & Winston.

————. (Ed.) (1967). *Challenges of humanistic psychology.* New York: McGraw-Hill.

Clevenger, C. (1982). *A middle range theory of power in universities.* Unpublished dissertation. State University of New York at Buffalo.

Coulson, W.R. (1972). *Groups, gimmicks and instant gurus.* New York: Harper & Row.

————. (1974). *A sense of community.* Columbus, OH: Merrill.

————. (1977). *The foreignness of feelings.* In Coulson, D.A.L., and Meador, B.S. (Eds.). *The La Jolla experiment: Eight personal views.* La Jolla, CA: Landmark Press. 45–58.

————. *The Socratic inquiry in medical school.* La Jolla, CA: Helicon House. In press.

Dinkmeyer, D., Pew, W., and Dinkmeyer, D., Jr. (1979) *Adlerian counseling and psychotherapy.* Monterey, CA: Brooks/Cole.

Dreikurs, R. (1950). *Fundamentals of Adlerian psychology.* New York: Greenberg Publishers.

————. (1957). "Group psychotherapy from the points of view of various schools of psychology: I. Group psychotherapy from the point of view of Adlerian psychology." *International Journal of Group Psychotherapy, 7,* 363–375.

————. (1971). "An interview with Rudolph Dreikurs." *The Counseling Psychologist, 3(1),* 49–54.

————, and Sonstegard, M. (1967). *The teleoanalytic approach to group counseling.* Chicago: Alfred Adler Institute.

Dusay, J., and Steiner, C. (1971). "Transactional analysis in group." In Kaplan, H.I., and Sadock, B.J. (Eds.). *Comprehensive group psychotherapy.* Baltimore: Williams & Wilkins.

Ellis, A. (1969). "A weekend of rational encounter." In Burton, Arthur (Ed.). *Encounter.* San Francisco: Jossey-Bass.

————. (1974a). "Rational-emotive therapy in groups." *Rational Living, 1,* 15–22.

————. (1974b). "The group as agent in facilitating change toward rational thinking and appropriate emoting." In Jacobs, A., and Spradlin, W. (Eds.). *The group as agent of change.* New York: Behavioral Publications.

————. (1975). *Reason and emotion in psychotherapy*. Secaucus, NJ: Lyle Stuart.

————, and Harper, R.A. (1975). *New guide to rational living*. Englewood Cliffs, NJ: Prentice-Hall.

————, and Whiteley, J. (1979). *Theoretical and empirical foundations of rational-emotive therapy*. Monterey, CA: Brooks/Cole.

Fagan, J., and Shepherd, I.L. (1970). *Gestalt therapy now*. Palo Alto, CA: Science and Behavior Books.

Forer, L. (1977). "Use of birth order information in psychotherapy." *Journal of Individual Psychology, 33*, 105–113.

Glasser, W. (1961). *Mental health or mental illness?* New York: Harper & Row.

————. (1965). *Reality therapy: A new approach to psychiatry*. New York: Harper & Row.

————. (1969). *Schools without failure*. New York: Harper & Row.

————, and Zunin, L.M. (1979). "Reality therapy." In Corsini, R. (Ed.). *Current psychotherapies (2nd Ed.)*. Itasca, IL: F.E. Peacock.

Goldhaber, G., and Goldhaber M. (1976). *Transactional analysis: Principles and applications*. Boston: Allyn & Bacon.

Greenberg, I.A. (1968). *Psychodrama and audience attitude change*. Beverly Hills: Behavioral Studies Press.

Gushurst, R. (1971). "The technique, utility, and validity of life style analysis." *The Counseling Psychologist, 3(1)*, 30–40.

Hansen, J., Warner, R., and Smith, E. (1976). *Group counseling: Theory and process*. Chicago: Rand-McNally.

Hansen, J.C., Stevic, R.R., and Warner, R.W. (1977). *Counseling theory and process*. Boston: Allyn & Bacon.

Harris, T. (1969). *I'm okay, you're okay: A practical guide to transactional analysis*. New York: Harper & Row.

James, M., et al. (1977). *Techniques in transactional analysis*. Reading, MA: Addison-Wesley.

Kiefer, H. (1980). *Some reflections on the philosophy of education*. Unpublished paper presented at a meeting of the Center for Philosophic Exchange. State University of New York, College at Brockport.

Koch, S. (1969). *Psychology: A study of a science, Vol. 3, Formulation of the person and the social context*. New York: McGraw-Hill.

LeShan, L. (1959). "Psychological states as factors in the development of malignant disease: A critical review." *Journal of the National Cancer Institute, 22*, 1–19.

————. (1966). "An emotional life-history pattern associated with neoplastic disease." *Annals of the New York Academy of Sciences, 125*, 780–793.

————. (1968). "Psychotherapy and the dying patient." In Peerson, L. (Ed.). *Death and dying*. New York: Macmillan.

Levitsky, A., and Perls, F.S. (1970). "The rules and games of gestalt therapy." In Fagan, J., and Shepherd, I.L. (Eds.). *Gestalt therapy now*. Palo Alto, CA: Science and Behavior Books.

Levitsky, A., and Simkin, J.S. (1972). "Gestalt therapy." In Solomon, L.N., and Berzon, B. (Eds.). *New perspectives on encounter groups*. New York: Jossey-Bass.

Manaster, G. (1977). "Birth order—an overview." *Journal of Individual Psychology, 33*, 3–8.

Mosak, H., and Mosak, B. (1975). *A bibliography for Adlerian psychology.* Washington, DC: Hemisphere.

O'Connell, W. (1971). "Sensitivity training and Adlerian theory." *Journal of Individual Psychology, 31,* 65–72.

Olden, C. (1943). "The psychology of obstinancy." *Psychoanalytic Quarterly, 12,* 252.

Osipow, S.H. (1973). *Theories of career development* (2nd Ed.). New York: Appleton-Century-Crofts.

Papanek, H. (1964) "Bridging dichotomies through group psychotherapy." *Journal of Individual Psychology.* May, 38–47.

Perls, F.S. (1969a). *In and out of the garbage pail.* Lafayette, CA: Real People Press.

———. (1969b). *Gestalt therapy verbatim.* Lafayette, CA: Real People Press.

———. (1969c). *Ego, hunger and aggression.* New York: Random House.

———. (1978). "Concepts and misconceptions of gestalt therapy." *Voices, 14(3),* 31–36.

———, Hefferline, R.R., and Goodman, P. (1951). *Gestalt therapy.* New York: Julian Press.

Polster, E., and Polster, M. (1973). *Gestalt therapy integrated.* New York: Brunner/Mazel.

Rachman, S. (1972). "Clinical applications of observational learning, imitation and modeling." *Behavior Therapy, 3(2),* 379–397.

Raubolt, R.R., and Bratter, T.E. (1976). "Beyond adolescent group psychotherapy: The caring community." *The Addiction Therapist, 1(4),* 10–17.

Reissman, F. (1965). "The helper therapy principle." *Social Work, 10(2),* 27–32.

Richards, I.A. (1942). *Principles of literary criticism.* New York: Harcourt Brace.

Rogers, C.R. (1942). *Counseling and psychotherapy.* New York: Houghton Mifflin.

———. (1959). "A theory of therapy, personality and interpersonal relationships, as developed in the client-centered framework." In Koch, S. (Ed.). *Psychology: A study of a science, Vol. 3, Formulation of the person and the social context.* New York: McGraw-Hill.

———. (1961). *On becoming a person.* New York: Houghton Mifflin.

———. (1965). *Client-centered therapy.* New York: Houghton Mifflin.

———. (1967). "The process of the basic encounter group." In Bugenthal, J.F.T. (Ed.). *Challenges of humanistic psychology.* New York: McGraw-Hill.

———. (1970). *Carl Rogers on encounter groups.* New York: Harper & Row.

Shulman, B., and Mosak, H. (1977). "Birth order and ordinal position: Two Adlerian views." *Journal of Individual Psychology, 33,* 114–121.

Siegel, J.M., and Spivack, G. (1976). "Problem-solving therapy: The description of a new program for chronic psychiatric patients." *Psychotherapy: Theory, Research And Practice, 13(4),* 368–374.

Simkin, J. (1974). *Mini lectures in gestalt therapy.* Albany, GA: Woodpress.

Solomon, L.N., and Berzon, B. (Eds.) (1972). *New perspectives on encounter groups.* San Francisco: Jossey-Bass.

Wagner, M.K. (1968a). "Comparative effectiveness of behavioral rehearsal and verbal reinforcement for effecting anger expressiveness." *Psychological Reports, 22,* 1079–1080.

———. (1968b). "Reinforcement of the expression of anger through role playing." *Behavior Research and Therapy, 2,* 91–95.

Wallen, R. (1970). "Gestalt therapy and gestalt psychology." In Fagan, J., and Shepherd, I.L. (Eds.). *Gestalt therapy now.* Palo Alto, CA: Science and Behavior Books.

Wolpe, J., and Lazarus, A.A. (1966). *Behavior therapy techniques: A guide to the treatment of neurosis.* New York: Pergamon Press.

Yalom, I.D. (1985). *The theory and practice of group psychotherapy (3rd Ed.).* New York: Basic Books.

Zinker, J. (1977). *Creative process in gestalt therapy.* New York: Brunner/Mazel.

# INDEX

ABC Theory, 44–45, 53 (*see also* Rational-Emotive Therapy)
Adler, A., 31–38
Adlerian therapy, 31–40 (*see also* Individual Psychology)
Ambiguity, 219 (*see also* Client-Centered Therapy)
tolerance for, 210
Anger, surrendering of, 190
Anzbacher, H., 32–33
Anzbacher, R., 32–33
Authenticity, 66, 71

Barriers to group growth, 14
Behaviors, self-defeating, 41–43, 52 (*see also* Rational-Emotive Therapy)
Beliefs, Rational-Emotive Therapy, 42
Belonging, 39, 204 (*see also* Individual Psychology)
Berne, E., 63–64, 66, 70–72, 74, 148, 176
Body language, 210
Bowen, M., 110
Bratter, T., 91–92, 109–110, 128–130, 146–147, 172–175, 192–195 (*see also* Reality Therapy)
Buber, M., 98
Bugenthal, J., 193
Burton, A., 50

Catalyst, therapist as, 120–121, 172
Clevenger, C., 2
Client-Centered Therapy, 9–22 (*see also* Coulson, W. R.)
ambiguity, tolerance for, 82
collusion, and the therapist, 212
critical constructs of, 10–12
crying, by the therapist, 118
empathy and, 117, 202
encounter groups and, 9, 13
feedback and, 13, 20–21
feelings, significance of, 116–117, 118, 157
group potential and, 222
group processes in, 18–22
group resistance and, 14

Client-Centered Therapy *(continued)*
group structure and, 12
group trust and, 202
healing capacity of group, 20, 119
*here and now* quality in, 19, 20
immediacy in, 20
individual therapy in, 157
interaction and, 18, 22
intimacy and, 13, 16
key concepts of, 12–14
members as therapists, 97, 136, 157
members' feelings and leader, 155–156
openness, 118
responses to Critical Incidents (*see* Critical Incidents)
responsibility and, 10
risk and risk-taking in, 13
self-concept, 10
role in therapy, 10
self-disclosure and, 202
and therapist, 16–17, 213
self-exploration and, 218
silence, management of, 82–83
subgrouping in, 21, 99
therapist:
  as active listener, 158
  as group member, 118, 202
  as leader, 97–99
  and modeling behavior, 202, 213–224
  primary objective of, 22
  role and techniques of, 14–18
  and self-disclosure, 16–17, 158
  *there and then* feelings, 19
  three key variables, 202
  trust and, 13
  and group therapist, 14
  trusting process and, 202
Cognitive methods and techniques, 47–48 (*see also* Rational-Emotive Therapy)
Cognitive power:
  in Individual Psychology, 204
Cohesion, 207, 211

Cohesiveness:
  and Individual Psychology, 39, 86, 129, 204
Commitment:
  Reality Therapy and, 61
  therapist and, 207
Comparison of theoretical practitioners' interventions, 209–224
  Critical Incident #1, 210–211
  Critical Incident #2, 211–213
  Critical Incident #3, 213–215
  Critical Incident #4, 215–217
  Critical Incident #5, 217–220
  Critical Incident #6, 220–221
Confidentiality, 91, 129
Confrontation, 17, 21, 25, 62, 72, 172, 194
  by group, 194
  Client-centered Therapy and, 17, 21
  Gestalt Therapy and, 25, 101, 162
  Reality Therapy and, 62, 172
  Transactional Analysis and, 72
Congruence, 37
  Individual Psychology and, 37
  Rational-Emotive Therapy and, 43
  of theory with practice, 201–208
    Client-Centered Therapy and, 202–203
    Gestalt Therapy and, 203
    Individual Psychology and, 204–205
    Rational-Emotive Therapy and, 205–206
    Reality Therapy and, 206–207
    Transactional Analysis and, 207–220
  of therapist, 16
Contracts, 92–93, 11, 128, 138–139
  negotiation of, 210–211
Core, of group therapy, 208
  definition of, 3
Coulson, W. R., 15, 82–83, 97–100, 116–119, 135–136, 155–158, 183–184
  (*see also* Client-Centered Therapy)

Creativity of therapist, 203–204
Critical Incidents, 79–198
  and Client-Centered Therapy,
    81–83, 97–100, 116–119, 135–136,
    155–158, 183–184
  definition of, 1–2
  and Gestalt Therapy, 83–85,
    100–103, 119–121, 136–139,
    158–163, 184–187
  and Individual Psychology, 85–86,
    103–105, 121–123, 139–141,
    163–166, 187–189
  management of, 3
  and procedures for students, 4
  and procedures for theoretical
    practitioners, 4
  and Rational-Emotive Therapy,
    87–91, 105–108, 123–128,
    141–146, 166–172, 189–192
  and Reality Therapy, 91–92,
    109–110, 128–130, 146–147,
    172–175, 192–195
  student guideline questions for, 80
  and Transactional Analysis, 92–94,
    110–113, 130–131, 147–151,
    175–179, 195–197

Death:
  acceptance of, 129
  and Adlerian psychology, 121
Diagnosis, internal, 217
Dialogue, 206
  example of, 283
  in Gestalt Therapy, 100–101, 121,
    138, 203, 215
Dialoguing, 206–207, 213, 216
Dinkmeyer, D., 32, 37, 39
Dinkmeyer, D., Jr., 37, 39
Directive therapist, 205
Dreikurs, R., 32–36

Ellis, A., 41–43, 45–50, 52, 87–91,
  105–109, 123–127, 141–146, 166–172,
  189–192 (see also Rational-Emotive
  Therapy)
Empathy, 37, 117, 218
Encounter groups, 9, 13

Fagan, J., 24
Fantasy:
  in Gestalt Therapy, 120, 213
  in Rational-Emotive Therapy, 42
Feedback, 13, 17, 20–21, 216
Feelings, in Rational-Emotive Therapy,
  126
Freud, S., 31
Front, of therapy, 208
  definition of, 2

Gestalt Therapy (see also Polster, M. F.):
  cohesion and, significance
    and achievement of, 84
  confrontation in, 25, 101, 162, 213
    use of, 162
  contact in, 101, 184
    definition and use of, 159–162
  contracts in, 138–139
  creative way of therapist and, 203

Gestalt Therapy (continued)
  deflection, value of, 102
  denial, confrontation of, 120
  dialogue in, 100, 215
    and introjection, 138
    use of, 100–101, 121, 203, 213
  experiment and, 210
    example of, 85
  expressive vs. resistant behavior,
    importance of, 101–102
  fantasy and, 120, 213, 215
    use of, 120
  focusing, 28
  games, 66, 70–71, 76, 203
  group:
    process, 29–30
    self-regulation, 102
    as social microcosm, 158–159
  how and why, 150
  I-boundaries and, 119
  incongruencies, 30
  individual growth and, 83
  introjection in, example of,
    137–138
  intuitive feel of therapist in, 203
  key concepts of, 24–26
  member differences, importance
    of, 84
  member interaction, 30
  projection in, example of, 186–187
  responses to Critical Incidents (see
    Critical Incidents)
  responsibility, 30
    in communication, 162
  risk-taking and, 27
  role-playing and, 85
  self-awareness and, 161
  specificity of communication and,
    importance of, 136
  structure and membership, 24
  therapist role and techniques,
    26–29
  top dog-underdog and, implied use
    of, 103
  unfinished business and, 27–28,
    103
  why and when to use, 136
  workshops and, 24
Glasser, W., 55–58, 61
Goals, 32, 34–35, 38, 40, 42, 43, 87–89,
  106
Goldstein, K., 23
Goodman, P., 24
Group:
  centered, 222
  exercises and, 18
  leadership in, 3–4 (see also
    Therapist)
  self-direction in, 14
  theory and practice of, 1
  as therapeutic tool, 174
  wisdom of, 175 (see also
    Client-Centered Therapy)
Group member variables, 13
Group mind (see Individual
  Psychology)
Group process, 3, 14
  cohesion in, 210

Group process (continued)
  cohesiveness and , 39, 86, 129, 204
  collusion by therapist in, 212
  confrontation in, 17, 21, 25, 62, 72,
    172, 174
  considerations in, 219
  deemphasis of, 146, 206, 212
  demystified, 228
  effective learnings from, 223
  emotional contagion and, 213, 221
  emotional stimulation and, 213
  extra-group socializing, 212, 213
    (see also Subgrouping)
  feedback in, 13, 17, 20–21, 216
  and group development, 222
  and group history, 212–213
  and group involvement, 218
  and group support, 214
  and here and now, 19, 20, 24, 172
  immediacy in, 20
  interactive nature of, 216
  intervention and, 216
  member involvement in, 211
  as mystery, 2
  resistance and, 14
    interpreted, 214
  student concern for, 222
  and theory development, 226
  and there and then, 19
Group structure, 75
  therapist responsibility for, 38 (see
    also Individual Psychology)
Group therapist:
  attitudes of, 13
  defined, 226
  effectiveness of, 14
  establishing emotional climate, 15
  as facilitator of process, 14
  nature of front and core and, 2–5
  need for experience of, 2–3
  philosophy of, 13
  qualities of, 3
  rationale for, 2–5
  as role model, 15
  and variables, 12

Hampshire, H., 92–94, 110–113,
  130–131, 147–151, 175–179, 195–197
  (see also Transactional Analysis)
Hansen, J., 39, 70
Hefferline, R., 24
Here and now, 19–20, 21–30, 61, 172,
  176, 179
Heuristic experience, 82
Homework, 108, 168, 192, 205, 206, 211,
  221
How and why question, 150 (see also
  Gestalt Therapy)

Imagery, 127, 146–147, 216
Immediacy, 20, 59
Incongruencies, 30
Individual focus vs. group focus, 213
Individual Psychology, 31–40 (see also
  Manaster, G. J.)
  belongingness and, 204
  cognitive power and, 34, 204
  comradery and, 86

Individual Psychology *(continued)*
  death, importance of in theory, 121
  family system and, 35
  and feelings of inadequacy and
    inferiority, 32, 36
  goals:
    life-style, 35
    as priority in therapy, 34
    revealed, example of, 103–104
    situational, 35
  goal-setting, 85–86
  group cohesion and, 39, 204
  group mind and, 141
  group processes in, 38–40
  and group therapy, 33
  and harmonious social living, 32
  identification in, and the therapist,
    35
  intuition and, 123
  key concepts of, 33–37
  maladjustment and, 33
  member responsibility in, 165–166
  one-to-one sessions and, 165
  one-to-one therapy and, 188
  paradox and, 205, 214
    example and use of, 121–122
  paradoxical intervention and, 204,
    205
  participant's goals in, 40
  personality in, 32
  and phases of Adlerian group
    therapy, 39
  private logics and, 35
  purposeful behavior of therapist
    and, 204
  responses to Critical Incidents *(see*
    Critical Incidents)
  responsibility and, 34
  risk in, 204
  self-concept in, 36
  self-esteem and, 38, 39, 40, 204
  self-worth and, 204
  sibling rivalry and, 35
  social interest and, 31–33, 36,
    38–39, 105, 139–140, 163–164
    development of, 105
    purpose of, 163–164
  societal reinforcement and, 36
  spontaneity and creativity of
    therapist in, 204
  summary as teaching technique in,
    165–166, 189
  and therapist:
    function of, 204
    as model of effective living, 40,
      204
    role and techniques of, 37–38
    self-disclosure of, 213
Installation of hope, 213
Instruction, 205
Interaction, 39, 51
Intervention:
  and group as a whole, 218
  intense affect and, 211
  member-centered, 222
  rationale for, 2
  therapist-centered vs.
    group-centered, 210–211

Intimacy, 13, 66, 129, 207
Intuition, 16, 123
  therapist use of, 203
Irresponsible behavior, 62

Kiefer, H., 2
Kohler, W., 23

La Jolla groups, 82
Lazarus, A., 193
Leadership, *(see also* Therapist):
  effective, 3–4, 209, 223
  style, 3
  techniques, 228
LeShan, L., 129
Levitsky, A., 26, 27

Manaster, G., 85–86, 103–105, 121–123,
  139–141, 163–166, 187–189 *(see also*
  Individual Psychology)
Modeling, 37, 40, 47–51, 59, 110,
  191–192, 205, 212–214

Olden, C., 193
Osipow, S., 2

Papanek, H., 32, 34
Paradox *(see* Individual Psychology)
Paradoxical intervention, 204, 205
Perls, F., 23–25, 27, 29, 83
Pew, W. L., 37, 39
Polanyi, M., 82
Polster, E., 27, 29
Polster, M. F., 27, 29, 83–85, 100–103,
  119–121, 136–139, 158–163, 184–187
  *(see also* Gestalt Therapy)
Primary intervention assessment,
  221–222
Primary intervention, types of, 222
Primary task, of therapist, 172
Problem solving, example of, 193
Profile for students' theoretical
  approach, 80
Programming *(see* Transactional
  Analysis)

Rational-Emotive Therapy, 41–53 *(see
also* Ellis, A.)
  ABC Theory and, 44–45, 53, 108,
    126–127, 142, 168–169, 170, 218
  appropriate feelings and, 126–128
  assumptions and, 109
  awfulizing behavior, 42
  awfulizing, musterbating, and
    whining:
    examples of, 141–144, 168
  behavioral change and, 43
  and beliefs:
    fantasized, 42
    irrational, 42
    rational, 42
  comparison with nondirective
    groups, 166
  congruence and, 43
  and dealing with irrational beliefs,
    124
  depression and, 126
  and dispute and challenge, 125

Rational-Emotive Therapy *(continued)*
  dialogue, individual, 206
  directives and, therapist-offered,
    205
  fantasy and, 42
  goals and, 42–43, 87–89, 106
  group processes and, 50–52
  groups and, kinds of, 42, 50
  homework and, examples of, 108,
    168, 192
  imagery and, 127, 145–146
  and irrational ideas and beliefs, 43,
    52
  key concepts of, 44–47
  objectives of, 43–44
  primary and secondary symptoms
    and, 168
  principles of, 89–91
    instruction of, 205
    and therapist, 168, 205
  responses to Critical Incidents *(see*
    Critical Incidents)
  and responsible behavior of
    members, 205
  self-defeating behaviors and,
    41–43, 52
  self-disclosure and:
    by member, 192
    by therapist, 212–213
  self-enhancing behaviors and, 42,
    52
  self-talk and emotional
    disturbance, 42
  sorrow and sadness vs. depression,
    126
  structure and, therapist role, 206
  surrendering anger and, 190
  therapist:
    qualities of, 47
    role of, 172
    as role model, 47, 51, 191–192
    use in self-disclosure, 191–192
  and three major musts of
    emotional disturbance, 52
  unconditional acceptance and, 107
  universality and, 211
Reality Therapy, 55–62 *(see also*
  Bratter, T.)
  assertiveness training and, 195
  collective wisdom of group and,
    175
  commitment and, 60–61
    of therapist, 110, 173
  confidentiality and, 91, 129
  confrontation and, 172
    by group, 194
  contract and, 128
  and correlation of behavior and
    feelings, 147
  death and, 129
  and developmental stages, 58–61,
    206
  dialoguing and, 206–207
  failure identities and, 60–61
  group:
    cohesiveness and intimacy of,
      129
    as therapeutic tool, 174

Reality Therapy (continued)
  group process and, 58–61
  key concepts of, 56–58
  primary objective of, 55
  problem solving, model, 193
  reason and, 206
  responses to Critical Incidents (see
    Critical Incidents)
  self-defeating behavior and, 59
  self-disclosure:
    by therapist, 91, 207, 212–213,
      216
  structuring in, 91, 128, 172
  success identity and, 60, 62
  tension and, 61
  therapist:
    as catalyst, 128, 130, 172
    pedagogical role of, 207
    primary task of, 172
    and respect of members, 146
    responsible behavior of, 59, 62,
      207
    as role model, 110, 191–192
    role and techniques of, 58–61
    vulnerability of, 128
    wisdom and, 175
  therapist-member relationship, 55
  trust and, 173
Reframing (in Transactional Analysis),
  112
Reinforcement, 36
  social, 13
Resistance (see Group process)
Respect, 37, 56
  by therapist for members, 146
Responsibility, 10, 25–26, 30, 34, 57, 148,
  175–176, 207, 210, 216
  as modeled by therapist, 110
Responsible behavior, 55, 62
  by members, 205
  by therapist, 175–176, 207
RET (see Rational-Emotive Therapy)
Risk, 204
  of self-disclosure, 19
Risk-taking, 13, 27, 30
Rogers, C., 9–20, 202
Role-playing, 210
  compared with Rational-Emotive
    and Gestalt Therapies, 210–211

Safety, need for, 13
Scripts, 77, 110, 150
Self-acceptance, 20
Self-awareness, 28
Self-concept:
  in Client-Centered Therapy, 10
  in Individual Psychology, 32, 36
Self-defeating behaviors, 41–43, 52, 59
  (see also Rational-Emotive Therapy)
Self-direction, 14
Self-disclosure:
  by group member, 19, 192
  by therapist, 16–17, 91, 191–192,
    202, 207, 210–213, 216, 218
Self-esteem, 64, 204
  in Individual Psychology, 3, 8, 40,
    204
Self-exploration, 19

Shepherd, I. L., 24
Siegel, J., 193
Simkin, J., 26
Skills, of therapist, 207
Smith, E., 39, 70
Social interest, 31–33, 36 (see also
  Reality Therapy)
Spivak, J., 193
Spontaneity of therapist, 204
Stages, 58–61 (see also Individual
  Psychology, phases)
  in Client-Centered Therapy, 8–22
  in Rational-Emotive Therapy,
    58–61
  in Reality Therapy, 58–61, 206
Structure, 12, 211
  leader responsibility for, 91, 128,
    172
  Rational-Emotive Therapy and, 51,
    53
  Reality Therapy and, 91, 128, 172
  and therapist role, 206
Student rationale for group therapy, 79
Subgrouping, 212, 213 (see also
  Client-Centered Therapy)

TA (see Transactional Analysis)
Termination, member responsibility in,
  216–217
Theoretical approaches, 3–4
Theoretical map:
  key elements of, 226–228
Theory:
  development of, 225–228
  and relationship to practice, 2
  role of, 2
  steps in developing, 225
  and therapist's personal style, 208
Theory Evaluation Forms, 5, 80, 94, 114,
  131–132, 151–152, 179–180, 197–198
Therapist:
  attitudes of, 37
  creativity and, 71, 203
  in Individual Psychology, 204
  primary task of, 172
  qualities of, 47
  in Reality Therapy, 62
  as role model, 191–192
Therapist-centered group, 29, 71, 222
Therapist role and techniques (see
  Client-Centered Therapy, Gestalt
  Therapy, Individual Psychology,
  Rational-Emotive Therapy, Reality
  Therapy, and Transactional Analysis)
Transactional Analysis, 63–78 (see also
  Hampshire, H.)
  ambiguity and, 92
  anger and, 113
  avoidance in:
    and stroking, 130
    and verbalization, 130
  basic position of, 63
  contextual shifts and, 197
    as mechanism of therapeutic
      change, 177
  and contracts, 92, 93, 111, 147, 148,
    175
    establishment of, 92–93

Transactional Analysis (continued)
  negotiations in, 93
  structure of, as therapeutic tool,
    148, 175
  and ego states, 67–68, 71, 77
    diagnosis of, 178
    treatment of, 178
  and emphasis of present, 64
  family dynamics and scripts in, 177
  game analysis in, 111
  goals of, 77
    early establishment of, 92
  group processes in, 74–76
  here and now, 176, 179
  how and why, 150
  individuality, 175
  individuation, 175
  key concepts of, 67–71
  and minimal structure, 92
  and nonverbal, behavior, 178
  pastiming in, 112–113
  personhood of therapist and, 207
  programming and, 113, 131,
    149–151, 175–177, 197, 212
  rackets in, 195
  recontextualizing:
    as interaction, 196
    as ways of achieving, 197
  reinforcement and, 65
  responses to Critical Incidents (see
    Critical Incidents)
  responsibility in, 175–176
    of members, 148
    of members during termination,
      216
    resistance to, 148
    and therapist, 207
    of therapist for group reality,
      176
  scripts and, 110, 150
    as reinforcers, 110
  self-esteem and, 64
  strokes in, 64–66, 76, 77
    definition of, 64–65
    method of receiving, 65–66
    success of, 64
    taboo topics and, 131
  termination in, 147, 148, 151
    as function of adult ego state,
      151
  theme identification in, 150
  therapist:
    and analysis, 208
    and collusion with members,
      130
    and commitment, 207
    primary task of, 131
    role and techniques of, 71–74
    skills of, 71, 77, 207
    and transactions, 63–65, 67, 71,
      76–77, 177, 211
    and transference, 150, 208
  treatment:
    philosophical and ethical
      problems in, 195–196
    purpose of, 94
Transactions (see Transactional
  Analysis)

Transference, 150, 208
Trust, 63
    in Client-Centered Therapy, 13
    and greater self-acceptance, 13
    and involvement, 173

Unconditional acceptance, 47
Unconscious vs. conscious, 124

Unconscious and subconscious, 215
Unfinished business, 30 (*see also*
    Gestalt Therapy)
Universality, 210, 211, 214, 216

Wallen, R., 24
Warner, R., 39
Werthermer, K., 23

Whitely, J., 45–46, 48
Why vs. how, 215
Wolpe, J., 193

Yalom, I., 2–3, 208, 228

Zinker, J., 26–27